VS COBOL II
FOR COBOL
PROGRAMMERS

VS COBOL II
FOR COBOL
PROGRAMMERS

Robert J. Sandler

WILEY

John Wiley & Sons

New York   Chichester   Brisbane   Toronto   Singapore

IBM is a registered trademark, and MVS, MVS/XA, System/360, System/370, Systems
Application Architecture, SAA, VM, and VM/XA are trademarks, of International Business Machines Corporation. ANSI is a registered trademark of American National Standards Institute, Inc.

Library of Congress Cataloging-in-Publication Data:
Sandler, Robert J.
   VS COBOL II for COBOL programmers / Robert J. Sandler.
     p. cm.
   Bibliography: p.
   1. VS COBOL II (Computer program language) 2. COBOL I. Title. II. Title:
VS COBOL 2 for COBOL programmers.
QA76.73.V77S25 1989
005.13′3—dc20   89-16520
                                                      CIP

ISBN 0-471-62226-5

Printed in the United States of America

10 9 8 7 6 5 4 3 2 1

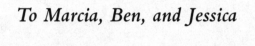

To Marcia, Ben, and Jessica

Contents

Preface

This book is intended to teach COBOL programmers what is new or different in VS COBOL II, the latest mainframe COBOL compiler from IBM. VS COBOL II introduces many changes and improvements to the COBOL language itself, as well as new compiler features and debugging tools. IBM has made it clear that VS COBOL II will be the base for its future development of COBOL.

This book covers only those statements and features that are new in VS COBOL II, not the entire COBOL language. The reader is assumed to be already familiar with OS/VS COBOL or some other earlier version of COBOL. (The primary basis for comparison to determine what is new is OS/VS COBOL with the LANGLVL(2) option.) I have also assumed that the reader has at least a general familiarity with the IBM mainframe environment. The book can be used as a basis for a training course, or for individual study. It is addressed primarily to programmers, rather than to managers or to the systems programmers who install the compiler. Some of the information will be of value to managers planning for the installation of and conversion to VS COBOL II, particularly chapters 10 and 17. The systems programmer may find Chapter 16 helpful in selecting default options, but will have to look elsewhere for further help with installation and tuning.

I have tried to cover the COBOL language as it is actually used by most programmers, and to avoid the distraction of odd or unusual elements that are used rarely, if at all. The text does not cover every last detail of every change or new feature. There are so many changes that no instructional book of a reasonable size (and price) could cover them all, and no one would want to read a book that did. To keep the book manageable, I have tried to concentrate on those things that will be important to most programmers, or are likely to affect a significant percentage of programs. Appendix A contains a complete list of all changes and new features.

Probably the biggest single factor influencing the changes in VS COBOL II is its support for COBOL 85. VS COBOL II is also the mainframe implementation of SAA COBOL. It is important to understand, however, that the subject of this book is not COBOL 85 versus COBOL 74, nor is it SAA COBOL. The subject is VS COBOL II and how it differs from OS/VS COBOL and older IBM versions of COBOL. Most commercial programmers, as a practical matter, use the IBM compiler as a complete package, and don't distinguish between the ANSI standard and IBM extensions. And very few people are using SAA as yet. I have therefore treated the language as a whole, as most programmers will use it, without distinguishing IBM extensions or SAA restrictions.

As a general rule, this book describes only what is new or changed in VS COBOL II. There are a few cases, though, where something that is not actually new will nevertheless be unfamiliar to most programmers in IBM COBOL installations. Where these items are important in using VS COBOL II, they are fully explained. Examples of this are COBTEST and some items in Chapter 10.

COBOL 85, and therefore VS COBOL II, allow the use of lowercase letters in source programs. It is too soon to tell what will become the common practice—that is, whether most programmers will use lowercase. For clarity of presentation, I have chosen to continue the existing practice and use only uppercase letters in the programming examples and for reserved words in the text.

This book has three parts. Part I is devoted to the changes in the COBOL language itself. Part II covers the new debugging features that are incorporated in the VS COBOL II compiler. Part III contains information on other changes that the programmer needs to be aware of in the operation of the compiler and of the object programs.

Part I begins with a review of structured programming concepts and a discussion of how they have been implemented in earlier versions of COBOL. Most readers will probably have at least some basic knowledge of these concepts, but may have forgotten, from lack of use, those constructs that are more difficult to implement in the older COBOL. Structured programming is so entwined with many of the major improvements in VS COBOL II that I feel a review is essential as a starting point. It is a brief review, and is not intended to teach the principles of structured programming to someone who has never been exposed to it. Even if you are familiar with structured programming, however, I recommend a quick reading of Chapter 1 to make sure that you understand the terminology that will be used in the subsequent chapters, and also for the review of the difficulties of structured programming in earlier versions of COBOL.

Chapters 2, 3, and 4 cover those statements and features that implement the structured programming concepts reviewed in Chapter 1. It is these new language elements that make VS COBOL II an up-to-date programming language that is entirely suitable for structured programming.

VS COBOL II greatly simplifies the writing of CICS programs in COBOL, particularly by eliminating the manipulation of BLL cells. Chapter 9 is devoted to the changes in the CICS COBOL environment. You should skip this chapter if you are not familiar with CICS programming in COBOL.

One of the biggest concerns of most programmers confronting VS COBOL II for the first time is that many language elements from earlier versions of COBOL have been eliminated, including some that were used quite often. Chapter 10 discusses what has been removed, and what new features can be used to accomplish the same things. I hope this information will set some minds at ease and encourage the use of the new compiler.

There are short programming exercises at the end of most of the chapters in Part I. If you have the VS COBOL II compiler available, I encourage you to set up a simple skeleton test program so that you can compile your answers to the exercises, and even try to run them. As you well know, the compiler may find errors in coding that you were sure was correct.

Part II discusses debugging. The most powerful of the improved debugging tools incorporated into the VS COBOL II compiler is COBTEST, which I have already mentioned as one of the things that will be unfamiliar to most readers. Although a similar facility was available as a separate product for OS/VS COBOL, it was not widely used. COBTEST will surely enjoy more widespread use, largely because it is sold as part of the compiler product, but also because it is needed as a replacement for some older debugging functions that have been eliminated. Because of the lack of popularity of the earlier product, I have not assumed familiarity with it. Chapter 13 gives complete instructions for using the basic functions of COBTEST, even where there is no change from the older version. I have chosen to concentrate on the full-screen interactive mode of COBTEST because this mode is the most powerful and the easiest to use, and it seems certain that this is the way that COBTEST will be used most of the time. The chapter on COBTEST is illustrated with a number of screen images to familiarize the reader with the appearance of the displays.

Part III covers other features of VS COBOL II that are outside of the COBOL language, including XA support and the sort feature. Compiler options often seem to be a source of considerable confusion. Many of the options are discussed in the chapters covering the functions that they affect, but some of the more important new options are covered separately in Chapter 16. All of the compiler options are summarized in Appendix E.

The book ends with a discussion of a subject that engenders a good deal of anguish: converting existing programs to VS COBOL II. Chapter 17 describes the tools that are available for conversion and ways of handling some of the more difficult problems that will be encountered. It also provides some suggestions for making the transition faster and smoother.

In the Appendices I have tried to gather some reference information that will be useful to the programmer who is new to VS COBOL II. This includes, among other things, a list of all of the differences between VS COBOL II and OS/VS COBOL, and all of the language formats that are new or changed.

I am indebted to my wife, Marcia Sandler, for giving me moral support and encouragement, and to the whole family for doing without me during the many days and evenings that I spent writing. Marcia also helped with the preparation of the flowcharts. I also thank Rosalie Keyes of IBM for a great deal of assistance in obtaining information, and Martin H. Tillinger of MHT Services, Inc. for providing information from which the lists of reserved words in Appendix C were developed.

COBOL is an industry language and is not the property of any company or group of companies, or of any organization or group of organizations.

No warranty, expressed or implied, is made by any contributor or by the CODASYL COBOL Committee as to the accuracy and functioning of the programming system and language. Moreover, no responsibility is assumed by any contributor, or by the committee, in connection therewith.

The authors and copyright holders of the copyrighted materials used herein

> FLOW-MATIC (trademark of Sperry Rand Corporation), Programming for the UNIVAC® I and II, Data Automation Systems copyrighted 1958, 1959, by Sperry Rand Corporation; IBM Commercial Translator Form No. F28-8013, copyrighted 1959 by IBM; FACT, DSI 27A5260-2760, copyrighted 1960 by Minneapolis-Honeywell

have specifically authorized the use of this material in whole or in part, in the COBOL specifications. Such authorization extends to the reproduction and use of COBOL specifications in programming manuals or similar publications.

ROBERT J. SANDLER

New Milford, New Jersey
May 1989

Introduction

VS COBOL II is the newest IBM version of the COBOL programming language. With this new version, it is now possible to write COBOL programs that fully comply with modern structured programming practice. The VS COBOL II compiler also incorporates many improvements in performance and debugging.

COBOL is by far the most widely used language for commercial data processing. It is also one of the oldest programming languages. Originally developed in 1959, it reflects the programming methodologies of that time. COBOL has been criticized in recent years for not being compatible with modern programming principles, especially structured programming. VS COBOL II answers these criticisms by adding to COBOL many of the features that are now considered necessary in a programming language.

In earlier versions of COBOL, there was no natural way to represent some of the basic logical structures used in structured programming. The only way to implement these structures was to use artificial combinations of COBOL statements, essentially coding "tricks," to imitate the desired structures. VS COBOL II incorporates in the language a way to directly implement every standard logical structure. These new language elements make it possible to write structured programs in a straightforward and natural way.

Besides the improvements for structured programming, other new language elements in VS COBOL II eliminate some of the inconveniences and limitations of earlier COBOL versions. There are many enhancements in data manipulation, table handling, and other areas. Communication between calling and called programs is also significantly improved with new ways of passing and sharing data.

VS COBOL II incorporates a number of enhancements that make it easier for the programmer to find and correct errors during compiling and testing. Diagnostic messages issued by the compiler can be embedded in the source listing at the location of the error. The maps and cross-reference listings produced by the compiler have also been improved. During execution, indexes and subscripts can be checked to make sure that they do not go beyond the defined range. More detailed information about unsuccessful I/O operations is available to the program, including actual VSAM error codes. A formatted dump is easily obtained, making it much easier to debug abends.

A complete source-level debugging tool is included in VS COBOL II, and can be used interactively or in batch. It provides traces, display of fields, breakpoints, and many other facilities that make debugging easier. This debugging tool is based on TESTCOB, which was previously sold as a separate product from the compiler.

VS COBOL II programs can take full advantage of extended storage in the MVS/XA operating system, and in VM/XA with some restrictions. Program data and files can be "above the 16-megabyte line," and the program itself can be loaded and run above the line. VS COBOL II programs can also be reentrant.

The impending decline or demise of COBOL is constantly proclaimed. Newer languages are said to be far superior and strong challengers to the old, cumbersome, and inelegant COBOL. One new language or another is reported to be making serious inroads against COBOL in the commercial world. But the new languages come and go, and 30-year-old COBOL remains by far the most widely used language for business applications. And VS COBOL II, IBM's newest COBOL product, will further solidify COBOL's place as the primary language for commercial programming.

HISTORY OF VS COBOL II

IBM announced VS COBOL II in February 1984. Release 1 was first delivered to users in December of that year. Although this first release contained many of the improvements discussed above, it lacked a number of important elements from earlier versions of COBOL. Among the most significant of the missing features were exponentiation, floating-point arithmetic, and certain arrangements of OCCURS DEPENDING ON clauses within a record. The absence of these features made it impractical, if not impossible, for many existing applications to be converted to the new version. The new language was even unsuitable for new programs in certain applications. Because of these limitations, acceptance of the new compiler was slow, and its use was often confined to just one or two projects in those installations that did purchase it.

Release 1 could be run under MVS only. Release 1.1, announced in July 1985 and first shipped that September, added support for VM, but did not add any language improvements or compiler features. It therefore did nothing to increase the general acceptance of the new product.

A full year later, in September 1986, IBM announced Release 2.0 of VS COBOL II. This release added to the language all of the significant missing features, including those mentioned above, that were, as IBM put it "key inhibitors to conversion." With the delivery of Release 2.0 beginning in December 1986, it became practical to use VS COBOL II for any new programs, and to convert existing COBOL programs. Release 2.0 also contained significant enhancements to the debugging tool, including a full-screen interface under ISPF.

A few major features of previous COBOL versions are still missing from VS COBOL II, most notably the Report Writer and the BDAM access method (direct organization). These features probably will not be restored, but even without them a new program can perform any desired function, and there are practical ways to deal with them in conversion. Chapter 10 discusses all of the features that are still missing and how they can be replaced.

IBM announced Release 3.0 of VS COBOL II in September 1988, two years, almost to the day, after Release 2.0. Easily surpassing the previous releases in the magnitude of the changes, Release 3.0 was first shipped to users in December 1988. Some of the changes in this release included support for Systems Application Architecture (SAA), improvements in VM support, enhancements in the compiler listings, some performance improvements, and other technical refinements. But by far the biggest innovation, and the source of most of the changes, was full support of COBOL 85.

VS COBOL II AND COBOL 85

Industry standards for the COBOL programming language are established by the American National Standards Institute (ANSI) in the United States, and by the International Organization for Standardization (ISO) internationally. The current standard for COBOL is formally identified as American National Standard for Programming Language COBOL X3.23-1985 and ISO Standard 1989-1985 for COBOL. (The ANSI and ISO standards are identical.) Informally it is commonly referred to as "COBOL 85."

The standard defines three levels or subsets of the language. A compiler must support one of these three levels to be considered in conformance with the standard. VS COBOL II, starting with Release 3.0, supports the highest level of COBOL 85, which means it includes all of the required language elements that are in the standard. The standard also defines some additional language elements as optional, such as Report Writer. VS COBOL II supports only some of the optional elements.

In addition to the full COBOL 85 language, VS COBOL II, like all earlier IBM compilers, includes many extensions to the standard. The extensions relax some of the restrictions in the standard, provide access to functions of the hardware or operating system that are not available in standard COBOL, and supply mechanisms for interfacing with other software such as the sort and CICS.

The COBOL 85 standard for the first time designates some older language elements as "obsolete." The intent of this innovation is to give early warning to programmers that these elements will be deleted from the COBOL language in the next revision of the standard. IBM, of course, might choose to continue supporting some deleted elements as extensions. There is even some doubt as to whether the standards committee will consider the "obsolete" designation in this standard to be binding on the future standard. Nevertheless it seems prudent to stop using these elements in order to minimize possible conversion problems in the future. This recommendation is repeated briefly wherever an obsolete element is mentioned in this book. Appendix D lists all of the obsolete elements in VS COBOL II.

VS COBOL II can be made to support the previous standard, COBOL 74, instead of COBOL 85, by specifying a compiler option. This book is based on the COBOL 85 support.

By supporting the full COBOL 85 standard, IBM has positioned VS COBOL II to keep up with new developments in COBOL and to remain a popular and effective programming language.

PART I

THE NEW COBOL LANGUAGE

Chapter 1

Structured Programming Concepts

Structured programming is a method of writing programs using a small set of simple logic structures or **constructs**, each of which has a single entry and a single exit. These structures can be combined like building blocks to perform any desired processing. Restricting the logic of the program to these predefined constructs reduces the likelihood of programming errors and makes the logical structure of the program easy to understand. A programmer can readily follow the logic of a structured program by reading it sequentially from beginning to end. The three basic constructs of structured programming are called **sequence**, **selection**, and **iteration**.

THE SEQUENCE CONSTRUCT AND BLOCKS

The simplest of the three basic constructs is sequence. This is merely the execution of instructions one after another in the order that they appear in the program. Figure 1.1 is a flowchart of the sequence construct. Several sequence constructs can be chained together, as illustrated by the flowchart in Figure 1.2.

A seemingly obvious but important concept is that the chain of sequence constructs in Figure 1.2 is itself a sequence construct that could be represented by a single box in a less detailed flowchart. If the individual steps are closely related, they can be grouped together into a single logical unit known as a **block**. Visually delineating such blocks

Figure 1.1   A sequence construct.

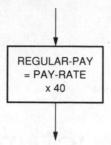

in the source program contributes heavily to making the program clear
and understandable. One basic method of grouping related statements
that has always been part of the COBOL language is the paragraph.
The processing in Figure 1.2 could be one paragraph like this.

```
CALCULATE-PAY.
     MULTIPLY PAY-RATE BY 40 GIVING REGULAR-PAY.
     COMPUTE O-T-PAY = PAY-RATE * 1.5 * O-T-HOURS.
     ADD REGULAR-PAY O-T-PAY GIVING GROSS-PAY.
```

Figure 1.2   Several sequence constructs chained together.

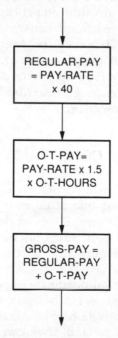

Each statement in this paragraph is a sequence construct, and the paragraph itself is a sequence construct. The paragraph name indicates the beginning of the block, and the indentation, which is required by the COBOL coding format, clearly indicates which statements are in the block. Note that this paragraph has only one point of entry, at the paragraph name, and a single exit, at the end of the paragraph. The single entry point is inherent in the COBOL language. There is no way to enter a paragraph other than at the beginning. COBOL does allow exiting from a paragraph before the end, but in order to adhere to the principles of structured programming we avoid doing so.

Another level of grouping in COBOL is the section, a group of paragraphs which provides a higher level block for a major segment of a program. Sections, paragraphs, sentences, and statements provide a hierarchy of structures **nested** within one another. This nesting extends the concept of blocks. The general structure and logic of the program can be understood by looking at the highest level blocks. Progressively lower levels give increasing amounts of detail within each block. For example, a rough idea of what a hypothetical program is doing can be seen in the following paragraph names.

```
READ-TRANSACTION.
CODE-TABLE-LOOKUP.
PRINT-REPORT-LINE.
```

The statements in one of these paragraphs would provide more detail on the processing that is being done.

VS COBOL II provides a new way of indicating blocks and hierarchy, which is discussed in detail in Chapter 2.

THE SELECTION CONSTRUCT

The second basic construct is called selection. The fundamental characteristic of the selection construct is that a choice of processing paths is made, depending on some condition. In the simplest type of selection, illustrated by the flowchart in Figure 1.3, the conditional test or decision has two possible outcomes, and different processing is associated with each of the two possibilities. The choice of one path or the other is typically associated with a stated condition being either true or false, as in the illustration. This simple type of selection is called an IF-THEN-ELSE construct, referring to the structure of the statement: IF the condition is true, THEN do such and such, ELSE (otherwise) do

Figure 1.3   A selection construct.

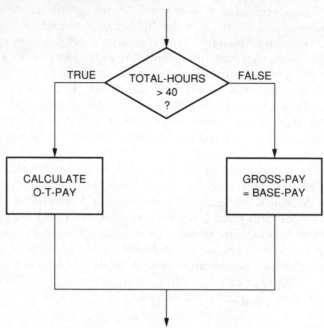

different processing. These keywords are actually used in many programming languages, including COBOL, to express this construct.

There does not have to be processing in both paths. One side or the other could be null, as illustrated in Figure 1.4. In this case, the one processing block is either executed or not, depending on the result of the conditional test.

Although there are two possible paths through each of these flowcharts, each flowchart still has only a single point of entry and a single exit. The two paths must rejoin at a common point. The processing in each path is shown as a sequence construct, but could be any valid construct, such as another IF-THEN-ELSE as illustrated in Figure 1.5. This would be written in COBOL like this.

```
IF TOTAL-HOURS > 40
THEN
     IF DOUBLE-TIME
     THEN
          COMPUTE O-T-PAY = PAY-RATE * 2 * O-T-HOURS
```

Figure 1.4   **A selection construct with one null path.**

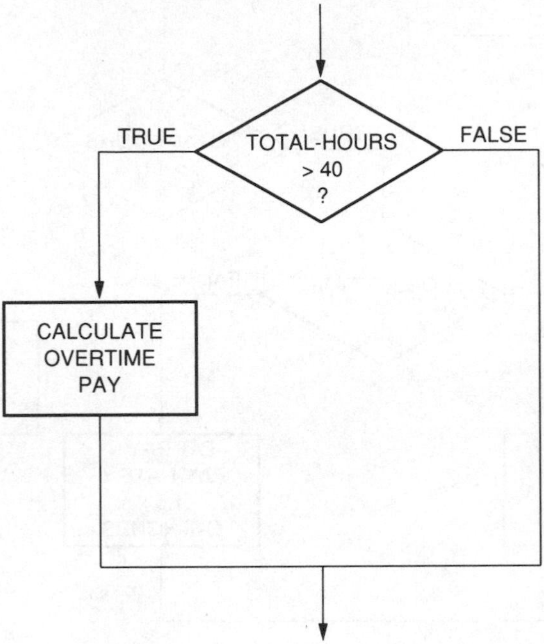

```
      ELSE
          COMPUTE O-T-PAY = PAY-RATE * 1.5 * O-T-HOURS
  ELSE
       MOVE 0 TO O-T-PAY.
```

In this example, the end of the inner IF-THEN-ELSE construct is marked by the second or outer ELSE, which is a continuation of the outer IF-THEN-ELSE. This is another example of nesting, which is essential to structured programming. Any construct or combination of constructs constitutes a block that can be used anywhere a single statement could be used.

Notice the use of the word THEN in the preceding example. This optional word is rarely used in practice, but there are two advantages to including it. When each path is preceded by the appropriate keyword, the statement is visually balanced and the THEN block is clearly identified. It also makes the statement an exact parallel of the IF-THEN-ELSE construct.

While the principles of structured programming allow unlimited combining of the various structures, some programming languages may be

Figure 1.5   Nested selection constructs.

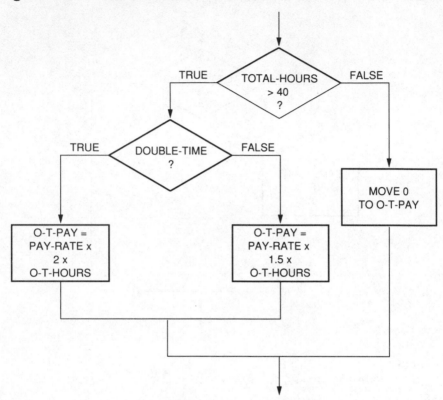

limited as to the kinds of structures or combinations they can represent. This is certainly the case with earlier versions of COBOL. There is a relatively simple nested arrangement of IFs that cannot be rendered directly in the older COBOL. Chapter 3 describes this in detail. The new language features in VS COBOL II solve this problem, and make it possible to use any combination of structured programming constructs in a straightforward manner.

A second type of selection construct provides for situations where there are more than two variations of the processing, and where the condition being tested is not simply true or false but can have more than two values or cases. This is called the **CASE** construct, and is illustrated in Figure 1.6. There is a separate path for each possible value or outcome of the test.

CASE is another construct for which there was no proper repre- sentation in prior versions of COBOL. The GO TO statement with the

Figure 1.6 **A CASE construct.**

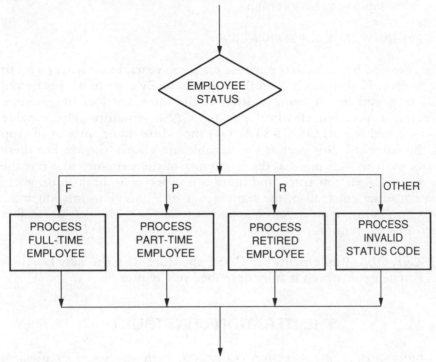

DEPENDING ON phrase bears some similarity to a CASE construct, but its use is very limited for two reasons. First, it cannot use ordinary conditional expressions. Instead, there must be a numeric field containing an integer from 1 to n, with each value corresponding to one of the n possible cases. This rarely occurs as a natural element of the application. Second, because it is a GO TO, the processing for each case must be a separate paragraph. The structure cannot, therefore, be readily nested within another construct.

The usual substitute for a CASE construct is a string of ELSE IFs. Using this method, the flowchart in Figure 1.6 would be implemented like this.

```
IF EMPLOYEE-STATUS = 'F'
    PERFORM PROCESS-FULL-TIME
ELSE
IF EMPLOYEE-STATUS = 'P'
    PERFORM PROCESS-PART-TIME
ELSE
```

```
IF EMPLOYEE-STATUS = 'R'
    PERFORM PROCESS-RETIRED
ELSE
    PERFORM INVALID-STATUS-CODE.
```

This method has served its purpose for some years, but it leaves a lot to be desired. First of all, it is artificial. It is actually a set of deeply nested IFs, disguised by all being written at the same level of indentation. Second, it does not clearly depict the CASE structure. The variable being tested (EMPLOYEE-STATUS) should be stated once at the top of the structure. Not only is the variable not clearly shown, but there is not even an indication at the beginning of the structure that it is the start of a CASE construct, and there is no specific indication of where the construct ends. Also, the significance of ELSE IF as introducing a selection option would not be apparent to anyone who was unfamiliar with this convention.

VS COBOL II implements the CASE structure with the new EVALU-ATE statement, which is fully described in Chapter 4.

THE ITERATION CONSTRUCT

In the sequence and selection constructs, each statement or block is executed once at most. The third basic construct, iteration, provides a means of executing one block repeatedly. This is commonly referred to as "looping." The repetition continues until some condition is satisfied.

There are two variations of the iteration construct. The more common one, generally called **DO WHILE**, is illustrated in Figure 1.7. In this example, the same calculation is executed for each line of an invoice. When the last line has been processed, the program exits from the construct. The usual implementation of DO WHILE in COBOL is the PERFORM statement. A serious disadvantage in the older versions of COBOL is that the processing done in the loop cannot be nested within the PERFORM statement. It has to be a separate paragraph elsewhere in the program, even if it is just one or two statements, which often breaks up the flow of the program to an undesirable degree. For example, the flowchart in Figure 1.7 might be implemented in an older version of COBOL like this.

```
PERFORM CALCULATE-INVOICE-LINE
      VARYING LINE-INDEX FROM 1 BY 1
      UNTIL LINE-INDEX > LAST-LINE.
   .    .    .
```

Figure 1.7   **A DO WHILE construct.**

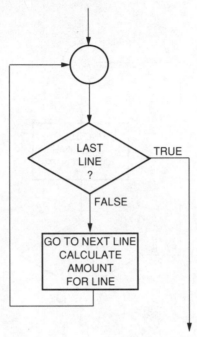

```
CALCULATE-INVOICE-LINE.
     MULTIPLY ITEM-QUANTITY (LINE-INDEX)
        BY ITEM-PRICE (LINE-INDEX)
           GIVING ITEM-AMOUNT (LINE-INDEX).
```

In the DO WHILE construct, the condition for ending the loop is tested before the processing is executed. This means that if the condition is true when the construct is entered, the processing will not be done even once. (This is how the PERFORM statement works.) In the other variation of iteration, **DO UNTIL**, the condition is tested after the processing. Figure 1.8 is a flowchart of a DO UNTIL construct. In this variation, the processing will always be done at least once, when the construct is first entered, even if the condition is already true.

There is no real implementation of DO UNTIL in the older versions of COBOL. The closest substitute is to write the processing once before the loop, and then use a regular PERFORM. For example,

```
PERFORM PROCESS-INVOICE-LINE.
PERFORM PROCESS-INVOICE-LINE
     UNTIL LINE-INDEX > LAST-LINE.
```

Figure 1.8   A DO UNTIL construct.

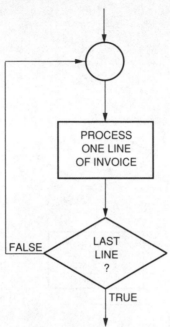

This has the same effect as DO UNTIL, but it is not a true DO UNTIL construct. Also, like any PERFORM, it suffers from the inherent disadvantage of not being able to nest other statements within the PERFORM statement.

Improvements to the PERFORM statement in VS COBOL II provide a true DO UNTIL construct, and allow blocks of coding to be written in-line, nested within the PERFORM. Chapter 2 describes these improvements.

Structured programming is now the generally accepted way of writing programs. Building programs from combinations of the three basic constructs—sequence, selection, and iteration—reduces the number of errors and makes programs easier to understand and maintain. Prior to VS COBOL II, programmers had to resort to tricks and artificial devices to force COBOL to meet the requirements of structured programming. In VS COBOL II, there is a direct and natural way of expressing each of the structured programming constructs. VS COBOL II thus revitalizes COBOL as an up-to-date programming language and assures its continued popularity. The next three chapters describe the improvements that make VS COBOL II wholly suitable for structured programming.

Exercises

1. Name and describe the three basic types of constructs used in structured programming.

2. Explain the difference between DO WHILE and DO UNTIL.

3. What is a block? Where can it be used?

Chapter 2

PERFORM Statement Enhancements

New forms of the PERFORM statement in VS COBOL II contribute to structured programming in several ways. They provide a new way to delineate blocks within a paragraph, allow PERFORMed routines to be written in line, and implement the DO UNTIL construct.

IN-LINE PERFORM

The **in-line PERFORM** statement allows the routine being PER-FORMed to be nested within the PERFORM statement itself, instead of being a separate paragraph somewhere else in the program. This can make it easier to follow the logic of the program because it elim-inates page-flipping when someone is trying to read through the program.

The simplest form of the in-line PERFORM statement merely brackets a group of statements that constitute a block. It looks like this.

```
PERFORM
    MULTIPLY PAY-RATE BY 40 GIVING REGULAR-PAY
    COMPUTE O-T-PAY = PAY-RATE * 1.5 * O-T-HOURS
    ADD REGULAR-PAY O-T-PAY GIVING GROSS-PAY
END-PERFORM
```

This PERFORM verb is not followed by the name of a paragraph to be PERFORMed. A PERFORM with no procedure name indicates

the beginning of an in-line PERFORM. The end of the in-line PER-
FORM is marked by the new reserved word **END-PERFORM**. This
special COBOL word is called an **explicit scope terminator**. An ordinary PERFORM statement would end at the next verb, but with an
in-line PERFORM, the subsequent statements are nested within the
PERFORM. These are the statements that are being PERFORMed.
END-PERFORM must be used to indicate where the PERFORMed
routine ends.

This very simple in-line PERFORM does not affect the execution of the
statements in any way. Look at it again, with other statements before
and after it.

```
MOVE EMPLOYEE-NAME TO EMPLOYEE-NAME-OUT
PERFORM
    MULTIPLY PAY-RATE BY 40 GIVING REGULAR-PAY
    COMPUTE O-T-PAY = PAY-RATE * 1.5 * O-T-HOURS
    ADD REGULAR-PAY O-T-PAY GIVING GROSS-PAY
END-PERFORM
ADD GROSS-PAY TO YTD-PAY
```

The execution of this routine would be exactly the same if all five
statements were written one after another, without the PERFORM.
The value of the PERFORM, in this simple case, is that it documents
the fact that the three statements it contains are closely related and
constitute a block.

You have probably noticed that there are no periods in these examples.
A period after the MULTIPLY statement, for example, would end not
only the MULTIPLY itself, but also the PERFORM and any other
statement within which the PERFORM was nested. In VS COBOL II
periods are generally omitted in the PROCEDURE DIVISION except
after a paragraph name and at the end of a paragraph. The period
is required in those two places. Chapter 3 explains how the need for
periods at the end of conditional statements is eliminated.

Also notice that the PERFORMed statements are indented under the
PERFORM verb. This indenting is not required, but is a good programming practice because it sets off the PERFORMed statements from the
surrounding statements and clearly shows which statements are within
the PERFORM.

The original type of PERFORM, which names a routine to be PER-
FORMed elsewhere in the program, still exists in VS COBOL II. To

distinguish it from the new in-line PERFORM, it is now referred to as an **out-of-line PERFORM**. This is just a new name for the same old thing: there is no change in the way it is written or used, and it has exactly the same format and meaning as before. END-PERFORM cannot be used with an out-of-line PERFORM.

OTHER FORMATS OF IN-LINE PERFORM

Simple in-line PERFORMs like the one above probably will not be used very often. The real value of the in-line PERFORM is in the more complex formats that create iteration constructs. The in-line PERFORM can use all of the formats that are available with the conventional out-of-line PERFORM: TIMES, UNTIL, and VARYING. They are written just like the out-of-line PERFORM, but without the procedure name, and are followed by the statements to be PERFORMed. Here are two ways of initializing totals in a table using different formats of the in-line PERFORM.

```
SET MONTH-INDEX TO 1
PERFORM 12 TIMES
    MOVE ZERO TO MONTH-TOTAL (MONTH-INDEX)
    SET MONTH-INDEX UP BY 1
END-PERFORM

SET MONTH-INDEX TO 1
PERFORM UNTIL MONTH-INDEX > 12
    MOVE ZERO TO MONTH-TOTAL (MONTH-INDEX)
    SET MONTH-INDEX UP BY 1
END-PERFORM
```

The example of iteration from Chapter 1 (Figure 1.7) could be rewritten using an in-line PERFORM like this.

```
PERFORM VARYING LINE-INDEX FROM 1 BY 1
          UNTIL LINE-INDEX > LAST-LINE
    MULTIPLY ITEM-QUANTITY (LINE-INDEX)
        BY ITEM-PRICE (LINE-INDEX)
          GIVING ITEM-AMOUNT (LINE-INDEX)
END-PERFORM
```

There is one restriction on the use of VARYING with an in-line PERFORM. The AFTER phrase for multiple subscripts or indexes is not permitted. A regular out-of-line PERFORM to sum all of the entries in a two-dimensional table might look like this.

```
PERFORM ADD-TABLE-ENTRY
    VARYING ROW-INDEX FROM 1 BY 1
        UNTIL ROW-INDEX > LAST-ROW
    AFTER ITEM-INDEX FROM 1 BY 1
        UNTIL ITEM-INDEX > LAST-ITEM
```

The same thing can be accomplished with the in-line PERFORM by nesting one in-line PERFORM within another.

```
PERFORM VARYING ROW-INDEX FROM 1 BY 1
        UNTIL ROW-INDEX > LAST-ROW
    PERFORM VARYING ITEM-INDEX FROM 1 BY 1
            UNTIL ITEM-INDEX > LAST-ITEM
        ADD TABLE-ITEM (ROW-INDEX, ITEM-INDEX) TO TABLE-SUM
    END-PERFORM
END-PERFORM
```

This nesting demonstrates that the PERFORMed block is not limited to a sequence construct or a series of imperative statements. Here one iteration construct is nested within another. The statements within an in-line PERFORM could include any construct.

WHEN TO USE IN-LINE OR OUT-OF-LINE PERFORM

While an in-line PERFORM can improve the readability of the program in many cases, it can actually hurt readability if the PERFORMed routine is too long or complex. The ability to nest one in-line PERFORM within another, carried to an extreme, makes it possible to write an entire program as a single paragraph. Rather than being easier to understand, such a program would be very difficult to follow because it would quickly become impossible to keep track of the level of nesting and what conditions were controlling deeply nested statements. Some limits have to be set on the depth of nesting and the length of in-line routines. Your installation may have some standards in this area, but it is difficult to make hard and fast rules. Some judgment is necessarily involved. The PERFORMed routine should certainly be moved out of line if nesting is already three or four levels deep, or if the routine is very long. What is too long? The IBM *Application Programming Guide* suggests that a paragraph should not exceed one page of the listing, approximately 55 lines, which is already quite long and should certainly be an upper limit.

One reason to use an out-of-line PERFORM rather than an in-line PERFORM is to improve readability when the PERFORMed routine is long. Another reason is to simplify maintenance when the same routine is PERFORMed in several different places. Having just one copy of the routine means that any future changes will have to be made in only one place. If you choose to put the same routine in line in more than one place, consider using COPY to avoid maintenance problems. The in-line PERFORM should always be used when the routine is PERFORMed in only one place and is not too long.

The decision to use the in-line or out-of-line PERFORM should be based on readability and maintainability rather than efficiency. With today's ever-faster computers at ever-lower prices, it is more important to save the programmer's time than to worry about small savings of computer time. Both forms of PERFORM are quite efficient, and the object code that the compiler generates may not follow your arrangement anyway. When the OPTIMIZE option is specified (and in production it always should be), the compiler will change out-of-line PERFORMed routines into in-line routines in the object code in a process called **procedure integration**. This makes execution slightly faster by eliminating the few instructions needed to link to a PERFORMed routine, and it reduces paging by avoiding some jumping around, possibly across page boundaries, in executing the object code. The cost is some increase in the size of the object program if the same routine is PERFORMed in more than one place. Programmers are sometimes unduly concerned about this, but program size is not an important consideration in virtual storage systems. This is especially true with VS COBOL II, since the programs can run above the 16-megabyte line. (Chapter 14 discusses running "above the line.")

The *Application Programming Guide* describes a method of coding to selectively prevent procedure integration. There are at least three good reasons not to use this method. First, there really should be no need to suppress this optimization. Second, the method uses segmentation, which is defined as an obsolete element in COBOL 85 (i.e., it will be deleted from the next ANSI standard). The use of segmentation should therefore be phased out rather than perpetuated. Third, this is a very artificial use of segmentation. The overlays implied by the source coding do not in fact exist, since VS COBOL II ignores segmentation. But it prevents procedure integration, an effect that is hidden and totally unexpected.

IMPLEMENTING DO UNTIL

All of the preceding PERFORM UNTIL and PERFORM VARYING examples, both in-line and out-of-line, have represented DO WHILE constructs. The PERFORM statement normally tests the condition specified in the UNTIL phrase before executing the PERFORMed routine. If the condition is true when the PERFORM is first entered, then the routine will not be executed at all.

The use of the word UNTIL in a statement that implements the DO WHILE construct unfortunately may cause some confusion. This use of the word goes back to the original COBOL language, which was designed before the advent of structured programming. VS COBOL II uses entirely new terminology to distinguish the two variations of the iteration construct. The new terminology clearly identifies the order of execution without relying on the terms WHILE and UNTIL.

To make any PERFORM with UNTIL into a DO UNTIL, put the phrase **WITH TEST AFTER** immediately after the name of the PER-FORMed procedure in an out-of-line PERFORM, or right after the word PERFORM in an in-line PERFORM. Here is an example of each type.

In-line:

```
PERFORM WITH TEST AFTER VARYING MONTH-INDEX FROM 1 BY 1
       UNTIL MONTH-INDEX = 12
    ADD MONTH-TOTAL (MONTH-INDEX) TO YEAR-TOTAL
END-PERFORM
```

Out-of-line:

```
PERFORM ADD-MONTH-TOTAL WITH TEST AFTER
       VARYING MONTH-INDEX FROM 1 BY 1
       UNTIL MONTH-INDEX = 12
```

There is a small but important change in these examples in addition to the WITH TEST AFTER phrase. The comparison in the UNTIL condition is for the index or subscript to be EQUAL TO, instead of GREATER THAN, the last occurrence number. When WITH TEST AFTER is used with VARYING, the UNTIL condition is tested after the PERFORMed routine is executed, but before the VARYING index or subscript is incremented. The flowcharts in Figure 2.1 illustrate the difference in the sequence of execution. The original DO WHILE form of PERFORM increments the index immediately after executing the routine, before testing the condition, so the index has to be incre-mented one extra time after the last item is processed. The WITH TEST AFTER, or DO UNTIL, form does not increment the index

Figure 2.1   Sequence of execution for PERFORM VARYING.

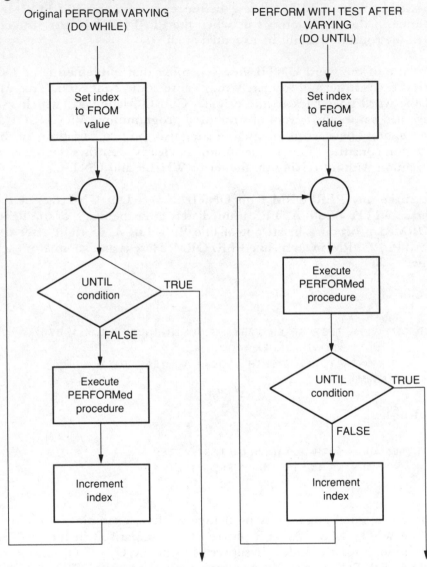

until after the condition is tested, so the exit from the loop is taken when the index still points to the last item.

To complement the WITH TEST AFTER phrase, **WITH TEST BEFORE** can be coded to explicitly indicate the original DO WHILE form of PERFORM. The format is the same as for WITH TEST AFTER. This is really just documentation; the result is exactly the same as if WITH TEST were not specified at all. But in a program where both forms are used, explicitly stating the type in each case can help avoid confusion. A PERFORM that specifies WITH TEST BEFORE, or that has no WITH TEST phrase, has the same execution logic that PERFORM has always had.

WITH TEST BEFORE and WITH TEST AFTER state, in very clear and natural English terminology, when the condition is tested in relation to executing the PERFORMed routine. This should eliminate any uncertainty about the logic of the PERFORM.

Exercises

1. Using the following data definitions, write an in-line PERFORM to calculate EQUIP-TAX for each of the 12 occurrences. To determine the tax, multiply EQUIP-AMOUNT by 0.06.

```
05   MONTH-BUDGET OCCURS 12 TIMES INDEXED BY MONTH-INDEX.
        10   EQUIP-AMOUNT   PICTURE S9(7)V99   COMP-3.
        10   EQUIP-TAX      PICTURE S9(6)V99   COMP-3.
```

2. Using the following data definitions, write an in-line PERFORM to add successive occurrences of A-QUANTITY to QUANTITY-SUM until QUANTITY-SUM exceeds 5000. The first occurrence of A-QUANTITY must always be added, even if QUANTITY-SUM is already over 5000.

```
05   QUANTITY-SUM   PICTURE S9(5)   COMP-3.
05   A-QUANTITY OCCURS 100 TIMES INDEXED BY QUANT-INDEX
        PICTURE S999   COMP-3.
```

Chapter 3

Nesting Conditional Statements

New language features in VS COBOL II eliminate most of the limitations in earlier versions of COBOL on combining or nesting various types of statements. With this increased flexibility, any structured programming construct or combination of constructs can be represented in COBOL.

A PROBLEM WITH IF

The flowchart in Figure 3.1 is a classic example of a logical structure that cannot be directly implemented in older versions of COBOL. This logic is perfectly valid structured programming, and is not uncommon in actual programs. The left side, the true path for the first decision, contains a selection construct followed by a sequence construct. REGULAR-PAY and O-T-PAY must be added together regardless of which overtime rate is selected at the second decision. The addition obviously must be done after the execution of whichever overtime calculation is chosen, but it is not to be done if the first condition is false (that is, there is no overtime). A typical first attempt at coding this structure might look like this.

```
IF TOTAL-HOURS > 40
    IF DOUBLE-TIME
        COMPUTE O-T-PAY = PAY-RATE * 2 * O-T-HOURS
```

**Figure 3.1   A logical structure that cannot be directly implemented in
older versions of COBOL.**

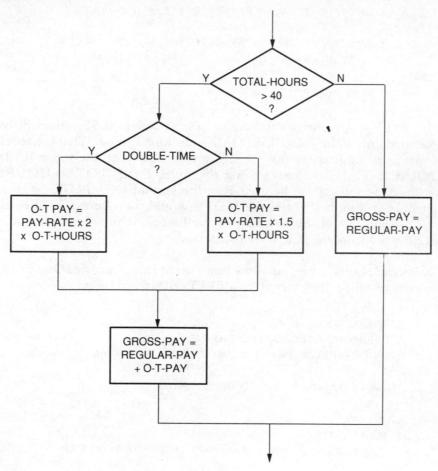

```
    ELSE
          COMPUTE O-T-PAY = PAY-RATE * 1.5 * O-T-HOURS
      ADD REGULAR-PAY O-T-PAY GIVING GROSS-PAY
  ELSE
      MOVE REGULAR-PAY TO GROSS-PAY.
```

Each statement is indented to the proper level to show its logical relationship to the rest of the structure. Unfortunately, the indenting fools
only the programmer. It doesn't fool the compiler, which ignores the
indenting and recognizes that the actual logic is the same as if it had
been written like this.

```
IF TOTAL-HOURS > 40
    IF DOUBLE-TIME
        COMPUTE O-T-PAY = PAY-RATE * 2 * O-T-HOURS
    ELSE
        COMPUTE O-T-PAY = PAY-RATE * 1.5 * O-T-HOURS
        ADD REGULAR-PAY O-T-PAY GIVING GROSS-PAY
ELSE
    MOVE REGULAR-PAY TO GROSS-PAY.
```

The ADD statement is subordinate to the inner ELSE, and will be
executed only if the DOUBLE-TIME condition is false. What is needed
to properly implement this logic is a way of ending the inner IF (IF
DOUBLE-TIME) without ending the outer IF (IF TOTAL-HOURS
> 40). A period cannot be used after the second COMPUTE because
it would end both IFs, and the MOVE would then be executed in all
cases, regardless of the outcome of the first IF. The second, or outer,
ELSE would not be valid after the period.

Various tricks have been used to implement this structure. One possibility is to move the inner IF to a PERFORMed paragraph.

```
    IF TOTAL-HOURS > 40
        PERFORM CALCULATE-OVERTIME
        ADD REGULAR-PAY O-T-PAY GIVING GROSS-PAY
    ELSE
        MOVE REGULAR PAY TO GROSS-PAY.
     .    .    .
CALCULATE-OVERTIME.
    IF DOUBLE-TIME
        COMPUTE O-T-PAY = PAY-RATE * 2 * O-T-HOURS
    ELSE
        COMPUTE O-T-PAY = PAY-RATE * 1.5 * O-T-HOURS.
```

Another method is to repeat the processing that is common to both
paths of the inner IF. In this example, the ADD is written twice, once
in each section of the IF.

```
IF TOTAL-HOURS > 40
    IF DOUBLE-TIME
        COMPUTE O-T-PAY = PAY-RATE * 2 * O-T-HOURS
        ADD REGULAR-PAY O-T-PAY GIVING GROSS-PAY
    ELSE
        COMPUTE O-T-PAY = PAY-RATE * 1.5 * O-T-HOURS
        ADD REGULAR-PAY O-T-PAY GIVING GROSS-PAY
```

```
ELSE
    MOVE REGULAR-PAY TO GROSS-PAY.
```

Although both of these methods achieve the desired results, neither one is really an exact implementation of the flowchart, and they both leave something to be desired in readability.

VS COBOL II provides just what is needed here: a way to end only the inner IF, without ending the whole structure. Like the in-line PER-FORM, described in Chapter 2, an IF statement can have an explicit scope terminator to mark the end of the IF-THEN-ELSE construct. As might be expected, the explicit scope terminator for an IF statement is **END-IF**. Any statement following the END-IF is outside the IF-THEN-ELSE construct, and will be executed regardless of the condition tested by that IF. The VS COBOL II coding for the flowchart in Figure 3.1 is

```
IF TOTAL-HOURS > 40
THEN
    IF DOUBLE-TIME
    THEN
        COMPUTE O-T-PAY = PAY-RATE * 2 * O-T-HOURS
    ELSE
        COMPUTE O-T-PAY = PAY-RATE * 1.5 * O-T-HOURS
    END-IF
    ADD REGULAR-PAY O-T-PAY GIVING GROSS-PAY
ELSE
    MOVE REGULAR-PAY TO GROSS-PAY
END-IF
```

This is an exact representation of the flowchart. There are several important points to observe in this coding. As with the in-line PER-FORM in Chapter 2, there are no periods. Both the inner and the outer IF statements are ended by END-IF instead of a period. Each END-IF is indented to the same level as the corresponding IF. The indenting is not required, and this is not how the compiler pairs END-IFs with IFs, but it is important for making the structure clear to anyone reading the program. The optional word THEN also helps to make the structure clear, as mentioned in Chapter 1. The action specified if the first condition is true (the THEN part of the outer IF) is a block consisting of a selection construct, the inner IF, followed by a sequence construct exactly as it is shown in the flowchart.

The use of the explicit scope terminator is not required for the IF statement, as it is for the in-line PERFORM. IF statements can still be

written the same as always. However, all statements following the IF
will be subordinate to it until it is ended by either a period or an END-
IF. Since greater use of nesting requires avoiding periods, you will use
END-IF a great deal.

If END-IF is used for some IF statements and not for others, it is
important to understand how END-IFs are matched with IFs. The rule
is that an END-IF terminates the last preceding IF that has not already
been terminated (either by a period or by an earlier END-IF). To avoid
confusion it is better to use an END-IF for every IF in the paragraph
whenever END-IF is used at all. This will clearly delineate the scope
of every IF, and can help to avoid unexpected problems when changes
are made to the program.

In the preceding example, both IF statements have ELSE phrases.
END-IF can also be used with an IF statement that does not have an
ELSE phrase.

```
IF ACCOUNT-TYPE = 'B'
    MOVE 0 TO DISCOUNT-PERCENT
    MOVE SUB-TOTAL TO NET-DUE
END-IF
```

OTHER CONSIDERATIONS FOR IF

The elimination of most periods in the PROCEDURE DIVISION can
cause problems with the use of the NEXT SENTENCE phrase in an
IF statement. NEXT SENTENCE means exactly what it says: go to the
beginning of the next *sentence*, not the next statement. The only thing
that ends a sentence is a period, and in VS COBOL II the next period
could be many lines down in the program. The following coding will
not work as intended.

```
IF THIS-WEEK-HOURS > 0
    IF EXEMPT
        NEXT SENTENCE
    ELSE
        COMPUTE O-T-PAY = O-T-HOURS * O-T-RATE
        ADD O-T-PAY TO GROSS-PAY
    END-IF
    ADD GROSS-PAY TO YTD-PAY
ELSE
    MOVE 'A' TO PAY-CODE
```

```
END-IF
PERFORM FICA-CALCULATION
```

The desired logic is to exit from the inner IF, skipping the over-time calculation, if the EXEMPT condition is true. However, NEXT SENTENCE will bypass the entire remainder of the structure that is shown here. Neither ADD GROSS-PAY TO YTD-PAY nor PER-FORM FICA-CALCULATION will be executed, nor will whatever additional statements follow the PERFORM.

What is needed instead of NEXT SENTENCE is a **null statement**, a statement that does nothing, but can occupy the true path of the IF, since something has to be there. A new statement in VS COBOL II, the **CONTINUE** statement, is a null statement. The one word CONTINUE is the entire statement. It can be used wherever any other statement can be used but is primarily useful in cases like this, where some statement is required but no processing is desired. Here is the same example, correctly written with CONTINUE.

```
IF THIS-WEEK-HOURS > 0
    IF EXEMPT
        CONTINUE
    ELSE
        COMPUTE O-T-PAY = O-T-HOURS * O-T-RATE
        ADD O-T-PAY TO GROSS-PAY
    END-IF
    ADD GROSS-PAY TO YTD-PAY
ELSE
    MOVE 'A' TO PAY-CODE
END-IF
PERFORM FICA-CALCULATION
```

With this correction, if the EXEMPT condition is true the inner IF sim-ply does nothing and processing continues with the statement follow-ing that IF (ADD GROSS-PAY TO YTD-PAY), which is the desired result.

Because of the problems that NEXT SENTENCE can cause, it should not be used in VS COBOL II.

There is one small change in the IF statement in VS COBOL II that should not cause any difficulties, but must be mentioned. The word OTHERWISE is no longer valid as a synonym for ELSE.

MORE EXPLICIT SCOPE TERMINATORS

There are two basic types of statements in COBOL, **conditional** statements and **imperative** statements. A conditional statement is one in which the action taken when the statement is executed depends on the result of testing some condition. An imperative statement specifies an action that is always taken. A few statements are always conditional. IF and SEARCH are in this category. Some statements, like MOVE and OPEN, are always imperative. Many statements can be either imperative or conditional, depending on whether or not certain conditional phrases are included. For example, a simple ADD statement such as ADD INV-AMT TO INV-TOTAL is an imperative statement, but if ON SIZE ERROR is added, it becomes a conditional statement.

VS COBOL II has an explicit scope terminator for every statement that is always or sometimes conditional. Here is a complete list of explicit scope terminators:

END-ADD	END-IF	END-SEARCH
END-CALL	END-MULTIPLY	END-START
END-COMPUTE	END-PERFORM	END-STRING
END-DELETE	END-READ	END-SUBTRACT
END-DIVIDE	END-RETURN	END-UNSTRING
END-EVALUATE	END-REWRITE	END-WRITE

This list includes the two that have already been discussed, END-IF and END-PERFORM, and also one new verb, EVALUATE, which is covered in the next chapter.

The explicit scope terminators make it possible to do some things in VS COBOL II that could not be done in the older versions of COBOL. For instance, one annoying limitation of COBOL has always been the difficulty of using READ in a series of statements within an IF statement. The problem was that any statements following the words AT END became part of the AT END processing and were executed only at end-of-file. The only way to terminate the AT END phrase was with a period, which would also terminate the IF. Explicit scope terminators solve this problem by providing a way to terminate just the READ statement, without ending the whole sentence. In the following example, MOVE TRANS-KEY TO OLD-KEY will be executed after the READ, whether or not end-of-file is reached.

```
IF TRANS-KEY < MASTER-KEY
    READ TRANS-FILE
```

```
        AT END
                MOVE 'Y' TO TRANS-EOF
    END-READ
    MOVE TRANS-KEY TO OLD-KEY
ELSE
    PERFORM TRANS-PROCESS
END-IF
```

The explicit scope terminator actually turns a conditional statement
into an imperative statement. This transformation is what makes it
possible to eliminate periods. Imperative statements can be strung
together one after another indefinitely and can be nested in conditional
statements. The ability to make any statement imperative means that
any statement can be used just about anywhere. It is now possible, for
example, to use an IF in an AT END or ON SIZE ERROR phrase,
where an imperative statement is required.

```
DIVIDE ORDER-DOLLARS BY ORDER-ITEMS GIVING AVERAGE-ITEM
    ON SIZE ERROR
        IF ORDER-ITEMS = 0
                MOVE 0 TO AVERAGE-ITEM
        ELSE
                PERFORM ERROR-ROUTINE
        END-IF
END-DIVIDE
```

The END-IF makes the IF into an imperative statement, so it is valid
in the ON SIZE ERROR phrase. Similarly, the END-DIVIDE makes
the DIVIDE an imperative statement, even though it includes the ON
SIZE ERROR phrase, so it in turn could be nested anywhere that an
imperative statement is allowed.

DETERMINING THE SCOPE OF A STATEMENT

By now what is meant by the **scope** of a statement should be evident.
It is a portion of the program embedded within the statement, the
execution of which is controlled by the statement. The scope of an
imperative statement is generally only itself. It ends at the next verb,
at its own explicit scope terminator if one is used, or at a period. For
a conditional statement, however, verbs that immediately follow it are
subordinate to it. They are within its scope. The scope of a conditional
statement ends at its explicit scope terminator or at a period. ELSE
terminates the scope of any statements that precede it within the IF

statement. The period and the word ELSE are called **implicit scope terminators**. PERFORM is considered an imperative statement, but the scope of an in-line PERFORM is determined in the same manner as for conditional statements. Only conditional statements and in-line PERFORM can have other statements nested within them.

Whenever the compiler finds an explicit scope terminator, it has to decide which statement is being terminated. The rule that it follows is a generalization of the rule that was given for pairing END-IFs with IFs. An explicit scope terminator ends the last preceding statement of the corresponding type that has not already been terminated either explicitly or implicitly. The biggest potential for mistakes occurs when imperative and conditional forms of the same verb are used in one structure.

```
ADD ORDER-QUANTITY TO TOTAL-QUANTITY
    ON SIZE ERROR
        ADD 1 TO ERROR-COUNTER
        MOVE MESSAGE-4 TO ERROR-MESSAGE
END-ADD
MULTIPLY ORDER-SUBTOTAL BY TAX-RATE GIVING SALES-TAX
```

In this example, the second or inner ADD statement, ADD 1 TO ERROR-COUNTER, is terminated by the MOVE verb that follows it. The END-ADD is therefore paired with the first ADD, and terminates the SIZE ERROR processing. The situation changes completely if we reverse the order of the ADD and the MOVE—a change that would not normally matter. A programmer might easily make this seemingly minor change without realizing its implications.

```
ADD ORDER-QUANTITY TO TOTAL-QUANTITY
    ON SIZE ERROR
        MOVE MESSAGE-4 TO ERROR-MESSAGE
        ADD 1 TO ERROR-COUNTER
END-ADD
MULTIPLY ORDER-SUBTOTAL BY TAX-RATE GIVING SALES-TAX
```

The END-ADD will now be paired with the second ADD statement, and the MULTIPLY will be part of the SIZE ERROR routine. This demonstrates that great care is needed in the use of explicit scope terminators.

In all of the examples in this chapter, indenting is used to show the level of nesting of each statement. Everything within the scope of a statement is indented under it. Each successively deeper level of nesting is indented from the level above it, and all statements at the same level are indented by the same amount. This provides a visual representation of the structure of the program. These indenting rules are not required by the COBOL language, but they should be required as a programming standard in every COBOL installation. As important as proper indenting is to a programmer's understanding of the program, it is important to remember that indenting is of no significance to the compiler, which treats the source code as a continuous stream of characters. The only way to indicate the logical structure of the program to the compiler is the proper use of nesting and scope terminators.

NOT CONDITIONAL PHRASES

Another new feature in VS COBOL II enhances the nesting capabilities of most of the statements that have conditional phrases, especially the I/O and arithmetic statements. For phrases such as AT END and ON SIZE ERROR, VS COBOL II includes corresponding NOT phrases that are executed if the condition is not true. For example, here is a READ statement with a **NOT AT END** phrase.

```
READ TRANS-FILE
    AT END
        MOVE 'Y' TO TRANS-EOF
    NOT AT END
        ADD 1 TO TRANS-COUNT
END-READ
MOVE TRANS-KEY TO OLD-KEY
```

The ADD statement will be executed each time a record is successfully read from the file and the AT END condition does not occur. When the end of the file is reached, MOVE 'Y' TO TRANS-EOF will be executed and the ADD will not be executed. MOVE TRANS-KEY TO OLD-KEY will always be executed after the READ, whether or not the AT END condition occurs.

The NOT AT END phrase is something like an ELSE phrase for the AT END condition. Unlike ELSE, however, NOT AT END is not the exact opposite of AT END. If an error occurs during the READ, neither the AT END nor the NOT AT END phrase will be executed. Consequently, if the program checks the FILE STATUS field to detect errors, the checking must be done outside the scope of the READ statement, not in the NOT AT END phrase.

NOT AT END can also be used in a RETURN statement in a SORT OUTPUT PROCEDURE. Note that unlike READ, every RETURN statement must have an AT END phrase, whether or not NOT AT END is included. The SEARCH statement has an AT END phrase, but it does not have a NOT AT END phrase.

Like NOT AT END for READ and RETURN, the new phrase **NOT INVALID KEY** can be used in any I/O statement that has an INVALID KEY phrase. The same precaution about errors applies as for AT END and NOT AT END.

Any arithmetic statement can have a **NOT ON SIZE ERROR** phrase in addition to or instead of ON SIZE ERROR. Other conditional phrases that are less frequently used also have new NOT forms. **NOT AT END-OF-PAGE** can be used in the WRITE statement in those situations where END-OF-PAGE can be used. For STRING and UNSTRING, **NOT ON OVERFLOW** complements the ON OVER-FLOW phrase. The CALL statement has an ON OVERFLOW phrase, but the NOT phrase for CALL is connected with a new conditional phrase that is discussed in Chapter 7.

The new language elements presented in this chapter, particularly explicit scope terminators, add tremendous power to the structuring capabilities of the COBOL language. They make it much easier to follow structured programming principles and to clearly show the structure of the program in the source code itself.

Exercises

1. Write the PROCEDURE DIVISION statements for the flowchart in Figure 3.2 in one COBOL sentence.

2. Consider this excerpt from a program.

```
PERFORM UNTIL TRANS-EOF = 'Y'
    PERFORM PROCESS-TRANSACTION
    READ IN-TRANS-FILE
        IF IN-TRANS-TYPE = HIGH-VALUE
            MOVE 'Y' TO TRANS-EOF
        END-IF
    END-READ
END-PERFORM
```

Figure 3.2   Flowchart for Exercise 1.

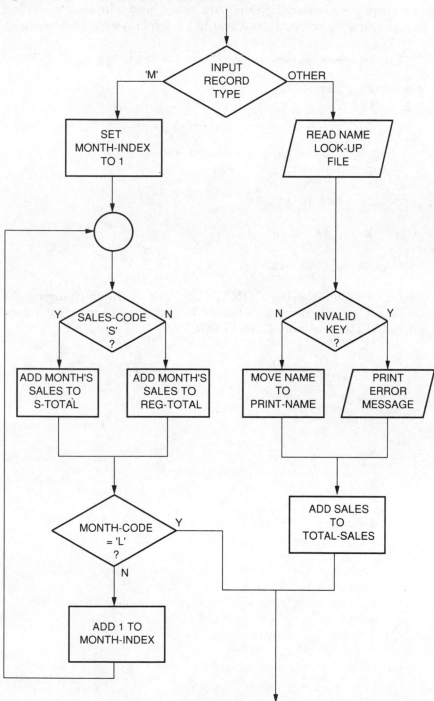

The compiler flagged the END-READ with this error message: "The explicit scope terminator 'END-READ' was found without a matching verb. The scope terminator was discarded." Explain why it was flagged.

3. Here is the example that was given for CONTINUE.

```
IF THIS-WEEK-HOURS > 0
    IF EXEMPT
        CONTINUE
    ELSE
        COMPUTE O-T-PAY = O-T-HOURS * O-T-RATE
        ADD O-T-PAY TO GROSS-PAY
    END-IF
    ADD GROSS-PAY TO YTD-PAY
ELSE
    MOVE 'A' TO PAY-CODE
END-IF
PERFORM FICA-CALCULATION
```

Rewrite this without using CONTINUE, and without changing the processing. Can you think of a nested IF structure in which it would be impossible to eliminate CONTINUE?

Chapter 4

The EVALUATE
Statement

The structured programming capabilities of VS COBOL II are completed by the **EVALUATE** statement. EVALUATE is a new statement that implements the CASE construct. CASE is similar to the IF-THEN-ELSE construct in that the flow of program logic will vary depending on some condition, but CASE has more than two possible outcomes. Figure 4.1 is a typical flowchart of a CASE construct. In earlier versions of COBOL there was no entirely satisfactory way to program a CASE construct, so EVALUATE is one of the features of VS COBOL II that adds significantly to the effectiveness of COBOL as a language for structured programming.

The EVALUATE statement is a very powerful tool with many options. The price of this power, of course, is a fair degree of complexity. This chapter introduces all of the facilities of the EVALUATE statement, but is certainly not exhaustive. As you gain experience with EVALUATE, you will undoubtedly discover new ways to use it.

EVALUATE WITH A SIMPLE SUBJECT

The simplest form of the EVALUATE statement tests a single field and executes different statements depending on the value in the field. Here is an example.

```
EVALUATE EMPLOYEE-STATUS
    WHEN 'F'
        MOVE 'FULL-TIME' TO PRINT-STATUS
```

Figure 4.1   A CASE construct.

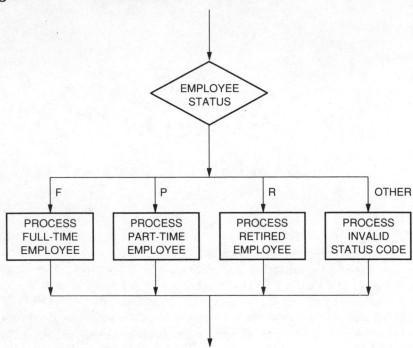

```
    WHEN 'P'
        MOVE 'PART-TIME' TO PRINT-STATUS
    WHEN 'R'
        MOVE 'RETIRED' TO PRINT-STATUS
END-EVALUATE
```

The name of the field that is being tested is written immediately after the verb EVALUATE. The value it is compared to is written after the word **WHEN**, and this is followed by a statement to be executed if the tested field is equal to the value in the WHEN phrase. There is a separate WHEN phrase for each value to be tested for. Each WHEN phrase represents one path in the flowchart of the CASE structure.

When this EVALUATE statement is executed, EMPLOYEE-STATUS is first compared to the literal 'F' in the first WHEN phrase. If they are equal, the MOVE statement immediately following that WHEN phrase will be executed. Execution of the EVALUATE statement is then complete. The remaining conditions are not checked. The next statement executed will be whatever statement follows the END-

EVALUATE scope terminator. Just as any path through the CASE flowchart passes through only one processing block, any EVALUATE executes only one WHEN action.

If EMPLOYEE-STATUS is not equal to 'F', it is next compared to the value 'P' in the second WHEN phrase. This process continues until an equal condition is found, at which point the statement following the WHEN phrase is executed and the EVALUATE statement is completed. If no match is found in any of the WHEN phrases, the EVALUATE statement does nothing and execution continues with the statement following END-EVALUATE.

The field that is tested, EMPLOYEE-STATUS in the example, is called the **selection subject**. The value to which it is compared in the WHEN phrase is called a **selection object**. Each of the objects must be a type of data that is valid for comparison to the subject. In the example, EMPLOYEE-STATUS in nonnumeric so the selection objects must be nonnumeric. If EMPLOYEE-STATUS were numeric, the objects would also have to be numeric.

There is a special form of the WHEN phrase that can be used to specify an action to be taken if none of the WHEN conditions is satisfied. This is illustrated in the following example.

```
EVALUATE EMPLOYEE-STATUS
    WHEN 'F'
        MOVE 'FULL-TIME' TO PRINT-STATUS
    WHEN 'P'
        MOVE 'PART-TIME' TO PRINT-STATUS
    WHEN 'R'
        MOVE 'RETIRED' TO PRINT-STATUS
    WHEN OTHER
        PERFORM INVALID-STATUS-CODE
END-EVALUATE
```

The PERFORM statement after **WHEN OTHER** will be executed if none of the conditions in the preceding WHEN phrases are true. WHEN OTHER must always be the last WHEN phrase in the EVALUATE statement.

It is a good idea to include WHEN OTHER in every EVALUATE statement, in order to clearly show the action to be taken if none of the WHEN conditions are satisfied. If no action is to be taken, it can be coded as

```
WHEN  OTHER
      CONTINUE
```

This is superfluous, but has the advantage of being explicit. Also, coding WHEN OTHER forces the programmer to consider the possibility that none of the expected conditions will be satisfied, and to think about what the program should do in that case.

The EVALUATE statement must be ended by either a period or the explicit scope terminator END-EVALUATE. Without one of these, every statement after the last WHEN would become part of the action for that WHEN condition. In keeping with the elimination of periods, as discussed in Chapter 3, END-EVALUATE is the preferred way to end the statement. Also note that no periods may be used in any of the statements within the EVALUATE, since any period would end the entire structure.

OTHER OPTIONS FOR THE WHEN CONDITIONS

Even with a single field as the subject, as in the preceding examples, the selection object in a WHEN phrase does not have to be just a single value. It can, for example, be a range of values specified by coding THROUGH or THRU. For example,

```
EVALUATE  MEMBER-AGE
     WHEN  13  THRU  19
          MOVE  'TEENAGER'  TO  AGE-GROUP  .   .   .
```

This WHEN condition will be true and the MOVE will be executed if MEMBER-AGE is any value from 13 to 19, inclusive.

Another option for specifying WHEN conditions is use of the word NOT to specify that the statement after the WHEN phrase should be executed if the field being tested is *not* equal to a particular value. For example,

```
EVALUATE  CUSTOMER-STATE
     WHEN  'NY'
          MOVE  4  TO  TAX-PERCENT
     WHEN  'MA'
          MOVE  5  TO  TAX-PERCENT
     WHEN  NOT  'PA'
          MOVE  3  TO  TAX-PERCENT
END-EVALUATE
```

Here, if CUSTOMER-STATE is anything other than NY, MA, or PA, the third MOVE statement will be executed.

The use of NOT raises the possibility that more than one of the WHEN conditions could be true. The rule in such a situation is that the WHEN conditions are tested in the order they are written, and the first true condition determines the action to be taken. Only one WHEN action is executed for any EVALUATE; execution of the EVALUATE then ends without even testing the remaining conditions. In the last example, if CUSTOMER-STATE is 'MA' then 5 will be moved to TAX-PERCENT, even though it is also true that CUSTOMER-STATE is NOT 'PA'.

MORE COMPLEX SELECTION SUBJECTS

The subject of an EVALUATE statement is not restricted to just a single field. One other type of subject that can be used is an arithmetic expression. The value of the expression is calculated and compared to the values in the WHEN phrases. In the following example, the product of UNIT-PRICE and ORDER-QUANTITY is compared to the range of values in each WHEN phrase.

```
EVALUATE UNIT-PRICE * ORDER-QUANTITY
    WHEN ZERO THRU 100
        PERFORM NO-DISCOUNT
    WHEN 100.01 THRU 500
        PERFORM DISCOUNT-1
    WHEN OTHER
        PERFORM DISCOUNT-2
END-EVALUATE
```

Since the value of an arithmetic expression is numeric, it must be compared to a numeric field or literal, or to another arithmetic expression. Notice that a figurative constant, such as ZERO, can be used as a selection subject or object in place of an identifier or literal.

An EVALUATE can also have more than one subject. Each WHEN phrase must then contain the same number of objects as there are subjects. The subjects and objects must be connected by the word ALSO. Here is an EVALUATE statement with two subjects.

```
EVALUATE EMPLOYEE-STATUS ALSO LOCATION-CODE
    WHEN 'P' ALSO 20
        PERFORM PAY-CALC-A
```

```
    WHEN 'P' ALSO 18
        PERFORM PAY-CALC-D
    WHEN 'F' ALSO 31
        PERFORM PAY-CALC-S
    WHEN OTHER
        PERFORM STANDARD-PAY-CALC
END-EVALUATE
```

Each object in one WHEN phrase is compared to the subject in the same relative position. That is, the first object in each WHEN phrase is compared to the first subject, and the second object to the second subject. The word ALSO can be thought of as being similar to AND. In order to satisfy the WHEN condition and execute the statement that follows it, all of the comparisons in one WHEN phrase must be true. In this example, PAY-CALC-A will be PERFORMed only if EMPLOYEE-STATUS is equal to 'P' *and* LOCATION-CODE is equal to 20.

In testing conditions with multiple subjects, there are sometimes cases where the value of one of the subjects does not matter for certain values of the other subject. Suppose, for example, that PAY-CALC-D is to be used for all employees in location 18, regardless of status. The **ANY** option of the WHEN phrase takes care of such situations. When the word ANY is used as a selection object, it is always considered equal to the corresponding subject. So the preceding example could be changed to

```
EVALUATE EMPLOYEE-STATUS ALSO LOCATION-CODE
    WHEN 'P' ALSO 20
        PERFORM PAY-CALC-A
    WHEN ANY ALSO 18
        PERFORM PAY-CALC-D
    WHEN 'F' ALSO 31
        PERFORM PAY-CALC-S
    WHEN OTHER
        PERFORM STANDARD-PAY-CALC
END-EVALUATE
```

LOGICAL EVALUATE

So far, the selection subjects and selection objects have been identifiers, literals, figurative constants, or arithmetic expressions. There is also a completely different category of subjects and objects consisting of logical conditions and truth values. Using these, the second example in this chapter could be recast as

```
EVALUATE  TRUE
    WHEN  EMPLOYEE-STATUS  =  'F'
        MOVE  'FULL-TIME'  TO  PRINT-STATUS
    WHEN  EMPLOYEE-STATUS  =  'P'
        MOVE  'PART-TIME'  TO  PRINT-STATUS
    WHEN  EMPLOYEE-STATUS  =  'R'
        MOVE  'RETIRED'  TO  PRINT-STATUS
    WHEN  OTHER
        PERFORM  INVALID-STATUS-CODE
END-EVALUATE
```

A conditional expression such as EMPLOYEE-STATUS = 'F' is evaluated and assigned a truth value of either 'true' or 'false'. The reserved words **TRUE** and **FALSE**, of course, represent the corresponding truth values. They can be thought of as something like figurative constants, although they cannot be used this way outside of the EVALUATE statement. A WHEN condition is satisfied if the truth values of the subject and object are the same.

Looking at the example above, suppose that EMPLOYEE-STATUS contains a P. The first WHEN condition, the conditional expression EMPLOYEE-STATUS = 'F', will have a truth value of 'false'. Since the selection subject is the constant TRUE there is no match, and the next WHEN condition will be tested. The second WHEN will, of course, have the truth value 'true', which matches the truth value of the subject, so the statement MOVE 'PART-TIME' TO PRINT-STATUS will be executed.

Two types of selection subjects and objects, numeric and nonnumeric, were mentioned earlier. Conditional expressions and truth values are a third type. Just as nonnumeric subjects must be compared only to nonnumeric objects, conditional expressions and truth values can be compared only to one another.

The conditional expression is not limited to a simple equal comparison. Any conditional expression that would be valid in an IF statement can be used. For instance, the readability of the last example could be greatly improved by using condition names. With appropriate 88-level definitions under EMPLOYEE-STATUS in the DATA DIVISION, this example could be rewritten as

```
EVALUATE TRUE
    WHEN FULL-TIME
        MOVE 'FULL-TIME' TO PRINT-STATUS
    WHEN PART-TIME
        MOVE 'PART-TIME' TO PRINT-STATUS
    WHEN RETIRED
        MOVE 'RETIRED' TO PRINT-STATUS
    WHEN OTHER
        PERFORM INVALID-STATUS-CODE
END-EVALUATE
```

The conditional expressions do not all have to refer to the same field, and they do not have to be the same type of expression. The next example illustrates some of the possibilities.

```
EVALUATE TRUE
    WHEN CUSTOMER-CODE IS NUMERIC
        PERFORM SPECIAL-CUSTOMER
    WHEN ACCOUNT-CODE = 'L' AND ACCOUNT-BALANCE > 1000
        PERFORM HIGH-BALANCE
    WHEN ACCOUNT-BALANCE IS NEGATIVE
        PERFORM CREDIT-BALANCE
    WHEN OTHER
        PERFORM REGULAR-ACCOUNT
END-EVALUATE
```

The first WHEN condition is a class condition that tests whether a field is numeric. The second WHEN condition is a complex condition consisting of two simple conditions connected by AND, but is still a single condition with a single truth value. Also notice that the first two conditions refer to different fields. The third WHEN condition is a sign condition. This type of EVALUATE does not require any similarity among the selection objects as long as each one can be evaluated to a truth value. It is hard to imagine this much variation in an actual application, however, and a hodgepodge of conditions could make the statement too confusing.

MULTIPLE LOGICAL SUBJECTS AND OBJECTS

Just as an EVALUATE can have two or more fields as subjects, it can also have two or more logical subjects. The format is the same as with field names, with the logical values connected by ALSO. For example,

```
EVALUATE TRUE ALSO TRUE
    WHEN PART-TIME ALSO LOCATION-CODE = 20
        PERFORM PAY-CALC-A
    WHEN PART-TIME ALSO LOCATION-CODE = 18
        PERFORM PAY-CALC-D
    WHEN FULL-TIME ALSO LOCATION-CODE = 31
        PERFORM PAY-CALC-S
    WHEN OTHER
        PERFORM STANDARD-PAY-CALC
END-EVALUATE
```

The word ANY can also be used as a logical selection object, and will always match the truth value of the corresponding subject. To ignore LOCATION-CODE for full-time employees, for example, we could write

```
EVALUATE TRUE ALSO TRUE
    WHEN PART-TIME ALSO LOCATION-CODE = 20
        PERFORM PAY-CALC-A
    WHEN PART-TIME ALSO LOCATION-CODE = 18
        PERFORM PAY-CALC-D
    WHEN FULL-TIME ALSO ANY
        PERFORM PAY-CALC-S
    WHEN OTHER
        PERFORM STANDARD-PAY-CALC
END-EVALUATE
```

Like the selection objects, the subjects of the EVALUATE can also be conditional expressions, instead of just the words TRUE or FALSE. Using conditional expressions as subjects and TRUE and FALSE as the objects, the EVALUATE statement can be written like a decision table.

```
EVALUATE TRANS-ITEM = MASTER-ITEM ALSO TRANS-TYPE = 'ADD'
    WHEN TRUE ALSO TRUE
        PERFORM ITEM-ALREADY-EXISTS
    WHEN TRUE ALSO FALSE
        PERFORM ITEM-UPDATE
    WHEN FALSE ALSO TRUE
        PERFORM ADD-NEW-ITEM
    WHEN FALSE ALSO FALSE
        PERFORM INVALID-ITEM-NUMBER
END-EVALUATE
```

This EVALUATE statement tests for all the combinations of conditions that can occur in a simplified matching of a transaction to a master file. Each WHEN phrase corresponds to what would be one rule in a decision table. Notice that WHEN OTHER is not used here, since every possible combination of conditions is explicitly tested for. It would be logically impossible for a WHEN OTHER phrase to ever be executed.

An EVALUATE statement can have a combination of fields and logical expressions as subjects. For example,

```
EVALUATE EMPLOYEE-STATUS ALSO TRUE
    WHEN 'P' ALSO LOCATION-CODE = 20
        PERFORM PAY-CALC-A
    WHEN 'F' ALSO LOCATION-CODE = 31
        PERFORM PAY-CALC-S
    WHEN OTHER
        PERFORM STANDARD-PAY-CALC
END-EVALUATE
```

When different types of subjects are mixed like this, each selection object must be the same type of data—numeric, nonnumeric, or logical—as the corresponding subject to which it is compared. In the example, the first subject, EMPLOYEE-STATUS, is a nonnumeric field, and the first object in each WHEN phrase is a nonnumeric literal. The second subject is the logical truth value TRUE, and the second object in each WHEN phrase is a conditional expression.

COMPLEX WHEN ACTIONS

Until now, only a single statement has been used as the action for each WHEN phrase. However it is not at all restricted to such simple statements. The action can be a series of statements or, in fact, any valid structure or nest of structures. Here are some possibilities.

```
EVALUATE PAY-CODE
    WHEN 'S'
        MOVE PAY-RATE TO GROSS-PAY
        ADD GROSS-PAY TO YTD-PAY
    WHEN 'H'
        IF TOTAL-HOURS > 40
            SUBTRACT 40 FROM TOTAL-HOURS GIVING O-T-HOURS
            COMPUTE O-T-PAY = PAY-RATE * 1.5 * O-T-HOURS
```

```
          ELSE
              MOVE ZERO TO O-T-HOURS
          END-IF
          MULTIPLY PAY-RATE BY 40 GIVING REGULAR-PAY
     WHEN 'P'
          MULTIPLY PAY-RATE BY TOTAL-HOURS GIVING GROSS-PAY
     WHEN OTHER
          PERFORM INVALID-PAY-CODE
END-EVALUATE
```

The first WHEN phrase contains two imperative statements. The second WHEN phrase contains an IF-THEN-ELSE structure and an imperative statement. The statements that follow each WHEN constitute a block of code that is executed if the conditions in that WHEN phrase are satisfied. The block is terminated by the next WHEN or the END-EVALUATE.

Since an EVALUATE statement is itself a valid structure, a WHEN phrase could even contain another complete EVALUATE statement. Such nesting of EVALUATE statements would, however, create a level of complexity that would make the program difficult to understand. Because of this, EVALUATE statements should not be nested.

Sometimes it might be appropriate to execute the same statements for two or more WHEN conditions. Instead of repeating the statements, the WHEN phrases can be grouped together like this.

```
EVALUATE ORDER-CODE ALSO ACCOUNT-TYPE
     WHEN 'S' ALSO 'A'
          PERFORM RUSH-ORDER
     WHEN 'N' ALSO 'B'
     WHEN 'E' ALSO 'R'
          PERFORM SPECIAL-ORDER
     WHEN OTHER
          PERFORM REGULAR-ORDER
END-EVALUATE
```

The statement PERFORM SPECIAL-ORDER will be executed if ORDER-CODE is 'N' and ACCOUNT-TYPE is 'B', or if ORDER-CODE is 'E' and ACCOUNT-TYPE is 'R'. If you want the program to do nothing for a particular condition, you can use CONTINUE as the action statement.

```
WHEN 'N' ALSO 'B'
     CONTINUE
```

This will end the execution of the EVALUATE statement if the condition is true. In effect, the "action" to be executed for this condition is "no action." The remaining WHEN conditions will not be tested, and no action statements will be executed.

The EVALUATE statement, with its many options and countless ways they can be combined, can be useful in a multitude of programming situations. The power of the EVALUATE statement seems to have a certain appeal for programmers to the extent that there is a tendency to overuse it. It is not intended as a replacement for the IF statement or nested IFs. In most cases, IF should still be used as it was in the past. EVALUATE is appropriate for a true CASE structure where one conditional test has more than two possible outcomes, each requiring different processing. If an EVALUATE statement would have only two WHEN phrases, IF should be used instead. Where genuine CASE logic exists, EVALUATE will produce well-structured coding that is easy to understand.

Exercises

1. Write an EVALUATE statement to implement this decision table.

PAST–DUE = 'Y'	Y	Y	Y	Y	N	N	N	N
BALANCE–DUE > 500	Y	Y	N	N	Y	Y	N	N
ACCOUNT–RATING = 'A'	Y	N	Y	N	Y	N	Y	N
Print regular statement					X	X	X	X
Print dunning letter	X		X	X				
Print collection notice		X						
Suspend account		X		X				

2. Consider this EVALUATE statement.

```
EVALUATE ACCOUNT-TYPE
    WHEN 'A'
        MOVE 4 TO DISCOUNT-PCT
    WHEN 'B'
        MOVE 2 TO DISCOUNT-PCT
    WHEN 'E'
        CONTINUE
    WHEN NOT 'G'
        MOVE 3 TO DISCOUNT-PCT
END-EVALUATE
```

After this statement is executed, what will be the value of DIS-COUNT-PCT if ACCOUNT-TYPE is D? If ACCOUNT-TYPE is E? If ACCOUNT-TYPE is G? Is there a way to code this without using CONTINUE? Does a set of conditions exist for an EVALUATE in which it would be impossible to eliminate CONTINUE?

Chapter 5

Defining and Manipulating Data

The preceding chapters described the new features of VS COBOL II that are specifically related to structured programming. There are many other improvements and new features in the language. The next five chapters cover these other areas.

In the past, COBOL has had some weaknesses in handling character data, especially variable-length or free-form character strings. This chapter discusses some enhancements in VS COBOL II that add significantly to its character-handling capabilities. It then examines improvements related to tables and to variable-length records.

USING SPECIAL CHARACTERS

Two enhancements in VS COBOL II make it easier for programs to handle special characters that are not on a standard keyboard. One of these enhancements is the ability to specify a nonnumeric literal in hexadecimal notation. A hexadecimal literal is indicated by an X preceding the opening quotation mark. Suppose, for example, a program has to look for a pair of control characters such as carriage return and line feed. It could use the literal X'0D25' to represent the two characters. The value of the literal is specified with the hexadecimal digits 0 through 9 and A through F, and every two hexadecimal digits specify one byte. A hexadecimal literal can be used anywhere that an ordinary nonnumeric literal is valid, including in a VALUE clause.

```
05   END-OF-SEGMENT-CODE   PICTURE XXX   VALUE X'1B9ADB'.

MOVE X'44ED1B' TO END-OF-SEGMENT-CODE
MOVE ALL X'E0' TO OUTPUT-RECORD
```

The other new way of representing special characters is to define a **symbolic character**. This is a name assigned by the programmer to any single character, and is defined in the SPECIAL-NAMES paragraph of the ENVIRONMENT DIVISION. If, for example, a program is to print solid horizontal and vertical lines, symbolic character names could be defined for the two line characters.

```
ENVIRONMENT DIVISION.
CONFIGURATION SECTION.
SPECIAL-NAMES.
    SYMBOLIC CHARACTERS HORIZONTAL-LINE IS 192
                        VERTICAL-LINE IS 251.
```

The character that will be represented by the symbolic character name is designated by giving its position in the complete EBCDIC character set. The first character in the character set, X'00' or LOW-VALUE, is position 1 and would be specified by the number 1. In the example, the vertical line character has the hexadecimal code FA, which is equal to the decimal value 250 and is the 251st character in the EBCDIC character set.

The symbolic character is actually a programmer-defined figurative constant, just like SPACES or HIGH-VALUE, and it can be used anywhere a figurative constant is allowed.

One obvious difference between a hexadecimal literal and a symbolic character is that the symbolic character is only one character, while the literal can contain multiple characters. There is another important difference that results from the symbolic character being regarded as a figurative constant. Consider the following statements, together with the preceding symbolic character definitions.

```
05   PRINT-FIELD   PICTURE X(4).

MOVE X'AE' TO PRINT-FIELD
MOVE HORIZONTAL-LINE TO PRINT-FIELD
```

After the first MOVE, PRINT-FIELD will contain X'AE404040' because the hexadecimal literal, like any nonnumeric literal, is left-

justified in the receiving field, and the remainder of the field is filled
with SPACES. After the second MOVE, PRINT-FIELD will contain
X'BFBFBFBF' because a figurative constant represents one or more
occurrences of the character, with a length equal to that of the associated field. This is exactly the same as filling a field with hexadecimal
FFs by MOVEing HIGH-VALUE to the field.

Hexadecimal literals and symbolic characters will eliminate the need for
coding tricks, awkward keying, or nonprinting characters in programs
that have to handle unusual characters.

DOUBLE BYTE CHARACTER SET

One new character-handling feature of VS COBOL II, the **Double
Byte Character Set (DBCS)**, deserves mention mainly because of the
many references to it throughout the VS COBOL II manuals, especially the *Language Reference* manual. The Double Byte Character Set
uses two bytes to represent a single printed or displayed character,
thus permitting the use of character sets containing many more than
the 256 characters available in EBCDIC. This capability is intended
primarily for Japanese Kanji character strings, which use a character
set containing more than 7,000 characters. Special hardware and additional software are required to enter, display, and print the double-
byte characters. Because of the limited application and the hardware
and software requirements, DBCS is rarely used outside of Japan, and
is not treated in detail in this book.

INSPECT STATEMENT IMPROVEMENTS

Several improvements in the INSPECT statement increase its power
and flexibility. The biggest change is the addition of a new format
with the **CONVERTING** phrase. This new phrase essentially has the
same function as the TRANSFORM statement in OS/VS COBOL.
It translates the characters in the INSPECTed field using two equal-
length strings of characters to specify the translation. Each character
in the INSPECTed field that matches a character in the first string is
replaced by the character in the corresponding position of the second
string. For example,

```
INSPECT KEY-FIELD CONVERTING 'PQRST' TO 'ABCDE'
```

Any P in KEY-FIELD will be changed to an A, any Q will be changed
to a B, and so on. Any characters in KEY-FIELD other than P, Q, R,

S, and T will not be changed. The strings could be specified by field names instead of literals. CONVERTING could be used, for example, to change lowercase letters to uppercase in manual input fields. The same thing can be accomplished with the REPLACING phrase, since VS COBOL II eliminates the limit on the number of REPLACING operands. However, with REPLACING, each pair of characters has to be listed separately. CONVERTING is a lot more concise.

The BEFORE and AFTER phrases can be used with CONVERTING, just as with TALLYING and REPLACING. This gives INSPECT CONVERTING some additional flexibility compared to TRANSFORM.

```
INSPECT MESSAGE-IN
    CONVERTING B-CODES TO LETTER-CODES AFTER '@'
```

An additional enhancement related to BEFORE and AFTER applies to all of the phrases of the INSPECT statement. Both BEFORE and AFTER can now be specified for the same operation.

```
INSPECT PRINT-DOLLARS REPLACING LEADING ZERO BY SPACE
    AFTER '$' BEFORE '.'
```

[handwritten: EXAMPLE:]
[handwritten: a/five/?six → A/FIVE/?six]

[handwritten: INSPECT DATA-FIELD CONVERTING]
[handwritten: 'abcdefghijklmnopqrstuvwxyz' TO]

DEFINING FIELDS

[handwritten: 'ABCDEFGHIJKLMNOPQRSTUVWXYZ']
*[handwritten: * MAY BE USED w/ AFTER OR BEFORE INITIAL 'whatever']*

VS COBOL II provides two new USAGE types for numeric fields: **BINARY** and **PACKED-DECIMAL**. These are not new types of data, but new names for existing types. BINARY is the same as COMPUTATIONAL or COMPUTATIONAL-4. PACKED-DECIMAL, as might be expected, is the same as COMPUTATIONAL-3. The main advantage of the new names is that they are more descriptive. They may also improve the portability of the program. While there is no guarantee that internal numeric representations will be the same in different systems, PACKED-DECIMAL will always mean some sort of compact decimal representation and BINARY will always mean some binary format. By contrast, different systems could use different bases for COMPUTATIONAL. In addition, BINARY and PACKED-DECIMAL are part of the ANSI standard, whereas COMPUTATIONAL-3 and COMPUTATIONAL-4 are IBM extensions, so the new terms will certainly be recognized by any COBOL 85 compiler. For all these reasons, you should use PACKED-DECIMAL and BINARY from now on, and stop using COMPUTATIONAL and its variations.

There is one small change in defining data that will be welcomed by any programmer who has ever tired of writing or typing the word FILLER

over and over again. That word can now be omitted. The other clauses
of the field definition can be coded without any name at all, like this.

```
05   PICTURE X(12).
```

Other changes in data definition, related to tables, are discussed later
in this chapter.

ACCESSING PART OF A FIELD
⌐→* ON THE ELEMENTARY LEVEL.

Reference modification is a new feature in VS COBOL II that provides a way to refer to part of a field. This is accomplished by specifying, in parentheses after the name of the field, the starting position and
length of the desired portion of the field. Here is an example.

```
05   ACCOUNT-CODE PICTURE X(10).

MOVE ACCOUNT-CODE (1:3) TO ACCOUNT-PREFIX
```

The reference modifier specifies a starting position of 1 and a length of
3, so this statement MOVEs the first three characters of ACCOUNT-
CODE to ACCOUNT-PREFIX. The first character of the field is position number 1. Notice the colon separating the starting position and
length. This distinguishes a reference modifier from a subscript.

Reference modification can only be used with fields that are USAGE
DISPLAY, either explicitly or by default. It has the effect of creating a
new field definition representing the specified part of the original field.
This new field is considered alphanumeric even if the original field
is numeric. Reference modification can be used anywhere an alphanumeric field is allowed.

The length can be omitted, in which case the length is assumed to
extend to the end of the field. For example,

```
IF ACCOUNT-CODE (9:) > '59' . . .
```

This compares the last two characters of ACCOUNT-CODE. The
colon is still required, even though the length is omitted.

The starting position and length do not have to be literals. They can
✳ be specified by data names or even arithmetic expressions.✳

```
MOVE ACCOUNT-CODE (CODE-POSITION : CODE-PART * 2) TO . . .
```

The value of the expression will be truncated if necessary to make it an integer. Reference modification cannot be used to access locations outside the named field. The length must not extend beyond the end of the field.

Reference modification can be used with subscripted or indexed data-names. The reference modifier is coded after the subscript or index.

```
                  ↳ field
MOVE SPACES TO TABLE-FIELD (TABLE-INDEX) (3:4)
```

Reference modification makes it possible to refer to parts of a field without resorting to a lot of redefining or to the very inefficient one-character OCCURS field.

DE-EDITING NUMERIC FIELDS

VS COBOL II makes it possible to convert the value in a numeric-edited field back to its internal numeric representation. This process is referred to as **de-editing**. The MOVE statement allows the numeric-edited field to be MOVEd to a numeric field.

```
05   PRINT-AMOUNT   PICTURE $ZZ,ZZ9.99-.
05   CALC-AMOUNT    PICTURE S9(5)V99  PACKED-DECIMAL.

MOVE PRINT-AMOUNT TO CALC-AMOUNT
```

If PRINT-AMOUNT contains '$1,427.05−' then the MOVE statement will put the value −1427.05 in CALC-AMOUNT.

ENHANCEMENTS FOR TABLES

There are a number of welcome improvements in VS COBOL II related to defining and processing tables. OCCURS clauses can now be nested to seven levels instead of only three. To correspond with this, a PERFORM statement can have up to six AFTER phrases in the VARYING phrase, for a total of up to seven levels. The OCCURS . . . DEPENDING ON clause can specify zero as the minimum number of occurrences, so the variable part of a record can be completely absent.

```
01   PERSONNEL-RECORD.
     . . .
     05   DEPENDENT-DATA OCCURS 0 TO 12 TIMES
             DEPENDING ON NUMBER-OF-DEPENDENTS . . .
```

If NUMBER-OF-DEPENDENTS is equal to zero, this record will not contain any occurrences of DEPENDENT-DATA.

Tables can be much larger than in the past. A single table can be up to 16 megabytes, compared to a maximum in OS/VS COBOL of 32K or 128K depending on the type of table. An OCCURS clause should therefore always define the true number of occurrences. There is no longer any need for "dummy" records after the definition to reserve space for a large table, and an index or subscript should never exceed the maximum shown in the definition.

There is also more latitude in the use of subscripts and indexes when referencing fields. Subscripting and indexing are no longer considered separate methods of reference. Indexing is now considered subscripting with an index-name, versus subscripting with a data-name or literal. This means that when the *Language Reference* manual refers to subscripting, it includes indexing as well. The practical effect of this change is that indexes and ordinary subscripts can be mixed in the same reference to a multidimension table.

```
ADD  TABLE-VALUE (TABLE-INDEX, ITEM-SUBSCRIPT) TO . . .
```

Relative subscripting, which is just like relative indexing, is also allowed in VS COBOL II. A data-name subscript can be followed by a + or − sign and an integer to change the effective value of the subscript for this reference only.

```
MOVE YEAR-SALES (YEAR-SUB + 1) TO YEAR-SALES (YEAR-SUB)
```

INITIALIZING FIELDS AND TABLES

VS COBOL II allows the entries in a table to be initialized by VALUE clauses in the table definition. That is, VALUE can be specified for items that have multiple occurrences.

```
05   REGION-ENTRY OCCURS 20 TIMES INDEXED BY REGION-INDX.
     10   REGION-NUMBER   PICTURE 99        VALUE ZERO.
     10   REGION-NAME     PICTURE X(20)  VALUE 'UNKNOWN'.
```

Every occurrence of the fields in the table will have the same initial value. If VALUE is used with OCCURS . . . DEPENDING ON, all of the occurrences, up to the specified maximum, are initialized with the VALUE.

A new statement in VS COBOL II, the **INITIALIZE** statement, provides a convenient way to initialize groups of fields, including tables, when VALUE clauses cannot be used. This would be the case with records in the FILE SECTION or LINKAGE SECTION, and when the fields must be reinitialized during execution.

In its simplest form, INITIALIZE moves a standard value to one field.

```
INITIALIZE TRANSACTION-COUNT
```

This statement will move an initial value to TRANSACTION-COUNT. The value that is moved depends on whether the field is numeric or nonnumeric. Since TRANSACTION-COUNT is presumably numeric, ZERO would be moved to it. If the field were alphabetic or alphanumeric, SPACES would be moved to it. The result is exactly the same as a MOVE of a figurative constant.

```
MOVE ZERO TO TRANSACTION-COUNT
```

More than one field can be INITIALIZEd in the same statement.

```
INITIALIZE TRANSACTION-COUNT ERROR-CODE
```

Again the effect is the same as if a MOVE statement had been written for each field, with the figurative constant ZERO or SPACES as appropriate for each one.

The examples given so far do not have any particular advantage over a MOVE statement. One of the features that makes INITIALIZE more powerful is the way it acts on a group item. An INITIALIZE of a group item is equivalent to an INITIALIZE of each elementary field in the group. Below is a group item with a few fields of different types, and an INITIALIZE statement for the group.

```
01  REGION-RECORD.
    05  REGION-NUMBER   PICTURE 99.
    05  REGION-NAME     PICTURE X(20).
    05  REGION-SALES    PICTURE S9(6)V99 PACKED-DECIMAL.
    .  .  .
    INITIALIZE REGION-RECORD
```

This statement will move ZERO to REGION-NUMBER and REGION-SALES, and SPACES to REGION-NAME. Since the action is the same as a MOVE of a figurative constant, each of the numeric fields will be INITIALIZEd to zero in the appropriate format. If a group contains many fields, this is an easy way to clear all of them with one source statement.

If a field that is being INITIALIZEd is redefined, only the first definition is used by the INITIALIZE. Here is the same group item, with a REDEFINES added.

```
01   REGION-RECORD.
     05   REGION-NUMBER   PICTURE 99.
     05   REGION-CODE REDEFINES REGION-NUMBER   PICTURE XX.
     05   REGION-NAME      PICTURE X(20).
     05   REGION-SALES     PICTURE S9(6)V99   PACKED-DECIMAL.
```

The statement INITIALIZE REGION-RECORD will still move ZERO to REGION-NUMBER, ignoring REGION-CODE. However, you can write

```
INITIALIZE REGION-CODE
```

This will move SPACES to REGION-CODE.

INITIALIZE will not move anything to a field with no name, or with the name FILLER, even if it is within a group that is being INITIAL-IZEd.

```
01   REGION-RECORD.
     05   REGION-NUMBER   PICTURE 99.
     05   REGION NAME      PICTURE X(20).
     05                    PICTURE X(5).
     05   REGION-SALES     PICTURE S9(6)V99   PACKED-DECIMAL.
```

The statement INITIALIZE REGION-RECORD will not change the contents of the PICTURE X(5) field. An INITIALIZE of a group item is the same as an INITIALIZE of each elementary item in the group, and there would be no way to write a statement referring to the unnamed field individually.

The biggest value of the group-level INITIALIZE is in clearing a table. Suppose we have the following table definition.

```
01   REGION-TABLE
     05   REGION-ENTRY OCCURS 20 TIMES INDEXED BY REGION-INDX.
          10   REGION-NUMBER   PICTURE 99.
          10   REGION-NAME      PICTURE X(20).
```

One short statement will clear the entire table. *SOMETIMES DOESN'T WORK TO CLEAR TABLE W/ SPACES

```
INITIALIZE REGION-TABLE
```

This will move ZERO to every occurrence of REGION-NUMBER, and SPACES to every occurrence of REGION-NAME. Notice that the INITIALIZE statement refers to the group-level name that contains the table entries, not to the name that has the OCCURS clause in its definition. One unfortunate limitation is that INITIALIZE cannot be used in this way to clear a variable-length table (i.e., a table defined with OCCURS . . . DEPENDING ON).

One entry in a table can be cleared by referring to the group-level name of the table entry, with the appropriate index or subscript. If REGION-INDX is set to 4, the following statement will INITIALIZE the fourth entry in the table.

```
INITIALIZE REGION-ENTRY (REGION-INDX)
```

It is permissible to refer to one entry in a variable-length table in this way. This means that a variable-length table can be cleared by using this INITIALIZE statement in a PERFORM loop.

You may not always want ZERO or SPACES as the initializing value for a field. The REPLACING phrase of the INITIALIZE statement provides a way to specify a different value for fields of a particular category, and looks like this.

```
INITIALIZE REGION-TABLE REPLACING NUMERIC DATA BY 1
```

With the table definition above, this statement will MOVE 1 to every occurrence of REGION-NUMBER. It will not change the contents of any of the occurrences of REGION-NAME. When an INITIALIZE statement contains the REPLACING phrase, it operates only on fields of the category specified in the REPLACING phrase. Any of the five standard data categories can be specified in the REPLACING phrase, namely,

```
ALPHABETIC
ALPHANUMERIC
NUMERIC
ALPHANUMERIC-EDITED
NUMERIC-EDITED
```

Remember that ALPHABETIC means fields with only the letter A in the PICTURE; fields with X in the PICTURE are ALPHANUMERIC.

More than one category can be specified in the same statement if the group that is being INITIALIZEd contains fields of different categories.

```
INITIALIZE REGION-TABLE
    REPLACING NUMERIC DATA BY 1
               ALPHANUMERIC DATA BY HIGH-VALUE
```

The value in the REPLACING phrase does not have to be a literal or figurative constant, but can be the name of a field containing the desired value.

```
05   UNKNOWN-REGION   PICTURE X(20)   VALUE 'UNKNOWN'.

INITIALIZE REGION-TABLE
    REPLACING ALPHANUMERIC DATA BY UNKNOWN-REGION
```

This statement will move the word "UNKNOWN" to each occurrence of REGION-NAME.

Note that specifying a single character in the REPLACING phrase does not fill an alphanumeric field with that character. INITIALIZE always follows the rules for MOVE. The following statement will put into each occurrence of REGION-NAME a single X followed by 19 spaces.

```
INITIALIZE REGION-TABLE REPLACING ALPHANUMERIC DATA BY 'X'
```

To fill REGION-NAME with Xs, use the ALL literal figurative constant like this.

```
INITIALIZE REGION-TABLE
    REPLACING ALPHANUMERIC DATA BY ALL 'X'
```

Also notice that a VALUE clause in the definition of a field in the DATA DIVISION has no effect on the INITIALIZE statement. The value moved to a field by INITIALIZE is whatever is specified in the REPLACING phrase, or the default of ZERO or SPACES.

LENGTH OF SPECIAL REGISTER

The new LENGTH OF special register contains the length (in bytes) of any field. Each elementary or group-level item in the DATA DIVISION has a LENGTH OF special register, which is referenced by writing

LENGTH OF identifier

The LENGTH OF special register can be used almost anywhere a numeric field or literal is allowed. However, it cannot be used as a receiving field or as a subscript. It is defined as a four-byte COMPUTATIONAL field with the implicit definition

PICTURE 9(9) COMPUTATIONAL.

Here is how it would look in some statements.

ADD LENGTH OF ITEM-PRICE TO BYTE-COUNT

MOVE LENGTH OF MASTER-RECORD TO RECORD-SIZE

The identifier in the LENGTH OF phrase does not have to be subscripted, even if it is defined with an OCCURS clause and would normally require a subscript. There is no need to identify the particular occurrence since all occurrences of a field are the same length.

LENGTH OF can refer to a variable-length area, that is, a group level that contains an item defined with OCCURS . . . DEPENDING ON. Remember, though, that the length is given in bytes, not the number of occurrences.

IMPROVEMENTS FOR VARIABLE-LENGTH RECORDS

The new **RECORD IS VARYING** clause can be used instead of RECORD CONTAINS in an FD or SD. It provides a new way of handling variable-length records, and looks like this.

RECORD IS VARYING FROM 96 TO 3874 CHARACTERS
                  DEPENDING ON TRANS-REC-SIZE

The biggest difference between RECORD IS VARYING and RECORD CONTAINS is the **DEPENDING ON** phrase. TRANS-REC-SIZE in the example is an unsigned numeric field defined by the programmer to contain the length of each record. For input, the READ (or RETURN for a SORT file) will put into this field the actual length, in bytes, of the record that was read. For output, the program must place in this field the length in bytes of the record to be written. This overrides the length of the 01-level record that is named in the WRITE, REWRITE, or RELEASE statement. The record length in the

▷ ALSO WRITTEN AS :
  FD TRANS-FILE
     RECORD CONTAINS 96 TO 3874 CHARACTERS .

  01 TRANS-REC
     05 FIXED-PORTION   PIC X(96).
     05 TRANS-REC-SIZE PIC X(2).
     05 RECORD OCCURS 0 TO 50
        depending on TRANS-REC-SIZE.

DEPENDING ON field is the length of the data portion of the record as the COBOL program sees it; it does not include the control fields that precede the data in variable-length records.

If RECORD IS VARYING is used, the file will have variable-length records regardless of the lengths of the 01-level record descriptions. The DEPENDING ON phrase provides a way to deal with unusual formats or with variations in size that cannot easily be described with OCCURS ... DEPENDING ON or with a few different record descriptions of different lengths. For the more common types of variable-length records, RECORD IS VARYING can be used without the DEPENDING ON phrase if the length in bytes is not needed. For that matter, RECORD IS VARYING and RECORD CONTAINS can be omitted altogether.

The interpretation of one form of the RECORD CONTAINS clause has been changed. OS/VS COBOL always determined the record size and format (fixed or variable) from the 01-level record descriptions, essentially disregarding the RECORD CONTAINS clause. VS COBOL II still works this way if RECORD CONTAINS *n* TO *m* CHARACTERS is coded. In VS COBOL II, however, RECORD CONTAINS *n* CHARACTERS (with only one length) makes the records fixed-length regardless of the lengths of the 01 levels. This is true even if there are 01s of different lengths or a record has an OCCURS ... DEPENDING ON. In most cases there is no warning message if the record descriptions do not agree with the RECORD CONTAINS clause.

A MOVE of a variable-length record is a little simpler in many cases because of another improvement in VS COBOL II. This involves the fairly common situation where the object of an OCCURS ... DEPENDING ON clause is part of the same group level as the OCCURS itself.

```
01   CUSTOMER-RECORD.
     05   CUSTOMER-NUMBER   PICTURE X(8).
          . . .
     05   OPEN-ORDERS.
          10   NUMBER-OF-ORDERS   PICTURE S99   BINARY.
          10   ORDER-NUMBER OCCURS 1 TO 50 TIMES
                    DEPENDING ON NUMBER-OF-ORDERS   PICTURE 9(6).
```

Suppose the program has to MOVE the order information from another record into OPEN-ORDERS. With earlier versions of COBOL, it would be necessary to first MOVE the number of occurrences from the other record to NUMBER-OF-ORDERS in order to set OPEN-ORDERS to the proper length. Only then could the group level be MOVEd. In this situation VS COBOL II does not use the number of occurrences in the receiving field to determine the length for the MOVE. Instead it assumes that the receiving field is the maximum length or, in other words, the maximum number of occurrences. This eliminates the need to MOVE the number of occurrences before moving the record.

when variable length field is last field of record.

If there is another field in the record after the OCCURS, however, the situation changes.

```
01   CUSTOMER-RECORD.
     05   CUSTOMER-NUMBER   PICTURE X(8).
          . . .
     05   OPEN-ORDERS.
          10   NUMBER-OF-ORDERS   PICTURE S99 BINARY.
          10   ORDER-NUMBER OCCURS 1 TO 50 TIMES
                    DEPENDING ON NUMBER-OF-ORDERS   PICTURE 9(6).
     05   CREDIT-RATING   PICTURE XX.
```

In this case, using the maximum number of occurrences could possibly overlay the data that follows the variable-length table. Therefore, the compiler goes back to the previous method and uses the actual number of occurrences specified by NUMBER-OF-ORDERS. This means that, as in the past, the program must set NUMBER-OF-ORDERS to the proper value before doing the group-level MOVE.

Exercises

1.   Define a symbolic character to represent the plus-or-minus sign, which has the hexadecimal code 9E.

2.   KEYED-INPUT is defined as PICTURE X(30). Write a statement to change any lowercase letters in KEYED-INPUT to uppercase, without changing any other characters in the field. Define any other fields that may be needed.

3.   Write one statement to initialize the following table, setting the PACKED-DECIMAL fields to zero and the state codes and state names to HIGH-VALUES.

```
05   STATE-DATA-TABLE.
     10   STATE-DATA OCCURS 50 TIMES INDEXED BY STATE-INDEX.
```

```
    15   STATE-CODE        PIC XX.
    15   STATE-NAME        PIC X(14).
    15   ST-TOTAL-SALES    PIC S9(7)V99   PACKED-DECIMAL.
    15   ST-SALES-QUOTA    PIC S9(7)V99   PACKED-DECIMAL.
    15   SALES-TAX-RATE    PIC SV999      PACKED-DECIMAL.
```

How could the data definition be changed to eliminate the need for an initializing statement if the table only has to be initialized once at the beginning of the job?

4. Write a statement or statements to clear the following table to zeros.

```
05   STORE-LIST.
    10   STORE-DATA OCCURS 1 TO 200 TIMES
            DEPENDING ON NUMBER-OF-STORES
            INDEXED BY STORE-INDEX.
        15   STORE-NUMBER       PICTURE 9999.
        15   STORE-ZIP-CODE     PICTURE 9(5).
        15   STORE-SQUARE-FEET  PICTURE 9(6).
```

Elementary Moves: When the data category of the receiving field is:
Alphabetic. left aligned. If size of sending < size of receiving, padding
of spaces to the right. If size of sending is > size of receiving,
truncation on right occurs. *

Alpha numeric / Alphanumeric edited
   Alignment of data to the left. Padding / Truncation occurs to
the right of field. *
* If specified, Justified clause overrides this rule.
   If sending has an operational sign, the unsigned value is used.
   If the operational sign occupies a separate character, that
character is not moved and the size of the sending item
is considered to be 1 less character than the actual size.

Numeric or Numeric Edited
   Alignment of data on decimal pt. truncation or padding
w/ zeros at either end. If no decimal is specified, it is assumed
to be specified immediately to the right.

If both sending and receiving items are signed, then the sign of
the sending item is moved (and converted in format if necessary)
to the receiving item.
If the receiving item is signed but the sending item is not
then a positive operational sign is generated for the
receiving item.

Chapter 6

Miscellaneous New Language Features

This chapter covers various new language features in VS COBOL II that provide some useful new capabilities. At the end of the chapter, some improvements in the *Language Reference* manual are described.

LOWERCASE LETTERS

Most computer systems today have the capability to enter, display, and print lowercase letters as well as uppercase. In keeping with this, VS COBOL II allows the use of lowercase letters anywhere in the program. They are considered equivalent to uppercase. For example, all of the following are the same data-name.

```
ACCOUNT-NUMBER
Account-Number
account-number
```

Reserved words can also be written in any combination of uppercase and lowercase.

```
GO TO
go to
GO to
```

Internally, the compiler translates the lowercase letters to uppercase. In the maps and cross-reference listings, names are shown in all uppercase.

In literals, of course, lowercase letters remain distinct characters, and are kept exactly as they are coded.

Programs can, of course, still be written in all uppercase. In this book, all of the programming examples and all COBOL words in the text are printed in uppercase for clarity.

If you choose to use lowercase, be careful about the CAPS mode in the ISPF/PDF Edit profile, and the position of the dual-case/mono-case switch on your CRT terminal. Edit translates lowercase input to uppercase if CAPS mode is on. If CAPS is off, it leaves lowercase letters alone. When Edit reads in a file or member, it automatically sets CAPS mode off or on depending on whether or not there are already lowercase letters in the file. Most CRTs have a dual-case/mono-case switch that determines how lowercase letters are displayed. It is typically marked "A" on one side and "A,a" on the other side. The "A" setting displays lowercase letters as uppercase, which affects only the display. In the file the letters are still lowercase. This switch should be set to "A,a" so that lowercase letters are displayed as such. Otherwise you may not realize that CAPS is off and you might inadvertently enter lowercase letters in literals or other places where you want uppercase.

CHANGES IN CLASS CONDITIONS

Now that COBOL recognizes lowercase letters, the ALPHABETIC class test (IF field-name IS ALPHABETIC) will consider a field to be ALPHABETIC if it contains any combination of uppercase letters, lowercase letters, and spaces. In earlier versions of COBOL, only uppercase letters and spaces were allowed. Two new class tests allow the program to distinguish between uppercase and lowercase. **ALPHABETIC-UPPER** is identical to what ALPHABETIC used to be. It is true if the field contains only uppercase letters and spaces. The **ALPHABETIC-LOWER** class condition is true if the field contains only lowercase letters and spaces.

Class conditions are no longer limited to just the few classes that are predefined in COBOL. The programmer can define new classes in the SPECIAL-NAMES paragraph of the ENVIRONMENT DIVISION, and these can be used in class conditions just like the standard classes. Here is an example of a class definition.

```
ENVIRONMENT DIVISION.
CONFIGURATION SECTION.
```

```
SPECIAL-NAMES.
    CLASS HEX-DIGITS IS '0123456789ABCDEF'.
```

With this definition, the HEX-DIGITS class test will be true if the field being tested contains only the characters listed in the definition: 0 through 9 and A through F. It could be used like this.

```
IF IN-FIELD-1 IS HEX-DIGITS
    PERFORM PROCESS-HEX-INPUT
END-IF
```

NOT can be used with a programmer-defined class name, just as it is with the standard classes.

```
IF HEX-FIELD-1 NOT HEX-DIGITS
    PERFORM ERROR-ROUTINE-1
END-IF
```

Programmer-defined class tests can only be applied to nonnumeric fields.

There are other ways to specify the characters that are included in the class. They can be listed as individual one-character literals instead of in a single string.

```
CLASS MATH-SYMBOLS IS '+' '-' '*' '/'.
```

A range of characters can be specified with THROUGH or THRU, as in a VALUE clause.

```
CLASS CODE-LETTERS IS 'S' THRU 'Z'.
```

Instead of literals, the characters can be specified by their positions in the complete character set, in the same way that a symbolic character is specified. (This is explained in detail in Chapter 5.) This can be useful when the class contains unusual characters.

```
CLASS SUPERSCRIPT-DIGITS IS 177 THRU 186.
```

This example defines a class that includes the characters with hexadecimal codes B0 through B9.

SET CONDITION-NAME TO TRUE

A new form of the SET statement provides a way to make a condition-name (an 88 level) true. Take the following definition of a field.

```
05   ACCOUNT-STATUS   PICTURE X.
     88   PAST-DUE   VALUE 'L'.
```

In order to make the PAST-DUE condition true, an 'L' must be moved to ACCOUNT-STATUS. In VS COBOL II, the following can be written instead of a MOVE statement.

```
SET PAST-DUE TO TRUE
```

This has the same effect as

```
MOVE 'L' TO ACCOUNT-STATUS
```

This SET statement does not really provide any new capability, but it does have two advantages over the MOVE. It references the condition name instead of the name of the field. This can make the program a little easier to understand because the same name is used in the statement that sets the condition and in the IF statement that tests it. Also, it avoids coding the value in more than one place in the program, so if the value is ever changed, the change has to be made only in the 88-level entry where it is defined.

If the condition name has more than one value, the first value is the one used by the SET statement. Here is the 88 level with some additional values.

```
05   ACCOUNT-STATUS   PICTURE X.
     88   PAST-DUE   VALUE 'D' 'L' 'Q'.
```

Now the statement

```
SET PAST-DUE TO TRUE
```

will move a 'D' to ACCOUNT-STATUS.

There is one situation in which the SET . . . TO TRUE statement does not work exactly the same way as a MOVE. Technically the SET makes the contents of the field what they would have been if the VALUE in the 88 level had been coded for the field. In most cases the result is the same as a MOVE of the literal to the field. The distinction makes a difference only in the rare case that the PICTURE for the field contains editing characters, because VALUE does not perform the editing when it assigns the value of the literal to the field.

NEW FILE STATUS CODES

New FILE STATUS codes in VS COBOL II provide more detailed information about I/O errors than the old codes. In OS/VS COBOL several different errors could produce the same value in the FILE STATUS field and it was often difficult to determine the precise cause. The new codes in VS COBOL II eliminate many of these situations. Nine of the 16 new codes represent conditions that all caused code 92 ("logic error") in OS/VS COBOL. One of these is code 38; the other eight all have 4 as the first digit. For example, code 46 is a READ after end-of-file and code 47 is a READ when the file is not open.

Table 6.1 lists the new codes with a brief statement of the meaning of each one. More detailed explanations of all the codes, new and old, appear in the *Language Reference* manual. Note that codes 05 and 07 might not be considered error conditions in particular situations. Code 04, even though it has zero as the first digit, is likely to be considered an error in most cases.

Even with these new codes there is not enough detail for some VSAM errors. As many as 15 different VSAM error codes can produce the same FILE STATUS code. In OS/VS COBOL there was no other information available. VS COBOL II provides an additional FILE STATUS field for VSAM files that makes the actual VSAM error codes available to the COBOL program. The additional field is specified by a second name in the FILE STATUS clause of the FILE-CONTROL entry for the file.

```
SELECT ACCOUNT-MASTER   ASSIGN TO ACTMAST
    ORGANIZATION IS INDEXED
    ACCESS IS RANDOM
    RECORD KEY IS ACCOUNT-NUMBER
    FILE STATUS IS   ACCT-MAST-STATUS-1   ACCT-MAST-STATUS-2.
```

The first FILE STATUS field, ACCT-MAST-STATUS-1 in the example, is the same two-byte field as before, and will contain the regular

Table 6.1   **New FILE STATUS Codes**

Code	Meaning
04	Wrong length record on READ
05	Successful OPEN of OPTIONAL file that is not present
07	OPEN or CLOSE with NO REWIND, REEL, UNIT, or FOR REMOVAL and file is not on a reel or unit medium
14	On sequential READ, relative record number too large for RELATIVE KEY field
35	Non-OPTIONAL file not present
37	Device will not support the type of file defined in the program
38	OPEN after CLOSE WITH LOCK
39	Program and file DCB parameters conflict
41	OPEN for file that is already open
42	CLOSE for file that is not open
43	REWRITE or DELETE not preceded by successful READ
44	REWRITE record with different length, or WRITE or REWRITE with length outside of RECORD IS VARYING limits
46	Sequential READ after end-of-file or after error on previous READ
47	READ with file not open for INPUT or I/O
48	WRITE with file not open for OUTPUT, I/O, or EXTEND
49	REWRITE or DELETE with file not open for I/O

two-digit FILE STATUS code. The second field, which is the new one, must be defined as a six-byte area containing three halfword BINARY subfields. An appropriate definition would look like this.

```
05  ACCT-MAST-STATUS-2  BINARY.
    10  ACCT-MAST-RETURN-CODE      PICTURE 99.
    10  ACCT-MAST-FUNCTION-CODE    PICTURE 9.
    10  ACCT-MAST-FEEDBACK-CODE    PICTURE 999.
```

These three codes are taken directly from a VSAM control block called the **request parameter list**, or **RPL**. All of the possible codes and their meanings are listed in the IBM reference manual describing the macros used for VSAM processing in assembler language in the particular operating system. For MVS/XA the manual is *MVS/Extended Architecture VSAM Administration: Macro Instruction Reference*. (There are different versions of this manual, with different order numbers, for the different versions of MVS/XA.) The codes are in Chapter 1, "Macro

Instruction Return Codes and Reason Codes." The COBOL manuals
and the VSAM manuals use different names for two of the codes. Here
is a list of the two sets of names, showing how they correspond.

COBOL Term	VSAM Term
return code	return code
function code	component code
feedback code	reason code

These new FILE STATUS fields are meaningful only if an error occurs.
If the first FILE STATUS field is zero, meaning that the I/O operation was successful, then the contents of the three new fields are not
meaningful. Also, if the return code is zero, then the function code
and feedback code are not meaningful. If the first FILE STATUS field
contains a non-zero error code, but the VSAM return code is zero, the
error condition was detected by COBOL before it called VSAM.

It is generally not necessary for the COBOL program to check or inter-
pret the codes in the second FILE STATUS field for VSAM. However,
the new area should be defined for every VSAM file, so that the information will at least be available in a dump if an unexpected problem
occurs. If the program prints error messages for VSAM errors, the new
codes should be included in the messages.

IMPROVEMENTS FOR SORT AND MERGE

In VS COBOL II, the INPUT PROCEDURE and the OUTPUT PRO-
CEDURE in a SORT statement, and the OUTPUT PROCEDURE in
a MERGE statement can be paragraphs instead of sections. (Actually,
OS/VS COBOL allowed the use of paragraphs, but issued a warning
message. VS COBOL II permits paragraphs officially.) Many programmers are unfamiliar with the rules for sections in the PROCEDURE
DIVISION, so sections tend to be a source of confusion. Removing
the requirement from the SORT and MERGE statements eliminates
the only place where most programmers have to use sections. This
should eliminate much of the confusion.

The SORT and MERGE statements in VS COBOL II allow more than
one file in the GIVING phrase. A copy of the sorted or merged file
is written to each output file, so multiple copies of the output can be
produced by a single SORT or MERGE.

Another improvement in the SORT statement is the new phrase **WITH DUPLICATES IN ORDER**. When this is specified in the SORT statement, records that have the same sort key will be kept in the same relative order as in the input. Without this phrase, records with equal sort keys can be in any order in the sorted file. A SORT with the new phrase looks like this.

```
SORT S-ITEM-FILE ON ASCENDING KEY S-ITEM-NUMBER
    WITH DUPLICATES IN ORDER
    INPUT PROCEDURE SELECT-RECORDS
    OUTPUT PROCEDURE PRINT-REPORT
```

The same thing could be accomplished in older versions of COBOL by specifying additional sort options in a control file. Having it in the source program is not only much simpler, but also puts all of the sort specifications in one place and clearly documents that the option is being used.

There are some improvements in the interface between VS COBOL II and the sort program that do not involve changes in the COBOL language. These are discussed in Chapter 15.

SOME SMALL PROCEDURE DIVISION IMPROVEMENTS

Two new relational operators can be used for comparisons in VS COBOL II. They are **LESS THAN OR EQUAL TO** and **GREATER THAN OR EQUAL TO**. These can also be written with the symbols $<=$ and $>=$ respectively. The new operators mean exactly what they say. They can sometimes simplify a condition or avoid the need for NOT where it might cause confusion. Here are some examples.

```
IF QUANTITY-ON-HAND <= REORDER-POINT
    PERFORM CREATE-PURCHASE-ORDER
END-IF

PERFORM READ-MASTER-FILE
    UNTIL MASTER-KEY >= TRANSACTION-KEY
```

The new relational operators can be used in any relation condition just like the older relational operators LESS THAN, EQUAL TO, and GREATER THAN. NOT cannot be used with the two new relational operators, but it isn't needed. Instead of NOT $<=$, which is invalid, simply use GREATER. For NOT $>=$, use LESS.

In an ADD statement with GIVING, the word TO can now be written before the last of the items being added. (This is another case of something that OS/VS COBOL allowed, but flagged with a warning message.) Here are a couple of examples.

```
ADD REGULAR-HOURS TO OVERTIME-HOURS GIVING TOTAL-HOURS
```

```
ADD JAN-SALES FEB-SALES TO MAR-SALES GIVING 1ST-QTR-SALES
```

This does not change the processing at all, but makes the statement read better.

The new **DAY-OF-WEEK** special register in the ACCEPT statement provides a number representing the day of the week. (Technically the sending fields in this form of ACCEPT are conceptual data items, not special registers. The distinction is not important.)

```
ACCEPT DAY-NUMBER FROM DAY-OF-WEEK
```

DAY-OF-WEEK has an implicit PICTURE 9. It contains a value from 1 through 7, representing Monday through Sunday.

MANIPULATING THE SOURCE

In earlier versions of COBOL, source coding brought in by a COPY statement was not allowed to contain another COPY statement. In VS COBOL II, COPYed coding may itself contain other COPY statements. This is called a **nested COPY**. This facility can be useful if, for example, a certain group of fields is contained in several differ-ent records. The group can be a separate member that is COPYed into each record description, and the record descriptions can still be COPYed into the programs that use them.

There is no fixed limit to the number of levels that COPYs can be nested. The REPLACING phrase cannot be used in any COPY state-ment involved in nesting—neither in the COPY in the program nor in any COPY statement in a COPYed member.

Unlike executable statements in the PROCEDURE DIVISION, a COPY statement must still end with a period in VS COBOL II.

A new compiler-directing statement, **REPLACE**, works like the REPLACING phrase of the COPY statement, but it operates on all of the source, not just COPYed code. The text to be replaced and the replacement text are specified in the same way as in a COPY. Replacement starts immediately after the REPLACE statement and continues to the next REPLACE statement or to the end of the program. REPLACE OFF can be used to end replacement without starting any new replacement. Like COPY, a REPLACE statement must end with a period.

The action of the REPLACE statement is very similar to doing global replacement with whatever text editor is used to write programs. With the editor, the change is permanent and the saved source appears just as it will be compiled. With REPLACE, on the other hand, the change is made on the fly each time the program is compiled, and the saved source does not reflect the changes. If a permanent change must be made to a program, it makes more sense to use the editor. REPLACE might be useful to make a temporary change for testing.

IMPROVEMENTS IN THE
LANGUAGE REFERENCE MANUAL

A few changes have been made to the IBM *Language Reference* manual for VS COBOL II. One change is a totally new type of diagram for language formats. Figure 6.1 shows Format 1 of the ADD statement in both the traditional and new styles. The new type of diagram, sometimes called a **railroad-track** diagram, is practically self explanatory. To read it, just follow the lines from left to right or as indicated by arrows. Anything on the main path, like the words ADD and TO, is required. A line that branches into a stack indicates either a choice or something optional, and any branch can be followed. For example, after the word ADD either identifier-1 or literal-1 may be chosen. The word ROUNDED is optional. The hooked arrows above the main path indicate that part of the format can be repeated. These new diagrams are much easier to use. One reason is that it is no longer necessary to match up pairs of brackets and braces to determine what part of a complex format is optional or can be repeated.

The format diagrams still show reserved words in uppercase letters and programmer-defined names in lowercase. But either type of word can be coded in any combination of uppercase and lowercase letters, as described at the beginning of this chapter.

In its COBOL language manuals over the years, IBM has tried various ways of marking IBM extensions to the ANSI standard. In the newest VS COBOL II *Language Reference*, IBM extensions are printed in blue.

Figure 6.1   Format diagrams. Top: Traditional style. Bottom: New IBM railroad-track style.

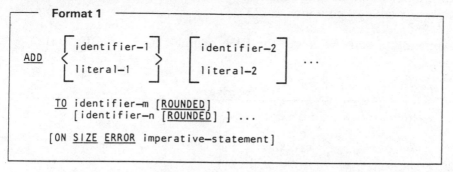

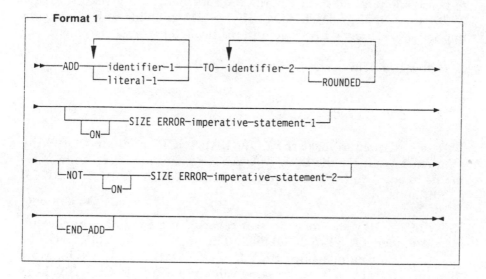

This avoids breaking up the text for the majority of COBOL programmers, who don't have to adhere to the standard, yet clearly identifies extensions for those who need to know.

The organization of the *Language Reference* manual has also been improved. A header at the top of every page indicates the statement, clause, or other topic covered on that page. All of the PROCEDURE DIVISION statements are in one alphabetical sequence instead of being grouped in categories. These changes make it much faster and easier to find information in the manual, often without having to refer to the index or table of contents.

Appendix F describes all of the IBM manuals for VS COBOL II.

Exercises

1. Below are two field descriptions.

```
05   EMPLOYEE-NAME   PICTURE X(20).
05   SOC-SEC-NUM     PICTURE X(11).
```

Write the statements needed to move EMPLOYEE-NAME to another field named PRINT-NAME if EMPLOYEE-NAME contains only uppercase letters and spaces. Write the statements to move SOC-SEC-NUM to PRINT-NUM if SOC-SEC-NUM contains only digits and hyphens. Code any CLASS definitions needed by these statements.

2. Below is a field defined with an 88-level condition name.

```
05   BALANCE-SWITCH   PICTURE X.
     88   LOW-BALANCE   VALUE 'L'.
```

Write a statement to make the LOW-BALANCE condition true. Write a statement to make the LOW-BALANCE condition false. Write statements to add 1 to LOW-BALANCE-COUNT if the LOW-BALANCE condition is true.

3. Write a SORT statement to sort records in ascending sequence on a field named CUST-ACCOUNT. The input to the SORT will be supplied by a routine named BUILD-CUSTOMER-RECORDS. More than one record will have the same value in CUST-ACCOUNT; keep such records in the same sequence in which BUILD-CUSTOMER-RECORDS produces them. Write two copies of the sorted file, one copy to a file named CUST-SORT-1 and the other to CUST-SORT-2.

Chapter 7

Subprograms and Sharing Data

Communication between calling and called programs is greatly enhanced in VS COBOL II with new features that make it possible to do some interesting things not previously possible in COBOL. In addition, a COBOL program can now access storage addresses and change the storage location referenced by a data description in the LINKAGE SECTION.

NEW TYPES OF PARAMETERS FOR CALL

Ordinarily, when a field is passed as a parameter in the USING phrase of a CALL statement, the field is in only one place in main storage. Both the calling program and the called program act on the same storage location when they reference the field. This method of passing parameters is usually called passing parameters **by reference**. If the called program changes the field and the calling program uses the field after the CALL, the calling program gets the new value that the called program put there.

Parameters are still usually passed by reference in VS COBOL II, but a new way of passing parameters is also available. With the new method, the CALL moves the contents of the parameter to a temporary work area, and the temporary work area is passed to the subprogram instead of the original field. This method is referred to as passing the parameter **BY CONTENT**. (In other programming languages this same method is often called passing a parameter **by value**.)

A CALL statement that passes a parameter BY CONTENT is written like this.

```
CALL 'SUBPROG' USING BY CONTENT ACCOUNT-NUMBER
```

This statement will pass to the subprogram a temporary field that is the same size as ACCOUNT-NUMBER and contains whatever was in ACCOUNT-NUMBER just before the CALL. When SUBPROG uses this parameter, it will get the same value as if the parameter had been passed by reference. However, if SUBPROG modifies the field, it changes only the temporary area, not the real ACCOUNT-NUMBER field in the calling program.

When the subprogram returns control to the calling program, the contents of the temporary area are *not* moved back to the original field. The called program was given the CONTENT of the field, but it is prevented from modifying the field in the calling program. When the calling program uses the field again, it will still have the same value that it had before the CALL, regardless of any changes the called program may have made.

A nonnumeric literal can now be used as a parameter in a CALL because passing parameters BY CONTENT prevents the called program from modifying the original field. A literal can be passed only BY CONTENT since the value of a literal must remain constant.

```
CALL 'SUBPROG' USING BY CONTENT 'AZ'
```

This statement will pass a two-byte field containing the letters AZ to the subprogram. In the LINKAGE SECTION of the subprogram, the definition of the field is the same for a literal as for a regular field. It might look like this.

```
LINKAGE SECTION.
77 STATE-CODE   PICTURE XX.

PROCEDURE DIVISION USING STATE-CODE.
```

If this subprogram MOVEs different characters to STATE-CODE and then uses STATE-CODE again during the same CALL, it will get the new characters. But the next time the calling program executes the CALL, the parameter will still be 'AZ'.

A figurative constant can also be used as a parameter passed BY CONTENT.

```
CALL 'SUBPROG' USING BY CONTENT HIGH-VALUE
```

A figurative constant is always passed as a one-byte field.

If BY CONTENT is not coded in the USING phrase, the parameters are passed by reference, as in the past. The words BY REFERENCE can be used to explicitly indicate that this is how the parameter is being passed.

```
CALL 'SUBPROG' USING BY REFERENCE ACCOUNT-NUMBER
```

In this case, the words BY REFERENCE are optional. This statement works exactly the same way as CALL always worked, whether or not BY REFERENCE is coded.

Fields passed BY REFERENCE, and fields, literals, or figurative constants passed BY CONTENT can be mixed in the same CALL statement. A BY REFERENCE or BY CONTENT phrase applies to all the parameters that follow it, until another such phrase appears.

```
CALL 'SUBPROG' USING BY CONTENT    'G'
                                   ITEM-COUNT
                 BY REFERENCE ACCOUNT-NUMBER
                              ITEM-NUMBER
```

In this statement, the one-byte literal 'G' and the field ITEM-COUNT are both passed BY CONTENT; ACCOUNT-NUMBER and ITEM-NUMBER are passed BY REFERENCE. If neither BY REFERENCE nor BY CONTENT is specified at the beginning of the list of parameters, BY REFERENCE is assumed. However, it is best to specify this explicitly, to avoid any possible confusion, when both types of parameters are used in the same CALL.

The subprogram that is CALLed by the preceding statement could define the parameters like this.

```
LINKAGE SECTION.
77  ACTION-CODE  PICTURE X.

01  ACCT-NUM.
    05  ACCT-BRANCH    PICTURE 99.
    05  ACCT-CUSTOMER  PICTURE 9(6).

01  ITEM-COUNT  PICTURE S999  PACKED-DECIMAL.

01  ITEM-NO  PICTURE 9(6).
```

```
PROCEDURE DIVISION
    USING ACTION-CODE ITEM-COUNT ACCT-NUM ITEM-NO.
```

Whether parameters are passed BY REFERENCE or BY CONTENT is irrelevant to the subprogram. There is no difference in the coding of the subprogram. For instance, the subprogram in this example would work just as well if the first parameter in the CALL were a one-byte field in the DATA DIVISION of the calling program instead of a literal. It could even be a literal in some CALLs and a field in other CALLs.

A LENGTH OF special register (described in Chapter 5) can be passed to a subprogram as a parameter. It must be passed BY CONTENT since it is not allowed to be modified. This can be particularly useful for CALLing a subprogram that can accept parameters of different lengths.

```
CALL 'SUBPROG' USING BY REFERENCE EMPLOYEE-NAME
                     BY CONTENT LENGTH OF EMPLOYEE-NAME
```

The subprogram would define the LENGTH OF parameter, the second parameter in the example, with the same specifications as the implicit definition of the LENGTH OF special register: PICTURE 9(9) COMPUTATIONAL. The parameter definitions in the subprogram for this CALL could be

```
LINKAGE SECTION.
77  STRING-LENGTH  PICTURE 9(9)  COMPUTATIONAL.

01  CHARACTER-STRING  PICTURE X(30).

PROCEDURE DIVISION USING CHARACTER-STRING STRING-LENGTH.
```

There is nothing in the subprogram that requires the second parameter to be a LENGTH OF special register. In the subprogram it is just a field in the LINKAGE SECTION, not a special register. The parameter in the CALL could just as well be a field passed BY REFERENCE, as long as the definition of the field is the same as what the subprogram expects.

ANOTHER CHANGE IN CALL

The CALL statement in VS COBOL II has a new conditional phrase, ON EXCEPTION. Statements in the ON EXCEPTION phrase will be executed if any error occurs in accessing the called program in a dynamic CALL. The error could be insufficient space to load the program, failure to find the program in the library, an I/O error in loading the program, and so on.

ON EXCEPTION also has a corresponding NOT phrase that is executed if no error occurs. Note that the NOT ON EXCEPTION phrase is executed after the called program returns control to the calling program.

In older versions of COBOL, the ON OVERFLOW phrase in the CALL statement used to be executed only for insufficient space. ON EXCEPTION covers not only insufficient space, but also any other error that can occur in accessing a called subprogram. ON OVER-FLOW can still be used, but in VS COBOL II it has the same meaning as ON EXCEPTION and will be executed for any error. However, ON OVERFLOW does not have a NOT form.

IMPROVEMENTS FOR SUBPROGRAMS

Normally, when a subprogram returns to the calling program and is later CALLed again, any data and files in the subprogram remain as they were when it returned. Sometimes, however, a fresh copy of the subprogram each time it is CALLed is preferred. When a dynamic CALL is used, this can be accomplished by executing a CANCEL for the subprogram before CALLing it again. VS COBOL II provides a way to achieve the same thing for either static or dynamic CALLs, and without the overhead of actually reloading the subprogram.

A subprogram can be given the **INITIAL** attribute by specifying INITIAL after the program name in the PROGRAM-ID paragraph.

```
IDENTIFICATION DIVISION.
PROGRAM-ID.   CALCRTNE   INITIAL.
```

When a subprogram has the INITIAL attribute, the subprogram is restored to its initial state each time it is CALLed, as if a new copy had been loaded. Any fields in WORKING-STORAGE for which a VALUE is specified will have that VALUE. This also means that no assumption can be made about the contents of fields that do not have a VALUE specified. They do not necessarily retain their contents from the last time the subprogram exited. If the INITIAL subprogram has any files, the files will not be open when the subprogram is CALLed again. Any open files are automatically CLOSEd by a GOBACK or an EXIT PROGRAM.

PERFORM statements in a VS COBOL II subprogram are always reinitialized each time it is CALLed, whether or not it is INITIAL.

There is an implicit EXIT PROGRAM following the last line of a VS COBOL II subprogram. If control falls through the end of the PROCEDURE DIVISION, control returns to the calling program as if an EXIT PROGRAM had been coded there.

A NEW WAY TO SHARE DATA AND FILES

In VS COBOL II, data and files can be shared among separately compiled programs without passing them from one program to another as parameters. This is accomplished by making the data area or file EXTERNAL. To make a data area EXTERNAL, the word EXTERNAL is coded in the 01-level entry.

```
01   CUSTOMER-RECORD EXTERNAL.
     05   CUSTOMER-NUMBER  .  .  .
```

Each program that is going to access this area must have an 01 with the same name with EXTERNAL specified. The 01 must be in the WORKING-STORAGE SECTION. Every program containing this definition will use the same area of storage when it refers to CUSTOMER-RECORD or to any field in the record. The storage is not actually in the WORKING-STORAGE SECTION of any of the programs, even though it is defined there in the source program. It is a separate area allocated at run time, truly EXTERNAL to all of the programs. The EXTERNAL area can be used in the main program as well as in subprograms.

There are some similarities and some differences between an EXTERNAL data area and a parameter defined in the LINKAGE SECTION of a called program. One similarity is that the program is accessing an area outside of its own storage. Another is that a field in an EXTERNAL area cannot have a VALUE. An important difference is that, unlike a parameter in a CALL, the name of an EXTERNAL 01 must be the same in every program that accesses it, because the association between the EXTERNAL data definition and the actual storage area is made by the data-name. Another difference is that programs that share an EXTERNAL area do not have to directly CALL one another. Any programs in the run unit can share the EXTERNAL area, regardless of where they fit in the hierarchy or flow of control.

Every program that uses an EXTERNAL area should have the same description for that area. A good way to assure this is to COPY the description into each program that uses it. A reference to any field in the 01, by any program, refers to the same storage location. (This is similar to a parameter passed BY REFERENCE.) However, if the area contains an OCCURS with INDEXED BY, the index is not shared. Each program has its own index, even though the index is named within the EXTERNAL record description, and even though each program uses the same name for the index. An index is not really part of the data area; it is part of the program. This means that if one program sharing the area leaves the index set to a certain value, another program cannot obtain that value.

As mentioned above, programs can share a file also. This is done by specifying EXTERNAL in the FD.

```
FD   MASTER-FILE   EXTERNAL
     BLOCK CONTAINS 0 RECORDS.
```

An EXTERNAL file allows a degree of sharing that cannot be achieved in any other way. Any program that contains the definition of the EXTERNAL file can perform any I/O operation on it. The OPEN could be in one program, the CLOSE in another, and READs or WRITEs in one or more others.

Making an FD EXTERNAL does not make the 01 record descriptions under it EXTERNAL. EXTERNAL for an 01 is valid only in the WORKING-STORAGE SECTION. In fact, each program that uses the EXTERNAL file could have different record descriptions. However, all of the clauses in the FD must be the same in every program. In addition, the FILE-CONTROL entries for the file must be the same in each program.

An EXTERNAL file in an INITIAL subprogram is not CLOSEd by the GOBACK or EXIT PROGRAM. Because the file is not within the subprogram, the state of the file is not considered part of the state of the subprogram.

NEW WAYS TO USE THE LINKAGE SECTION

The LINKAGE SECTION contains descriptions of storage areas without any storage allocated to them in the program. These descriptions are normally applied to storage areas that are passed to the program as parameters. The actual storage areas are located in other programs. An actual storage location is assigned to an 01- or 77-level item in the LINKAGE SECTION by naming the item in the USING phrase in the PROCEDURE DIVISION header or in an ENTRY statement. The assignment of the location takes place when the program is entered. The actual area that a LINKAGE SECTION description represents can be different each time the program is CALLed.

VS COBOL II provides a new way to assign a storage area to a LINK-AGE SECTION description. For each 01- or 77-level item in the LINK-AGE SECTION, there is an **ADDRESS OF** special register. This special register contains the main storage address of the item. The ADDRESS OF special register can be accessed and even changed by certain statements in the program. This can be done in a main pro-gram as well as in a subprogram. Below is the beginning of a record definition in the LINKAGE SECTION of a program.

```
LINKAGE SECTION.
01   TRANSACTION-IN.
     05   TRANSACTION-TYPE   PICTURE X.
     05    . . .
```

The ADDRESS OF special register for this record is referred to by writing

```
ADDRESS OF TRANSACTION-IN
```

If an 01- or 77-level item REDEFINES another item in the LINKAGE SECTION, there is only one ADDRESS OF special register for the two items since they always define the same location. Any reference to the ADDRESS OF either name will refer to the same special register.

To aid in manipulating addresses, VS COBOL II also includes a **pointer data item,** a new type of data field that can contain a main storage address. It is mainly used to save the value of an ADDRESS OF special register, and is defined by specifying the USAGE as POINTER, like this.

```
05   SALES-RECORD-ADDRESS   POINTER.
```

A POINTER data item has no PICTURE — it is always four bytes long. It is considered nonnumeric and therefore cannot be used in arithmetic statements or expressions. A POINTER data item can be defined any-where in the DATA DIVISION.

The implicit definition of an ADDRESS OF special register is POINTER. In other words, an ADDRESS OF special register is a special type of POINTER data item. The ADDRESS OF special register not only contains a storage address, but also associates a LINKAGE SECTION data description with the storage beginning at that address.

(Readers familiar with the way COBOL object programs address data areas, or who have used base address manipulation in CICS, may have noticed the similarity of the ADDRESS OF special register to a Base Locator for Linkage, or BLL, which is in fact exactly what it is. The BLL for a record is the ADDRESS OF special register for that record.)

The use of POINTER data items and ADDRESS OF special registers is restricted to a very few statements. One place they can be used is in relation conditions. That is, they can be compared, but only in certain ways. A POINTER data item or ADDRESS OF special register can be compared only to another POINTER data item or ADDRESS OF special register, and cannot be compared to any other type of field. Furthermore, the only comparison allowed is EQUAL or NOT EQUAL. As far as COBOL is concerned, the order or sequence of storage locations is of no significance. Using the definitions above, one could write

```
IF SALES-RECORD-ADDRESS = ADDRESS OF TRANSACTION-IN . . .
```

Besides IF statements, a comparison of addresses can be used in the WHEN phrase of an EVALUATE or SEARCH statement and in the UNTIL phrase of a PERFORM statement. It is not allowed in a SEARCH ALL.

THE SET STATEMENT FOR ADDRESSES

POINTER data items and ADDRESS OF special registers cannot be used in MOVE statements. There are three ways to put an address into an ADDRESS OF special register. The first occurs when the LINKAGE SECTION item is used to describe a parameter passed to the program, and the ADDRESS OF that item is set by the COBOL linkage routines when the program is entered.

The second way to put an address into an ADDRESS OF special register is a new form of the SET statement. The following statement will make the TRANSACTION-IN record description in the LINKAGE SECTION refer to the storage address that is in the POINTER data item.

```
SET ADDRESS OF TRANSACTION-IN TO SALES-RECORD-ADDRESS
```

When SET is used to establish the address of an item in the LINKAGE SECTION, the item does not have to be a parameter or appear in any USING phrase.

An ADDRESS OF special register can also be SET equal to another ADDRESS OF special register. If SALES-IN is another 01- or 77-level item in the LINKAGE SECTION, the following statement can be used.

```
SET ADDRESS OF TRANSACTION-IN TO ADDRESS OF SALES-IN
```

After this statement, both record descriptions, TRANSACTION-IN and SALES-IN, will refer to the same record in main storage.

The SET statement can also be used to put an address into a POINTER data item. For example, this statement could be used to save the address of SALES-IN in the POINTER data item SALES-RECORD-ADDRESS.

```
SET SALES-RECORD-ADDRESS TO ADDRESS OF SALES-IN
```

A POINTER data item can also be SET equal to another POINTER data item. If ITEM-AREA-ADDRESS is also a POINTER data item, the following can be written.

```
SET SALES-RECORD-ADDRESS TO ITEM-AREA-ADDRESS
```

There are times when it would be useful to be able to SET an ADDRESS OF special register or a POINTER data item to a special value that is not a valid address, but that could, for example, be used as an indicator to show that a record is not available or to mark the end of a list of POINTER data items. The figurative constant NULL serves this purpose, and it can be used only with ADDRESS OF special registers and POINTER data items. For example,

```
SET ADDRESS OF TRANSACTION-IN TO NULL
SET SALES-RECORD-ADDRESS TO NULL
```

NULL can also be used in comparisons, in order to test whether a valid address is present.

```
IF ADDRESS OF TRANSACTION-IN NOT = NULL . . .

PERFORM UNTIL NEXT-RECORD-POINTER = NULL . . .
```

A POINTER data item can be defined with an initial value of NULL by specifying it in the VALUE clause.

```
05  NEXT-RECORD-POINTER  POINTER  VALUE NULL.
```

This is the only VALUE that can be specified in the definition of a POINTER data item. A pointer data item cannot have a condition name (an 88 level) associated with it.

One of the ways these addressing capabilities can be used is in processing a type of data structure known as a **chained list, linked list,** or **threaded list.** In this type of structure, each entry in the list is a separate area in main storage. The entries are not contiguous, but each entry contains a POINTER to the next entry. A single list entry might look like this.

```
LINKAGE SECTION.
01  ITEM-ENTRY.
    05  NEXT-ITEM-POINTER POINTER.
    05  ITEM-NUMBER        PICTURE 9(6).
    05  ITEM-PRICE         PICTURE 999V99  PACKED-DECIMAL.
```

In the last entry in the list, NEXT-ITEM-POINTER would be NULL. A simple PERFORM loop can step through every entry in the list.

```
PERFORM UNTIL ADDRESS OF ITEM-ENTRY = NULL
    IF ITEM-NUMBER > 799999
        MULTIPLY ITEM-PRICE BY 1.05
    END-IF
    SET ADDRESS OF ITEM-ENTRY TO NEXT-ITEM-POINTER
END-PERFORM
```

Up to this point, the ADDRESS OF special register has been treated as referring only to 01- or 77-level items. There are two places, however, where it is valid to refer to the ADDRESS OF an item at any level in the LINKAGE SECTION, not just an 01 or 77. One such place is in the sending field, or second operand, of a SET statement. The other is in a relation condition. For example, if TRANSACTION-ITEM is an 05-level item in the LINKAGE SECTION, these statements could be used.

```
SET ITEM-AREA-ADDRESS TO ADDRESS OF TRANSACTION-ITEM

SET ADDRESS OF TRANSACTION-IN TO ADDRESS OF TRANSACTION-ITEM

IF ADDRESS OF TRANSACTION-ITEM = ITEM-AREA-ADDRESS . . .
```

None of these statements changes ADDRESS OF TRANSACTION-ITEM. In a statement where the ADDRESS OF special register is not being modified, it can refer to any level; where the statement is changing it, it can refer only to an 01 or 77 level. The ADDRESS OF a subordinate item can be changed only indirectly, by changing the ADDRESS OF the 01 level that contains it.

Notice that the second example SETs the ADDRESS OF an 01 level to the ADDRESS OF a subordinate item contained in that same 01. This technique can be used when a set of fields is repeated in one record or area.

The third way of putting an address into an ADDRESS OF special register is to pass the special register to a subprogram as a parameter. It must be passed BY REFERENCE. Since this allows the subprogram to change the value in the ADDRESS OF special register, it must refer to an 01 or 77 level. Here are a few lines from a calling program.

```
LINKAGE SECTION.
01   TRANSACTION-IN.
     05   TRANSACTION-TYPE   PICTURE X.
        . . .
     CALL 'SUBPROG'
         USING BY REFERENCE ADDRESS OF TRANSACTION-IN
```

The subprogram should define the parameter as a POINTER data item.

```
LINKAGE SECTION.
77  TRANS-ADDRESS   POINTER.

PROCEDURE DIVISION USING TRANS-ADDRESS.
     . . .
     SET TRANS-ADDRESS TO . . .
```

The SET statement will SET the ADDRESS OF TRANSACTION-IN in the calling program.

A POINTER data item can also be passed as a parameter in the USING phrase of a CALL, either BY REFERENCE or BY CONTENT, just like any other field.

Exercises

1. Subprogram EXM100 requires the following parameters in this order.

- An alphanumeric field that it will process.

- A PICTURE 9(9) BINARY field containing the length of the alphanumeric field.

- A one-byte code, which must be the letter C. (Use a literal.)

Write a statement to CALL this subprogram. If an error occurs accessing the subprogram, DISPLAY an error message and end the run. Write
the LINKAGE SECTION and the PROCEDURE DIVISION header
for the subprogram.

2. In order to get the address of the first entry in the example of a
chained list, it is necessary to CALL subprogram CHAIN01, passing
the following parameters.

- A three-character code identifying the chain to be processed. Use the
  letters ITM.

- A field (ADDRESS OF special register or POINTER data item) in
  which the subprogram will put the address of the first entry in the
  chain.

Write one statement to CALL the subprogram and make ITEM-
ENTRY represent the first entry in the list.

3. In order to process the chained list again, without having to CALL
CHAIN01 a second time, define a field to save the address of the first
entry in the chain. Write a statement to save the address of the first
entry in this field. Write a statement to make ITEM-ENTRY represent
the first entry again, using the saved address.

Chapter 8

Nested Programs

Nested programs bring to COBOL a concept of program structure that is completely new to the language, having just been introduced with COBOL 85. The basic idea is that a subprogram is contained within the program that CALLs it, instead of being compiled separately.

Figure 8.1 is an outline of what a nested program looks like. The main program, PAYROLL, CALLs the subprogram, FICA-CALCULATION, to calculate the FICA deduction. FICA-CALCULATION is referred to as a **contained program;** PAYROLL is the **containing program.** Although they are physically joined, FICA-CALCULATION is a separate program from PAYROLL, not just a subroutine. It has its own DATA DIVISION and PROCEDURE DIVISION. Notice, however, that it does not have an ENVIRONMENT DIVISION, which is optional in VS COBOL II. If the program has files it obviously will have to have FILE-CONTROL entries, but a subprogram with no files may very well have no need for an ENVIRONMENT DIVISION. In a contained program, the CONFIGURATION SECTION is not even allowed. The CONFIGURATION SECTION of the outermost containing program applies to all the programs contained within it. If the outermost program does not have a CONFIGURATION SECTION, the default specifications apply to all of the contained programs. So unless the contained program has files, it will not need an ENVIRONMENT DIVISION.

Figure 8.1 also shows that the contained program, FICA-CALCULATION, is at the very end of the PAYROLL program, after the last statement of the PROCEDURE DIVISION for PAYROLL. There can be more than one contained program, but they must be grouped together at the end of the containing program. The end of

Figure 8.1   A nested program.

```
IDENTIFICATION DIVISION.
PROGRAM-ID. PAYROLL.
ENVIRONMENT DIVISION.
      .   .   .

DATA DIVISION.
      .   .   .

01  FICA-FIELDS.
    05  . . .
PROCEDURE DIVISION.
      .   .   .

    CALL 'FICA-CALCULATION' USING FICA-FIELDS
      .   .   .

IDENTIFICATION DIVISION.
PROGRAM-ID. FICA-CALCULATION.
DATA DIVISION.

LINKAGE SECTION.
01  DATA-FIELDS.
    05  . . .
PROCEDURE DIVISION USING DATA-FIELDS.
    COMPUTE  . . .
END PROGRAM FICA-CALCULATION.
END PROGRAM PAYROLL.
```

each program, contained or containing, must be marked by END PRO-
GRAM program-name. In spite of its position at the end of a program,
this is called the **END PROGRAM header.** The program name in
the END PROGRAM header must be the same as the program name
in a preceding PROGRAM-ID paragraph, and the END PROGRAM
marks the end of the source for that program.

The CALL statement in the containing program is written in exactly the
same way as if the two programs were compiled separately. However,
the object code is not the same. The nested programs are not separate
object modules, so the linkage between them can be much simpler.
CALLing a nested program can be considered a reasonable alternative
to a PERFORM, without concern about the difference in performance.
The object code for a CALL to a nested program approaches the
efficiency of a PERFORM.

The contained program returns control to the CALLing program with
a GOBACK or EXIT PROGRAM, just like any subprogram. If the

contained program has no out-of-line code, and particularly if it is very short, an appropriate way of returning control is simply to rely on the implicit EXIT PROGRAM at the end of the program, as described in chapter 7.

The name FICA-CALCULATION is noticeably quite a bit longer than the usual eight-character program name. Names of nested programs, like any name in COBOL, can be up to 30 characters long. Since a nested program is not a separate unit to the operating system, the name is not limited by the restrictions of the operating system. The entire name is used to identify the program anywhere that it is referred to, so FICA-CALCULATION-1989 and FICA-CALCULATION-1990, for example, could be names of different contained programs in the same compilation.

Programs can be nested to any depth. A contained program can, in turn, contain other programs. Overdoing the nesting could, however, become confusing. For one thing, the use of indenting to set off the different levels is severely restricted by the normal COBOL require-ment that division headers, paragraph names, and the like begin in Area A. The first level of contained programs could be indented two or three spaces and still meet the Area A requirements, but that is the limit. Since all of the contained programs have to be grouped together at the end of the outermost containing program, it could become very difficult to tell which ones are at which level. The compiler tries to help by printing a number representing the nesting level alongside each line of the source listing (see Figure 11.3 in Chapter 11), but this does not have anywhere near the visual effect of indenting. If the contained programs are large they look just like part of the main program in the listing, and any sense of levels is completely lost.

SHARING DATA AMONG NESTED PROGRAMS

One of the major advantages of nested programs over PERFORMed subroutines is the ability to limit what data the subprogram can change. A PERFORMed routine can reference and change any field in the entire program. This freedom often leads to what are called **side effects:** changes by a routine to fields other than those in which it stores the results it is primarily intended to calculate. Unexpected side effects can make even a well-structured program very confusing and prone to errors when changes are made.

A contained program has its own DATA DIVISION, separate from the DATA DIVISION of the containing program that CALLs it. The contained program can, of course, reference anything in its own DATA DIVISION, but it can access fields in other programs only if those fields are explicitly made available to it. There are two ways that this can be done.

The first way is to pass fields in the containing program as parameters in the CALL statement. This is done in exactly the same way as when a separately compiled subprogram is called. The contained program defines the parameters in its LINKAGE SECTION and lists them in the USING phrase of its PROCEDURE DIVISION header. The contained program uses the name in its LINKAGE SECTION, but it is actually accessing the field in the containing program.

The other way to make data in a containing program available to a contained program is to declare an 01-level in the containing program as **GLOBAL**. This is done simply by writing GLOBAL after the data-name in the 01-level entry, like this.

```
01   INVENTORY-RECORD GLOBAL.
     05   INV-ITEM-NUMBER . . .
```

When a record in a containing program is GLOBAL, a contained program can directly reference the record or any subordinate fields within the record, including indexes and condition names. The contained program does not have its own definition of the record, but uses the data-names defined in the containing program.

An FD also can be declared as GLOBAL.

```
FD   INVENTORY-FILE GLOBAL
     BLOCK CONTAINS 0 RECORDS.
01   INVENTORY RECORD.
     05   INV-ITEM-NUMBER . . .
```

This makes the FD itself, as well as all its records and all subordinate fields, accessible to a contained program. This means that the contained program can perform I/O operations on the file, as well as access the records.

When there is more than one level of nesting, the meaning of GLOBAL is not quite what might be expected based on the normal meaning of the word. It does not make the record accessible to any program in the whole compilation. A GLOBAL name is accessible only by programs contained, directly or indirectly, in the program where the GLOBAL item is defined. Figure 8.2 illustrates this. The outer-

most program, PAYROLL, contains COMPUTE-DEDUCTIONS
and PRINT-CHECKS. COMPUTE-DEDUCTIONS in turn con-
tains FEDERAL-TAXES, which contains FICA-CALCULATION.
DEDUCTION-FIELDS is defined as GLOBAL in COMPUTE-DE-
DUCTIONS. It can be referenced in COMPUTE-DEDUCTIONS,
FEDERAL-TAXES, and FICA-CALCULATION. But DEDUCTION-
FIELDS cannot be referenced in PRINT-CHECKS or in PAYROLL.

Since each nested program is a separate program with its own DATA
DIVISION, the same name can be used for data items in two or more
of the programs. As long as the name is not made GLOBAL in any
of the programs, there is no confusion. Any use of the name refers to
the definition of that name in the same program. A name that is not
GLOBAL is called **local.** A local name can be referenced only in the
program in which it is defined.

It is possible for a GLOBAL name in one program to be the same as a
local name in another program, or even for two GLOBAL names to be

Figure 8.2   Nested programs with a GLOBAL record.

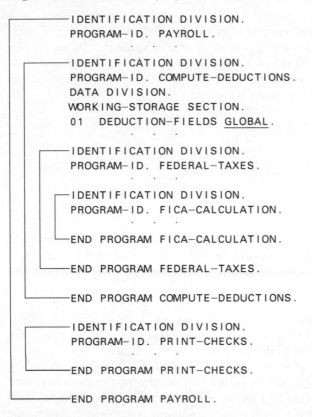

```
         ┌────────IDENTIFICATION DIVISION.
         │        PROGRAM-ID. PAYROLL.
         │                 .    .    .
         │  ┌─────────IDENTIFICATION DIVISION.
         │  │        PROGRAM-ID. COMPUTE-DEDUCTIONS.
         │  │        DATA DIVISION.
         │  │        WORKING-STORAGE SECTION.
         │  │        01  DEDUCTION-FIELDS GLOBAL.
         │  │                 .    .    .
         │  │  ┌──────IDENTIFICATION DIVISION.
         │  │  │      PROGRAM-ID. FEDERAL-TAXES.
         │  │  │               .    .    .
         │  │  │  ┌───IDENTIFICATION DIVISION.
         │  │  │  │   PROGRAM-ID. FICA-CALCULATION.
         │  │  │  │            .    .    .
         │  │  │  └──END PROGRAM FICA-CALCULATION.
         │  │  │
         │  │  └─────END PROGRAM FEDERAL-TAXES.
         │  │
         │  └────────END PROGRAM COMPUTE-DEDUCTIONS.
         │  
         │  ┌─────────IDENTIFICATION DIVISION.
         │  │        PROGRAM-ID. PRINT-CHECKS.
         │  │                 .    .    .
         │  └────────END PROGRAM PRINT-CHECKS.
         │
         └────────END PROGRAM PAYROLL.
```

the same. In the *Application Programming Guide* there are rules for determining which one is being referenced when such multiple definitions
exist, but this situation obviously has a high potential for confusion and
mistakes. The best policy is to make sure that all GLOBAL names are
unique, including subordinate names in GLOBAL records.

Defining an 01 or FD as EXTERNAL, as described in Chapter 7,
does not make it GLOBAL. EXTERNAL is intended primarily for
sharing among separately compiled programs. The definition of an
EXTERNAL item must appear in each program that references it.
GLOBAL provides sharing among nested programs, and all of the
programs use the definition that appears in only one of the programs.
If the file or record must be both GLOBAL and EXTERNAL, they can
both be specified.

At the beginning of this chapter it was mentioned that the ENVIRON-
MENT DIVISION is optional. The DATA DIVISION and PROCE-
DURE DIVISION are also optional in VS COBOL II. A contained
program might not need a DATA DIVISION if, for example, the only
fields it uses are GLOBAL fields in containing programs. On the other
hand, there might be a situation where it would be convenient for a
nested program to define GLOBAL records for use by contained programs, but not do any processing itself. It would then not need a PRO-
CEDURE DIVISION.

WHO CAN CALL WHOM

Just as there are rules for references to data among nested programs,
there are restrictions on which programs can CALL which other
programs. One of the complications of multiple levels of nesting is
making sure that each program can CALL whatever subprograms it
needs.

All of the following rules refer to CALLs among nested programs in
the same compilation. Any program, at any level of nesting, is free to
CALL any separately compiled subprogram, just as in the past.

Normally a program can CALL only a contained program at the very
next level down. It cannot CALL a program that contains it, nor a
program contained by a program that it contains. Figure 8.3 illustrates these rules. PAYROLL can CALL COMPUTE-DEDUCTIONS,
which is directly contained in PAYROLL. PAYROLL cannot CALL
FEDERAL-TAX or STATE-TAX, because it contains them only
indirectly. These two lower-level programs can be CALLed by

Figure 8.3   A program with several contained subprograms.

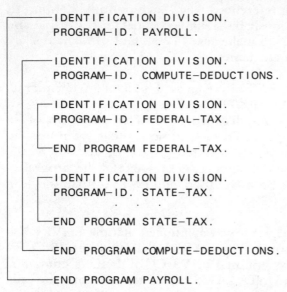

```
          IDENTIFICATION DIVISION.
          PROGRAM-ID. PAYROLL.
                       .   .   .

          IDENTIFICATION DIVISION.
          PROGRAM-ID. COMPUTE-DEDUCTIONS.
                       .   .   .

          IDENTIFICATION DIVISION.
          PROGRAM-ID. FEDERAL-TAX.
                       .   .   .
          END PROGRAM FEDERAL-TAX.

          IDENTIFICATION DIVISION.
          PROGRAM-ID. STATE-TAX.
                       .   .   .
          END PROGRAM STATE-TAX.

          END PROGRAM COMPUTE-DEDUCTIONS.

          END PROGRAM PAYROLL.
```

COMPUTE-DEDUCTIONS, which directly contains them. They cannot call each other, because neither one contains the other. FEDERAL-TAX cannot CALL COMPUTE-DEDUCTIONS or PAY-ROLL, because a program can never CALL a program that contains it.

A subprogram can be made available to a broader range of programs by declaring it as **COMMON.** This is done by writing COMMON after the program name in the PROGRAM-ID paragraph, like this.

```
IDENTIFICATION DIVISION.
PROGRAM-ID. COMPUTE-DEDUCTIONS COMMON.
```

COMMON is valid only in a contained program. A COMMON program can be called by the program that contains it, and also by any other program contained in the program that contains the COMMON program, except for itself and any programs that it contains. Figure 8.4 should help to clear up these somewhat confusing rules. COMPUTE-DEDUCTIONS and PRINT-CHECKS can be CALLed by PAYROLL, whether or not they are COMMON. Because COMPUTE-DEDUCTIONS is COMMON, it can also be CALLed by PRINT-CHECKS and by UPDATE-CHECK-REGISTER, since they are contained in PAYROLL, the program that contains the COMMON program. COMPUTE-DEDUCTIONS still cannot be CALLed by FICA-CALCULATION. The rule that a program can never CALL a program that contains it still applies, even to a COMMON program.

Figure 8.4   A COMMON contained program.

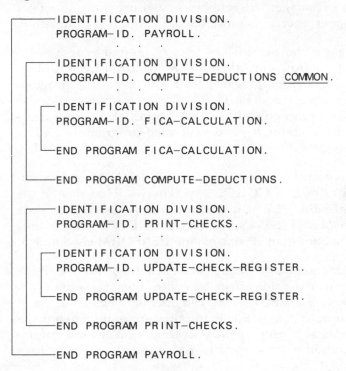

```
IDENTIFICATION DIVISION.
PROGRAM-ID. PAYROLL.

IDENTIFICATION DIVISION.
PROGRAM-ID. COMPUTE-DEDUCTIONS COMMON.
    .   . .
IDENTIFICATION DIVISION.
PROGRAM-ID. FICA-CALCULATION.
    .   . .
END PROGRAM FICA-CALCULATION.

END PROGRAM COMPUTE-DEDUCTIONS.

IDENTIFICATION DIVISION.
PROGRAM-ID. PRINT-CHECKS.
    .   . .
IDENTIFICATION DIVISION.
PROGRAM-ID. UPDATE-CHECK-REGISTER.
    .   . .
END PROGRAM UPDATE-CHECK-REGISTER.

END PROGRAM PRINT-CHECKS.

END PROGRAM PAYROLL.
```

There is one more, simpler rule for CALLs, which takes precedence over all of the other rules: a recursive CALL is never allowed. A program can never CALL itself, nor can it CALL another program that will directly or indirectly CALL the first program.

It is possible for a run unit to end up with two or more programs that have the same name, as long as at least one of them is a contained program. The *Language Reference* manual has some rules for determining which program is being CALLed when there are duplicate names, but the best solution is to avoid this very confusing and error-prone situation by having a standard for program names that prevents duplication.

PROS AND CONS OF NESTED PROGRAMS

Nested programs are sometimes presented as a structured programming methodology, but they do not fit comfortably into any particular structured programming construct. The fact that they require code to be out of line is a serious drawback. They do contribute to modular programming by offering a facility that is in between a subroutine and a separately compiled subprogram. But they add a level of complexity that may outweigh any advantages. Although a nested program resembles a subprogram in appearance, it is more like a PERFORM in function.

If a routine is going to be out of line anyway, nested programs do restrict the flow of control more than an out-of-line PERFORM. A PERFORMed routine is not segregated from the rest of the program the way a nested program is. The PERFORMed routine could also be executed by falling through to it, and the ranges of different PER-FORMs could overlap, although good structured-programming practice forbids such things.

A nested program requires more writing than a PERFORM, and wordiness is often cited as one of COBOL's weaknesses. However, if the nested program, like the PERFORMed routine, is just a procedure with no ENVIRONMENT DIVISION or DATA DIVISION, it only requires a few more lines than an out-of-line PERFORMed routine.

Probably the biggest potential advantage of nested programs over PER-FORM is the ability to avoid side effects by controlling access to data. It is unfortunate, therefore, that GLOBAL can only be specified at the 01 level. Making an entire record available to other programs when probably only a few fields are really needed severely weakens the control of access to data and dilutes the advantage that might otherwise have been attained.

Separately compiled subprograms provide very effective control of access to data. There may be some benefit to using nested programs for very small subprograms, where the overhead of a CALL to a separately compiled program would be disproportionate. On the other hand, if a subprogram is CALLed by many other programs it would generally make more sense to compile it separately. For large subprograms the benefits of nesting are nebulous. It is probably better to compile large programs separately.

Exercises

1. Write a skeleton for a main program containing two subprograms. For each program code all of the division headers, the PROGRAM-ID paragraph, and the END PROGRAM header. Indicate where the main program's PROCEDURE DIVISION statements are.

2. In Figure 8.5, which programs can reference CUSTOMER-RECORD? Which programs can reference ACCOUNT-MASTER?

3. In Figure 8.5, which programs can CALL PRINT-REPORTS?

Figure 8.5   Nested programs for Exercises 2 and 3.

```
IDENTIFICATION DIVISION.
PROGRAM-ID. ACCTRECV.
ENVIRONMENT DIVISION.
        .    .

DATA DIVISION.
        .    .

WORKING-STORAGE SECTION.
01   ACCOUNT-MASTER GLOBAL.
        .    .

PROCEDURE DIVISION.
        .    .


   IDENTIFICATION DIVISION.
   PROGRAM-ID. UPDATE-FILE.
   DATA DIVISION.
   WORKING-STORAGE SECTION.
   01   CUSTOMER-RECORD GLOBAL.
           .    .

      IDENTIFICATION DIVISION.
      PROGRAM-ID. ADD-CUSTOMER.
              .    .

      END PROGRAM ADD-CUSTOMER.

      IDENTIFICATION DIVISION.
      PROGRAM-ID. ADD-ORDER.
              .    .

      END PROGRAM ADD-ORDER.

   END PROGRAM UPDATE-FILE.

   IDENTIFICATION DIVISION.
   PROGRAM-ID. PRINT-REPORTS COMMON.
           .    .

      IDENTIFICATION DIVISION.
      PROGRAM-ID. PRINT-INVOICE.
              .    .

      END PROGRAM PRINT-INVOICE.

      IDENTIFICATION DIVISION.
      PROGRAM-ID. PRINT-PAST-DUE-NOTICE.
              .    .

      END PROGRAM PRINT-PAST-DUE-NOTICE.

   END PROGRAM PRINT-REPORTS.

END PROGRAM ACCTRECV.
```

Chapter 9

CICS

VS COBOL II introduces some significant changes in the way that CICS programs are coded. The coding is simpler and therefore easier than it was in the past. It is no longer necessary to resort to tricks to make COBOL interface with CICS. Also, some of the restrictions on the use of COBOL statements and features have been eliminated.

This chapter assumes that the reader is already familiar with command level CICS programming in an older version of COBOL. If you do not know command level programming, skip this chapter since it contains nothing relevant to non-CICS programming.

VS COBOL II supports only command level programming in CICS. Macro level programming cannot be used.

Some editions of the IBM programming reference manuals for CICS are only partially updated for VS COBOL II. They discuss the changes for VS COBOL II in an introductory section, but the main body of the manual, where the commands and options are described, does not reflect the differences. If you are using such an edition, be assured that the information in the VS COBOL II section, and in this book, supersedes the command and option descriptions, even though those descriptions do not mention the existence of any variations.

NO MORE BLLS

Probably the biggest change for a CICS programmer is the elimination of BLL cells. The ADDRESS OF special registers, described in Chapter 7, are used to perform the functions formerly done with BLL cells.

Since BLL cells are not used, there is no longer any need to define them. The list of BLL cells in the LINKAGE SECTION (sometimes referred to as the address list or parameter list) is therefore no longer coded.

In any CICS command with a SET option, ADDRESS OF the data area in the LINKAGE SECTION is now specified in the SET option instead of the name of a BLL cell. For example, suppose an OS/VS COBOL program contains the following definitions.

```
LINKAGE SECTION.
01  BLL-CELLS.
    05  FILLER          PICTURE S9(8)  COMPUTATIONAL.
    05  MAST-REC-BLL    PICTURE S9(8)  COMPUTATIONAL.
01  EMPLOYEE-MASTER.
    05  . . .
```

In OS/VS COBOL, the command to read a record from the master file might look like this.

```
EXEC CICS READ
        DATASET('MASTER')
        RIDFLD(EMPLOYEE-NUMBER)
        SET(MAST-REC-BLL)
END-EXEC.
```

With VS COBOL II, the LINKAGE SECTION would contain only the definition of the record itself.

```
LINKAGE SECTION.
01  EMPLOYEE-MASTER.
    05  . . .
```

The definition of the BLL cells is omitted. In the READ command, the reference to the BLL cell is replaced by the ADDRESS OF special register.

```
EXEC CICS READ
        DATASET('MASTER')
        RIDFLD(EMPLOYEE-NUMBER)
        SET(ADDRESS OF EMPLOYEE-MASTER)
END-EXEC
```

Also notice in this example that, as with regular VS COBOL II statements, the period is omitted at the end of the command. The CICS command delimiter END-EXEC functions like an explicit scope terminator (but it is always required). A CICS command can be nested anywhere an imperative statement is allowed.

An additional benefit of using ADDRESS OF instead of BLL cells is that the program no longer has to do anything special if a record is longer than 4096 bytes. There is only one ADDRESS OF special register for a record, no matter how long it is. VS COBOL II automatically establishes addressability for the entire record any time that the ADDRESS OF special register is changed. The incrementing and setting of additional BLL cells is eliminated.

A POINTER data item can be used instead of an ADDRESS OF special register in a SET option. This might be done, for example, to obtain an area of main storage that will be not be used until later. The following command will obtain storage and save the address of the area in the POINTER data item named WORK-AREA-ADDR.

```
EXEC CICS GETMAIN
          SET(WORK-AREA-ADDR)
          LENGTH(WORK-LENGTH)
END-EXEC
```

When addressability is needed for the work area, a SET statement can be used to place the saved address into the ADDRESS OF special register. The result is the same as if the ADDRESS OF special register had been specified in the command, including the handling of an area larger than 4096 bytes if necessary.

VS COBOL II also recognizes whenever an ADDRESS OF special register is changed, and adjusts its internal addressing without any special coding. The SERVICE RELOAD statement is not used in VS COBOL II. There is also no need for artificial paragraph names after an ADDRESS OF special register is changed.

A new statement, SERVICE LABEL, is generated by the CICS COBOL translator under certain circumstances. There is never any need for the programmer to code this statement.

The ADDRESS OF special register must also be used, instead of BLL cells, for processing chained storage areas. The technique for doing this is explained in detail in Chapter 7.

DATA AREA LENGTHS

The LENGTH option can be omitted in many commands in which it was previously required. In any command using a FROM or INTO option, CICS will use the LENGTH OF special register to obtain the length of the record. A REWRITE command, for example, could be written like this.

```
EXEC CICS REWRITE
         DATASET('MASTER')
         FROM(EMPLOYEE-MASTER)
END-EXEC
```

The length of the record that will be written is LENGTH OF EMPLOYEE-MASTER. This can eliminate the need for the program to calculate record lengths in bytes. However, to write a different length, the LENGTH option must be specified in the command.

Use care when omitting the LENGTH option in a READ command. For READ, the LENGTH option specifies the maximum number of bytes that CICS will read into the data area. A longer record will be truncated. If the record is defined with an OCCURS . . . DEPENDING ON clause, the value in the LENGTH OF special register is based on the current value of the DEPENDING ON object. Suppose the employee master record includes the following fields.

```
05  NUMBER-OF-DEPENDENTS  PICTURE S99  BINARY.
05  DEPENDENT-DATA OCCURS 1 TO 20 TIMES
          DEPENDING ON NUMBER-OF-DEPENDENTS.
   10  DEPENDENT-NAME  PICTURE X(30).
   10   . . .
```

If the last record processed contained three dependents, then NUMBER-OF-DEPENDENTS still contains 3. At this point, a READ with the LENGTH option omitted will read in only enough bytes to contain three dependents, even if the new record has more. To avoid truncating the record, set the DEPENDING ON field to its maximum value before doing the READ.

```
MOVE 20 TO NUMBER-OF-DEPENDENTS
EXEC CICS READ UPDATE
         DATASET('MASTER')
         INTO(EMPLOYEE-MASTER)
```

```
            RIDFLD(EMPLOYEE-NUMBER)
END-EXEC
```

Similarly, if the file contains records of different lengths, defined by separate 01-level record descriptions, always use the longest record in the INTO option if the LENGTH option is omitted.

The LENGTH option in a READ command also makes available to the program the actual length in bytes of the record that was read. This information is not available if the LENGTH option is omitted. However, if you rely on the LENGTH OF special register and let COBOL do all of the calculation of record lengths, you normally will not need access to the length.

Where the LENGTH option is still required, it may sometimes be convenient to use the LENGTH OF special register in the option. For example, a GETMAIN could be written like this.

```
EXEC CICS GETMAIN
            SET(ADDRESS OF WORK-AREA)
            LENGTH(LENGTH OF WORK-AREA)
END-EXEC
```

When using variable-length areas that are defined with OCCURS . . . DEPENDING ON, it is no longer necessary to move the DEPEND-ING ON object to itself in order to make sure that the correct number of occurrences is used. VS COBOL II always uses the current value of the DEPENDING ON field, no matter how it was changed.

EASED RESTRICTIONS ON CALL

A VS COBOL II program in CICS can CALL a VS COBOL II sub-program, and the subprogram can issue CICS commands. The CICS execution interface is maintained for the subprogram as well as for the main program. The CALL can be either static or dynamic. The first two parameters passed by the CALL must be DFHEIBLK and DFHCOMMAREA. These can be followed by application-program parameters.

```
CALL 'CICSSUB' USING DFHEIBLK
                     DFHCOMMAREA
                     STATE-CODE
                     WORK-AREA
```

In the subprogram, the CICS COBOL translator will automatically insert the EIB and COMMAREA into the LINKAGE SECTION and the USING phrase of the PROCEDURE DIVISION header. Therefore, the PROCEDURE DIVISION header written by the programmer for the subprogram CALLed by the statement above would contain only the application parameters.

```
PROCEDURE DIVISION USING STATE-CODE WORK-AREA.
```

If a dynamic CALL is used, it must be a CALL identifier. A CALL literal is always static in CICS because CICS programs must be compiled with the NODYNAM option. A dynamic CALL essentially has the same effect as a CICS LINK command, but there is one difference. LINK reinitializes the WORKING-STORAGE SECTION of the subprogram each time it is executed, whereas CALL normally leaves WORKING-STORAGE in its last-used state. If reinitialization is necessary, the subprogram can be given the INITIAL attribute, as described in Chapter 7. This will make the dynamic CALL produce the same effect as LINK. CALL is more efficient than LINK if the same subprogram is CALLed more than once in the same task.

Whether the CALL is static or dynamic, both the calling and called programs must be VS COBOL II. CICS does not support CALLs between VS COBOL II and OS/VS COBOL programs. CICS also does not allow a VS COBOL II subprogram to be CALLed by a program written in any other language. As with OS/VS COBOL, a static CALL from a VS COBOL II program to an assembler-language subprogram is permitted, provided that the subprogram does not use any CICS commands.

OTHER RESTRICTIONS

CICS programs written in VS COBOL II can use some of the statements that were not allowed with earlier versions of COBOL. The INSPECT, STRING, and UNSTRING statements can be used in CICS programs. STOP RUN can also be used, but it has the same effect as an EXEC CICS RETURN command, so there is really no reason to use it. Other restrictions remain in effect, primarily those forbidding the use of the SORT statement and COBOL I/O statements.

VS COBOL II also allows the use of certain COBOL debugging facilities in CICS. Debugging declarative sections (USE FOR DEBUGGING) are permitted. Two of the new VS COBOL II debugging features can be used: range checking for subscripts and indexes, which is described in detail in Chapter 16, and the formatted dump (an improved version of the SYMDMP abend dump), described in Chapter 12. When a CICS program produces a formatted dump, the dump is written to a temporary storage queue named CEBRxxxx, where xxxx is the terminal ID of the terminal that initiated the transaction. The CEBR transaction can be used to browse the formatted dump.

COBTEST, the VS COBOL II debug tool described in Chapter 13, can be used for a CICS program, but there are significant restrictions. It cannot be used interactively, but only in a batch-like mode with all of the debugging commands being read from a file that is set up before the transaction is executed. COBTEST also cannot be used with any program that contains a CICS LINK command. EDF and third-party packages for testing and debugging can still be used with VS COBOL II programs in CICS. Because of the limitations on the use of COBTEST, you will probably prefer to use one of these other tools.

Some of the new language features that were introduced in Release 3 of VS COBOL II are not supported by the CICS/OS/VS translator, and can be used only with CICS/MVS Version 2. The most prominent features in this category are the use of lowercase letters, reference modification, nested programs and symbolic characters.

TRANSACTION ABEND CODES

For certain error conditions, VS COBOL II produces its own transaction abend codes. Unlike regular CICS transaction abend codes, the VS COBOL II codes are numeric. They are in the range 1001 to 1099, and are the same as user abend codes U1001 to U1099 issued by batch VS COBOL II programs. Each abend code corresponds to a run-time message number IGZnnnI, where nnn is the last three digits of the abend code. For example, abend code 1006 means that message IGZ006I was issued. The message is written to the CEBRxxxx temporary storage queue, and can be viewed with the CEBR transaction. These messages are documented in Appendix C of the VS COBOL II *Debugging* manual. Two abend codes, 1090 and 1091, do not have corresponding messages and are documented in Appendix D of the *Debugging* manual.

The improvements in the interface between COBOL and CICS make the coding of CICS programs simpler and less error-prone, and make the program easier to understand. The easing of some restrictions makes COBOL a more powerful language for CICS programming. In particular, the increased flexibility of the CALL statement offers new options for modularizing and organizing CICS programs.

Exercise

Below are portions of a CICS program written in OS/VS COBOL. Make the changes necessary to convert it to VS COBOL II.

```
WORKING-STORAGE SECTION.
77  WS-ORDER-NUMBER  PICTURE 9(7).
77  ORDER-REC-LEN  PICTURE S9(4)  COMP.

LINKAGE SECTION.
01  BLL-LIST  COMPUTATIONAL.
    05  FILLER            PICTURE S9(8).
    05  ORDER-REC-ADDR    PICTURE S9(8).
    05  ORDER-REC-ADDR2   PICTURE S9(8).

01  ORDER-RECORD.
    05  ORDER-NUMBER      PICTURE 9(7).
    05  ORDER-CUSTOMER    PICTURE X(6).
    05  ORDER-DATE        PICTURE 9(6).
    05  ORDER-ITEM-COUNT  PICTURE S999  COMP.
    05  ORDER-ITEM OCCURS 1 TO 500 TIMES
                DEPENDING ON ORDER-ITEM-COUNT.
        10  ITEM-NUMBER    PICTURE X(10).
        10  ITEM-PRICE     PICTURE S9(4)V99   COMP-3.
        10  ITEM-QUANTITY  PICTURE S9(4)      COMP-3.

PROCEDURE DIVISION.

    EXEC CICS READ UPDATE
            DATASET('ORDERS')
            RIDFLD(WS-ORDER-NUMBER)
            SET(ORDER-REC-ADDR)
            LENGTH(ORDER-REC-LEN)
    END-EXEC.

    IF ORDER-REC-LEN > 4096
        ADD ORDER-REC-ADDR 4096 GIVING ORDER-REC-ADDR2.
    SERVICE RELOAD ORDER-RECORD.

    MOVE ORDER-ITEM-COUNT TO ORDER-ITEM-COUNT.

    COMPUTE ORDER-REC-LEN = 21 + 17 * ORDER-ITEM-COUNT.
    EXEC CICS REWRITE
            DATASET('ORDERS')
            FROM(ORDER-RECORD)
            LENGTH(ORDER-REC-LEN)
    END-EXEC.
```

Chapter 10

What's Missing?

The preceding chapters show the programming capabilities that are provided by the statements and other language features that are new in VS COBOL II. These new language elements add considerable power and flexibility to the COBOL language. However, some language elements and features that were available in OS/VS COBOL are not included in VS COBOL II. When programmers first learn about VS COBOL II, they are often quite concerned about the things that are omitted. Among the omitted items are some that programmers relied on and used often. The purpose of this chapter is to allay any anxiety about lost functions by showing how the same ends can be accomplished in VS COBOL II.

All of the major missing features are covered in this chapter, and a substitute is suggested for each one. Some very minor missing elements are not mentioned, especially if the appropriate replacement is obvious. Also not discussed are some changes that only affect the format of a statement, but do not reduce the function. There is a complete list of all language changes in Appendix A. Remember that many language features omitted from Release 1 of VS COBOL II were added in Release 2. If an important language element is rumored to be missing, but is not discussed in this chapter, it is probably because that element is now included in the language. This can be confirmed by referring to Appendix A.

The focus of this chapter is on how to achieve the desired results in new programs being written in VS COBOL II. A different approach is required in some cases when converting existing programs that use the omitted features. Conversion is discussed in Chapter 17.

The other chapters of this book, as a rule, describe only those language elements and features that are new in VS COBOL II. Most of the language elements described in this chapter, however, existed in OS/VS COBOL and in some cases even in earlier versions of COBOL. They are described briefly here to illustrate how they can be used in place of other elements that are not present in VS COBOL II. The descriptions here may also be a useful starting point for programmers unfamiliar with these language elements because they are accustomed to using the older language elements that have now been eliminated. If more detail is needed, refer to the *Language Reference* manual.

CURRENT-DATE AND TIME-OF-DAY

VS COBOL II does not have the CURRENT-DATE and TIME-OF-DAY special registers that were included in earlier versions of COBOL. The date and time are available in the DATE, DAY, and TIME special registers, which can only be accessed by the ACCEPT statement. To get the date, define a field or area in the format of the DATE special register.

```
05  RUN-DATE.
    10  RUN-YEAR    PICTURE 99.
    10  RUN-MONTH   PICTURE 99.
    10  RUN-DAY     PICTURE 99.
```

The ACCEPT statement MOVEs the date into the field.

```
ACCEPT RUN-DATE FROM DATE
```

This may be all that is needed if the date is being placed in a record or used for internal processing. If the mm/dd/yy format of CURRENT-DATE is necessary, then an additional data area and some MOVEs will have to be coded.

The TIME special register is eight digits, the first six of which are the same as TIME-OF-DAY, so any difference in convenience of coding is insignificant. The DAY special register provides the Julian date.

WRITE AFTER POSITIONING

The AFTER POSITIONING phrase of the WRITE statement is not included in VS COBOL II. The ADVANCING phrase can perform all of the functions of POSITIONING, and provides simple and direct equivalents for all the POSITIONING options. There are no changes in the ADVANCING phrase itself.

Instead of AFTER POSITIONING 1, 2, or 3 LINES, simply write AFTER ADVANCING 1, 2, or 3 LINES. For AFTER POSITIONING 0 LINES, the equivalent is AFTER ADVANCING PAGE.

AFTER POSITIONING with an identifier allows the program to use actual ANSI control characters. There is no provision in VS COBOL II for the program to directly supply the actual control character. All of the same spacing and skipping functions can, however, be specified with AFTER ADVANCING. The object program will write ANSI control characters in the output file if the DCB parameters for the file specify ANSI control characters. For single, double, or triple spacing, use AFTER ADVANCING 1, 2, or 3 LINES, or AFTER ADVANCING identifier, where identifier is a numeric field containing the number of lines. To suppress spacing, use AFTER ADVANCING 0 LINES, or an identifier containing a value of zero. A skip to channel 1 is most easily accomplished by AFTER ADVANCING PAGE.

To skip to other channels, a mnemonic-name must be used. The mnemonic-name is defined in the SPECIAL-NAMES paragraph of the ENVIRONMENT DIVISION. For example, if the program will require a skip to channel 9, the CONFIGURATION SECTION could include the following.

```
SPECIAL-NAMES.
    C09 IS TOTALS-LINE.
```

TOTALS-LINE is a name made up by the programmer to represent channel 9 in the ADVANCING phrase. The following WRITE statement will print the line at the channel 9 location.

```
WRITE STATEMENT-TOTALS AFTER ADVANCING TOTALS-LINE
```

Mnemonic-names can also be used to skip to channel 1 and to suppress spacing, but the other methods suggested above are simpler.

EXAMINE AND TRANSFORM

The INSPECT statement performs all of the functions of both the EXAMINE and TRANSFORM statements, which are not implemented in VS COBOL II. INSPECT is actually much more powerful than either EXAMINE or TRANSFORM because it has more options and allows more combinations of options.

The syntax of INSPECT and EXAMINE are analogous and the equivalent coding for most situations will readily be apparent. In some common cases the statement will be exactly the same except for the verb. For example,

```
EXAMINE INPUT-FIELD REPLACING ALL SPACES BY ZERO.
INSPECT INPUT-FIELD REPLACING ALL SPACES BY ZERO
```

The equivalent of EXAMINE . . . UNTIL FIRST can be achieved with INSPECT . . . CHARACTERS BEFORE INITIAL. When TALLYING is specified, EXAMINE always uses the TALLY special register. INSPECT specifies in the statement the count field to be used for TALLYING; it can be TALLY or any numeric integer field defined in the DATA DIVISION.

The functions of the TRANSFORM statement can be performed by the INSPECT statement with either the REPLACING phrase or the CONVERTING phrase. If only one or a small number of characters is being changed, REPLACING will generally do the job. For example, instead of

```
TRANSFORM Y-N-FIELD FROM 'YN' TO '10'
```

the following could be written.

```
INSPECT Y-N-FIELD REPLACING ALL 'Y' BY '1'
                              'N' BY '0'
```

To change a larger number of characters, such as changing all lowercase letters to uppercase, CONVERTING will be more concise. CONVERTING is also more like the TRANSFORM statement than REPLACING is. The CONVERTING phrase is described in Chapter 5.

REMARKS AND NOTE

The REMARKS paragraph in the IDENTIFICATION DIVISION is not valid in VS COBOL II, and the NOTE verb is eliminated. Both of these can be easily replaced by comment lines (an * in column 7).

All of the other paragraphs of the IDENTIFICATION DIVISION, except PROGRAM-ID, are obsolete elements in COBOL 85, and will be dropped from the next standard. Therefore, it is advisable to start putting all of the desired information in comment lines and stop using the paragraph names.

REPORT WRITER

The Report Writer is not included in VS COBOL II, and IBM has given no indication that it is likely to be included in the future. Of course, everything that can be done by the Report Writer can also be done by writing out the appropriate logic. The "pure" VS COBOL II solution is to do just that, and stop using Report Writer. However, for installations that want to continue using Report Writer source coding, IBM markets the COBOL Report Writer Precompiler. This package converts Report Writer coding to COBOL source acceptable to the VS COBOL II compiler. It can be used together with the compiler in a way that makes it appear as though the program with the Report Writer language is being compiled in a single step. The Report Writer Precompiler can also be used as a conversion tool. This is described in Chapter 17.

ISAM AND BDAM

VS COBOL II does not support the ISAM and BDAM access methods. All of the function of ISAM can, of course, be implemented using a VSAM indexed file (a KSDS). The COBOL coding for equivalent functions is almost exactly the same as for ISAM. A BDAM relative file can be replaced by a VSAM relative file (an RRDS), defined in the COBOL program as ORGANIZATION IS RELATIVE. There is no exact equivalent of a BDAM direct file, but the same functions could certainly be accomplished with either an indexed or a relative file, although the details of the file design would be somewhat different.

These equivalent access methods are fine for new files. But what if a program being written in VS COBOL II has to access an existing ISAM or BDAM file? Depending on the nature of the file and the number of existing programs that use it, it might be possible to convert the file to VSAM and modify the existing programs. For ISAM the changes would be relatively simple because of the high degree of similarity in the COBOL coding for the two access methods. If the program were converted to VS COBOL II at the same time (and it might as well be), the automated conversion program would take care of almost all of the changes. This is discussed in more detail in Chapter 17. If it is not practical to convert the file, there are only two other options. One is to CALL a program written in assembler language or OS/VS COBOL to do the I/O operations on the file. The other is to write the new program in OS/VS COBOL, and not use VS COBOL II at all. However, either of these alternatives is simply putting off the inevitable conversion, and is in fact increasing the eventual magnitude of that conversion.

DEBUGGING

Many of the debugging features of earlier versions of COBOL have been eliminated in VS COBOL II. Actually, all of the debugging functions are still available, but are provided in different ways. The primary vehicle for debugging in VS COBOL II is the COBTEST debugging tool, which is external to the program and the compiler. Debugging functions are specified at execution time by COBTEST commands, rather than by source statements or compiler options. Some COBTEST commands are mentioned briefly here as equivalents of omitted features. COBTEST, including these commands, is described in detail in Chapter 13.

The READY TRACE, RESET TRACE, EXHIBIT, and ON statements have all been dropped. The functions of these statements are performed by COBTEST, with no source coding.

The TRACE command in COBTEST is the closest parallel to READY TRACE, but other commands can provide a trace in a way that is even easier to use. The STEP or VTRACE commands, used interactively, allow the programmer to actually watch the flow of control in the PROCEDURE DIVISION source as the program executes, and to stop it at any point.

The simpler forms of EXHIBIT can easily be replaced by DISPLAY. There is no source-language equivalent of EXHIBIT CHANGED, other than writing out the necessary comparison logic. Using the WHEN command in COBTEST is like having an EXHIBIT CHANGED before every statement in the program. By putting a LIST command in the command list of the WHEN, the contents of a field can be displayed or printed when it changes, similar to EXHIBIT CHANGED. Auto monitoring (the AUTO LIST command) might accomplish the purpose of EXHIBIT CHANGED in some cases.

The COUNT option of the AT command in COBTEST is equivalent to the ON statement for debugging purposes. Although ON was always identified as a debugging statement, programmers sometimes used it in the regular production logic of a program because it was a very convenient way to implement a first-time switch or a counter. For these purposes a switch or counter, and the related logic, must now be explicitly defined in the program.

VS COBOL II does not support debugging packets. The best way to accomplish the same purpose is to put the debugging statements in their proper place in the PROCEDURE DIVISION as debugging lines. For structured programming this is a more appropriate approach, since it puts the debugging routine in line where it will be executed. Debugging lines have two other advantages over debugging packets. First, they can be placed anywhere, not only after a paragraph name. Second, they can be left in place for future use and can easily be activated or deactivated by the WITH DEBUGGING MODE clause, instead of having to be removed. Another possible substitute for debugging packets is to put the statements in a debugging section (a USE FOR DEBUGGING declarative section). Like a debugging packet, this keeps the debugging statements out of line. However, debugging sections are identified as an obsolete element in COBOL 85 and will be removed from the next standard, so it would be a good idea to get out of the habit of using them. In many cases what was previously accomplished with a debugging packet can be done in COBTEST by using the AT command with a command list.

While USE FOR DEBUGGING is still included in VS COBOL II, some of its capabilities have been dropped. It can no longer be used for references to identifiers or files, only for references to procedure names. Since it is best to phase out debugging sections altogether, the reduction of capability should not be viewed as a problem. The WHEN command in COBTEST can trap all references that change the contents of a field and take whatever action is desired at each reference.

The VS COBOL II compiler does not have the debugging options STATE, FLOW, COUNT, and SYMDMP. The information provided by STATE, the statement that was being executed at the time of the abend, is available in the formatted dump produced by the new FDUMP option. COBTEST provides the same information automatically. The FLOW command in COBTEST performs the same function as the FLOW option in OS/VS COBOL. The FREQ command provides counts of the execution of each verb, like COUNT. FREQ has some additional capabilities, since the counts can be viewed or printed at intermediate points, and can be reset to zero during execution. The new FDUMP option produces a dump similar to that produced by SYMDMP when the program abends, and it is easier to use. FDUMP is discussed in detail in Chapter 12. The COBTEST commands AT, LIST, and TRACE ENTRY can be used to perform the equivalent of the dynamic dump and other functions that were available with SYMDMP.

SUMMARY

Table 10.1 briefly summarizes the items that have been discussed in this chapter. A complete list of all language changes is in Appendix A.

Table 10.1   OS/VS COBOL Elements Not in VS COBOL II

Old Element or Feature	VS COBOL II Replacement
AFTER POSITIONING	AFTER ADVANCING
BDAM	VSAM RELATIVE
COUNT option	COBTEST FREQ
CURRENT-DATE	ACCEPT . . . FROM DATE
DEBUG packet	Debugging lines
DEBUGGING ON identifier	COBTEST WHEN
EXAMINE	INSPECT
EXHIBIT	DISPLAY
EXHIBIT CHANGED	COBTEST WHEN
FLOW option	COBTEST FLOW
ISAM	VSAM INDEXED
NOTE	Comment line
ON	COBTEST AT . . . COUNT
READY TRACE	COBTEST TRACE
REMARKS	Comment line
Report Writer	Report Writer Precompiler
STATE option	FDUMP
SYMDMP option	FDUMP, COBTEST
TIME-OF-DAY	ACCEPT . . . FROM TIME
TRANSFORM	INSPECT

PART II

DEBUGGING

Chapter 11

Improved Compiler Listings

There are many improvements in VS COBOL II in the content and format of the listings that the compiler produces. These improvements provide more information and make that information easier to find. This makes the listings a more useful and efficient tool for debugging and maintaining the program.

THE OPTIONS LIST

The first page of the listing shows all of the compiler options. Figure 11.1 is an example of the options list. In order to show the source of the option specifications for this compilation, it first lists the "Invocation parameters," if there are any. These are the options in the PARM field of the EXEC statement, or on the ISPF panel for running the compiler, or from some equivalent source depending on the environment. Options can also be specified in a PROCESS statement in the source program. (The PROCESS statement is discussed in Chapter 16.) If this statement is used, it is listed next. Then all of the options in effect for this compilation are listed. They are in alphabetical order in one column, making it much easier to find a particular option than in the unordered list produced by OS/VS COBOL.

DIAGNOSTIC MESSAGES

The designations of severity levels for diagnostic messages in VS COBOL II are different from previous IBM compilers. The following table shows the old and new levels.

Figure 11.1   An options list.

```
PP 5668-958 IBM VS COBOL II Release 3.0 09/13/88 8808

Invocation parameters:
NOTERM,SIZE(768K)

PROCESS(CBL) statements:
000100 PROCESS RES,NODYNAM,

Options in effect:
    ADV
     APOST
     AWO
     BUFSIZE(15360)
  NOCMPR2
  NOCOMPILE(S)
     DATA(31)
  NODBCS
  NODECK
  NODUMP
  NODYNAM
  NOEXIT
     FASTSRT
     FDUMP
     FLAG(I,E)
  NOFLAGMIG
  NOFLAGSAA
  NOFLAGSTD
     LANGUAGE(EN)
     LIB
     LINECOUNT(59)
  NOLIST
     MAP
  NONAME
  NONUMBER
     NUMPROC(NOPFD)
     OBJECT
     OFFSET
     OPTIMIZE
     OUTDD(SYSOUO)
  NORENT
     RESIDENT
  NOSEQUENCE
     SIZE(786432)
     SOURCE
     SPACE(1)
     SSRANGE
  NOTERM
  NOTEST
     TRUNC(OPT)
     VBREF
  NOWORD
     XREF
     ZWB
```

OS/VS Level	VS II Level	VS COBOL II Meaning	Return Code
	I	Informational	0
W	W	Warning	4
C	E	Error	8
E	S	Severe error	12
D	U	Unrecoverable	16

So the well-known "E-level diagnostic" is not what it used to be. The letter E now has the meaning that C used to have, and the new designation S replaces E. There is a new level, I, for informational messages. These do not affect the return code from the compiler. The VS COBOL II compiler does a more thorough analysis of the program than previous compilers. As a result you will notice an increase in the number of messages, particularly a lot of I-level messages.

When the same message is issued for more than one line in the source
program, the message is printed in the list of messages only the first
time it occurs. The first occurrence is followed by a list of other lines
for which the same message was issued. This helps to reduce the size
of the listing, particularly in situations that generate many repetitions
of the same message, such as when a single coding error in the DATA
DIVISION causes the same error on every reference to a field. Figure
11.2 is an example of the diagnostic message listing.

Notice that the messages, as well as headings in the compiler listing,
are printed in upper- and lowercase. The new **LANGUAGE** compiler
option can make these all uppercase if necessary. Specifying LAN-
GUAGE(ENGLISH) produces mixed-case listings, like those in the
examples in this chapter.

LANGUAGE(UENGLISH) prints the headings and messages in all
uppercase but does not affect the printing of the source program itself.
If the program is written with lowercase letters, it will be printed that
way. The LANGUAGE option, as its name suggests, also provides
for printing messages and headings in languages other than English.
For example, LANGUAGE(JAPANESE) will produce messages in
Japanese. A special software feature must be purchased to use other
languages. The LANGUAGE values can be abbreviated to the first two
characters: EN, UE, or JA.

At the end of the listing of messages is a summary showing the total
number of messages issued, and a breakdown by severity level.

The format of the FLAG option has been changed to provide more
selective control over which messages are printed. Any of the five
severity levels can be specified as the lowest level to be printed. For
example, FLAG(E) means that only messages with severity E or worse
will be shown in the listing. FLAG(I) will print all messages. If some
messages are not printed because of the FLAG option, the summary
will have an additional line showing the number of messages that were
suppressed.

THE SOURCE LISTING

There are a number of improvements in the listing of the source
program. The most obvious, and perhaps the most useful, is that diagnostic messages can be embedded in the source listing. If this option is
used, each message is printed directly under the source line in which

Figure 11.2 A diagnostic message listing.

```
PP 5668-958 IBM VS COBOL II Release 3.0 09/13/88 8808          PHONREPT  Date 01/19/89  Time 15:27:02    Page  11

LineID  Message code   Message text

        IGYSC3002-I    A severe error was found in the program.  The "OPTIMIZE" compiler option was cancelled.
    14  IGYGR1216-I    A "RECORDING MODE" of "F" was assumed for file "CALL-DETAIL".
    32  IGYGR1216-I    A "RECORDING MODE" of "F" was assumed for file "PHONE-REPORT".
    64  IGYGR1080-S    A "VALUE" clause literal was not compatible with the data category of the subject data item.  The "VALUE"
                       clause was discarded.
    86  IGYPS2121-S    "REPT-RATE" was not defined as a data-name.  The statement was discarded.

                       Same message on line:    99   101

    91  IGYPS2121-S    "REPT-EXTENTION" was not defined as a data-name.  The statement was discarded.


Messages     Total    Informational    Warning    Error    Severe    Terminating
Printed:       8            3                                  5


*  Statistics for COBOL program PHONREPT:
***     Source records = 122
***     Data Division statements = 38
***     Procedure Division statements = 36

End of compilation 1, program PHONREPT, highest severity 12.

Return code 12
```

the error was found. This saves a lot of page turning, and is especially convenient for viewing the listing on a CRT. Figure 11.3 shows one page of a source listing, with an example of an embedded message. All of the messages are still collected together at the end of the listing as well, even if they are also embedded.

A second value in the FLAG option specifies the lowest level of messages to be embedded in the source listing. FLAG(I,E) would be a reasonable choice to avoid embedding of unimportant messages. This specifies that all messages will be printed at the end of the listing, but only messages with severity E or worse will be embedded in the source listing. One exception is that messages connected with options or COPY statements, because they are processed in an early phase of compilation, are always printed at the beginning of the listing. If this happens, an informational message at the end of the listing will refer to the messages at the beginning.

Another option that may make the listing easier to look at on a CRT is **LINECOUNT(0)**. (LINECOUNT is just a new name for LINECNT.) Specifying zero for the number of lines eliminates all page breaks in the compiler listing, so the source listing, cross-references, and maps are not broken up by extra headings.

A heading line has been added to the source listing. It has column headings, and a scale showing the column numbers for the source statements. The scale also indicates the beginning of Area A and Area B.

A new compiler-directing statement in VS COBOL II allows the programmer to specify a title to be printed in the page heading. This can help to identify the program, or sections of a large program. The **TITLE** statement looks like this.

```
TITLE 'ACCOUNTS RECEIVABLE MASTER FILE UPDATE'
```

A TITLE statement can be anywhere in the program. It is not printed itself, but causes a new page to be started, and the specified title replaces the compiler identification and release level on the left side of the page heading. The PROGRAM-ID, date, time, and page number on the right side of the heading line remain as they were. The new title stays in effect until there is another TITLE statement, or to the end of the listing.

Figure 11.3   A page of a source listing.

```
000061  006100       05  REPT-COST              PICTURE Z,ZZ9.99.
000062  006200                                  PICTURE X(73).
000063  006300
000064  006400  WORKING-STORAGE SECTION.
000065  006500  77  MORE-INPUT PICTURE X  VALUE 'Y'.
000066  006600  88  END-OF-INPUT VALUE 'N'.
000067  006700
000068  006800  01  RATE-CODE-TABLE.
000069  006900      05  RATE-CODE-VALUES PIC XXX VALUE 'DEN'.               69
000070  007000      05  REDEFINES RATE-CODE-VALUES.
000071  007100        10  RATE-CODE OCCURS 3 TIMES INDEXED BY RATE-X PIC X.
000072  007200
000073  007300  PROCEDURE DIVISION.
000074  007400      OPEN INPUT CALL-DETAIL OUTPUT PHONE-REPORT             14 32
000075  007500      READ CALL-DETAIL                                      14
000076  007600         AT END SET END-OF-INPUT TO TRUE                    66
000077  007700      END-READ
000078  007800      PERFORM UNTIL END-OF-INPUT                            66
000079  007900         PERFORM PRINT-REPORT-LINE                          86
000080  008000         READ CALL-DETAIL                                   14
000081  008100            AT END SET END-OF-INPUT TO TRUE                 66
000082  008200         END-READ
000083  008300      END-PERFORM
000084  008400      CLOSE CALL-DETAIL PHONE-REPORT                        14 32
000085  008500      STOP RUN.
000086  008600  PRINT-REPORT-LINE.
000087  008700      MOVE SPACES TO REPORT-LINE                            IMP 35
000088  008800      MOVE CALL-MM TO REPT-MONTH                            18 36
000089  008900      MOVE '/' TO REPT-SLASH                                37
000090  009000      MOVE CALL-DD TO REPT-DAY                              19 38
000091  009100      CALL 'FORMAT-TIME'                                    104
000092  009200      MOVE CALL-EXTENSION TO REPT-EXTENSION                 23 UND

==000092==> IGYPS2121-S  "REPT-EXTENSION" was not defined as a data-name.  The statement was
            discarded.

000093  009300      IF CALL-RATE-CODE NUMERIC                             28
000094  009400         AND CALL-RATE-CODE >= 1                            28
000095  009500         AND CALL-RATE-CODE <= 3                            28
000096  009600         MOVE RATE-CODE (CALL-RATE-CODE) TO REPT-RATE       71 28 56
000097  009700      ELSE MOVE CALL-RATE-CODE TO REPT-RATE                 28 56
000098  009800      END-IF
000099  009900      MOVE CALL-MINUTES TO REPT-MINUTES                     29 58
000100  010000      IF CALL-MINUTES > 0 MOVE CALL-COST TO REPT-COST       29 30 61
000101  010100      WRITE REPORT-LINE AFTER ADVANCING 1 LINE.             35
000102  010200  IDENTIFICATION DIVISION.
000103  010300  PROGRAM-ID. FORMAT-TIME.
000104  010400  PROCEDURE DIVISION.
000105  010500      EVALUATE CALL-HH                                      21
000106  010600         WHEN 00
000107  010700            MOVE 12 TO REPT-HH                              41
000108  010800            MOVE 'AM' TO REPT-AM-PM                         45
000109  010900         WHEN 01 THRU 11
000110  011000            MOVE CALL-HH TO REPT-HH                         21 41
```

Another very useful improvement, an **embedded cross-reference**, is on the right side of the source listing under the heading "Cross Reference." On each line, the compiler lists the line number where the definition is located for any name that is used in this line. This is not what we usually think of as a cross-reference. It does not list other lines that refer to something in this line. Nevertheless, it can be very handy and saves flipping to the cross-reference part of the listing to get the information. The embedded cross-reference covers both data-names and procedure-names. For example, line 88 in Figure 11.3 shows that CALL-MM is defined on line 18 and REPT-MONTH is defined on line 36. The cross-reference on line 79 shows that PRINT-REPORT-LINE is defined on line 86.

There are some codes in the embedded cross-reference in addition to line numbers. IMP is shown for a name, such as a special register or figurative constant, that has an implicit definition in COBOL. UND means that a name is undefined, and DUP means that it is duplicately defined. EXT is an abbreviation for external, but it does not mean that a name is EXTERNAL. EXT is used only for the program name in a CALL when the called program is separately compiled. The cross-reference for an EXTERNAL name points to the line where it is defined in this program, just as for any other name. If full compilation (generation of object code) is stopped because of errors, some references may be unresolved and an asterisk will be shown in the embedded cross-reference.

The embedded cross-reference is selected by the same option, XREF, that controls the full cross-references that follow the source listing. Either all of the cross-reference output is produced, or none of it.

On the left side of the source listing, under the headings "PL" and "SL," the compiler shows the nesting level of each line. SL is the nesting level of statements in the PROCEDURE DIVISION. PL is the program nesting level for contained programs. The level is blank for the outermost level of either statements or programs. A statement nested within an outermost statement, like the PERFORM on line 79 in Figure 11.3, is level 1. Deeper levels of nesting have progressively higher numbers. If there is more than one verb on a line, as in line 101, the level shown is for the first verb on the line. Both a verb and its matching scope terminator have the same nesting level. ELSE has the same level as its associated IF and END-IF. Examining the nesting levels can be very helpful in identifying coding errors where an ELSE or a scope terminator is not matched with the intended verb, or a statement is not at the intended level. Statement nesting levels are only applicable to the PROCEDURE DIVISION. The program nesting level is the same for every line of a contained program, in any DIVISION.

CROSS-REFERENCES

The cross-reference listings have also been significantly improved. The cross-references are always sorted in VS COBOL II. There is only one option for cross-references, XREF, and it produces sorted cross-reference listings.

A major improvement is that the cross-references do not just show where a name is referenced; they also show the type of reference. For example, in the data-name cross-reference in Figure 11.4, some of the references have an M before the line number. This means that the field is modified by that reference. The references without the M use the field but do not change it. There is one unfortunate exception, however. An M is not shown where the name is passed BY REFER-ENCE as a parameter in the USING phrase of a CALL statement, even though the called program might change the field.

In the procedure-name cross-reference, there are seven different types of references. Figure 11.5 shows a procedure cross-reference. Every reference has a letter before the line number indicating the type of reference. The legend at the beginning explains the meaning of each letter. If the name is used as an INPUT PROCEDURE or OUTPUT PROCEDURE in a SORT statement, the reference is shown with a P, as though it were a PERFORM.

The data-name cross-reference in VS COBOL II includes references to special registers. These were not shown in earlier compilers.

Another improvement involves references in a statement that extends over more than one line. The cross-reference in VS COBOL II shows the number of the line on which the name actually appears, whereas OS/VS COBOL would always show the line number of the verb that begins the statement.

There is one new type of cross-reference in VS COBOL II. Figure 11.6 shows a **program cross-reference** listing for a program with several nested programs. It lists the PROGRAM-ID of each program, the line number of the PROGRAM-ID paragraph (under "Defined"), and the line numbers where the program name is referenced. Separately com-piled called programs are also listed, with the word "EXTERNAL" in

Figure 11.4 Part of a data-name cross-reference listing.

PP 5668-958 IBM VS COBOL II Release 3.0 09/13/88 8808   ADA001   Date 12/29/88   Time 15:54:59

An "M" preceding a data-name reference indicates that the data-name is modified by this reference.

Defined	Cross-reference of data names	References
165	ABORT-CODE	1155
197	AVG-COST	M928 929 M939
510	COB2-CURRENT-DATE	551 552
513	COB2-CURRENT-DD	M529
511	COB2-CURRENT-MM	M527
515	COB2-CURRENT-YY	M531
506	COB2-YYMMDD	M525
509	COB2-YYMMDD-DD	528
508	COB2-YYMMDD-MM	526
507	COB2-YYMMDD-YY	530
351	D-AM-PM	M863
359	D-CALL-NUMBER	
360	D-CALL1	M869
362	D-CALL2	M870
364	D-CALL3	M871
336	D-CARR-CODE	M855
357	D-COST	M865
342	D-DASH	M858
363	D-DASH1	M872
347	D-DATE	M861
355	D-DURATION	M864
349	D-HOUR	M862
353	D-PERIOD	M874 M881 M888
340	D-SPACE	
361	D-SPACE1	
345	D-STAGE1	M860
338	D-TELEPHONE	M856
341	D-TEL1	M857
343	D-TEL2	M859
109	D-TEL3	669
108	D-TIME-END	668
182	D-TIME-START	M875 904 M936 951 984
191	DAY-CALLS	M879 907 M937
188	DAY-COST	M877 906 M938
333	DAY-DURATION	M854 894
112	DETAIL-LINE	671
111	E-TIME-END	670
176	E-TIME-START	709
175	END-OF-FILE	M715
178	END-OF-FILE-FLAG	826 832
172	END-OF-SORT-RECS	M819 M831
172	END-OF-SORT-RECS-FLAG	565 569 656 1056 1062
171	END-OF-TABLE	M556 M566 M570 M583 M597 M653 M664 M1053 M1058 M1088 M1105
189	END-OF-TABLE-FLAG	595 1102
494	END-OF-TYPE-SW	M592 M610 M1099 M1122
184	EOF-VAL-FILE	M620 M659
192	EVE-CALLS	M882 911 M936 953 986
189	EVE-COST	M886 914 M937
497	EVE-DURATION	M884 913 M938
242	FOUND-SWITCH	M755
	HEAD-1	1029

Figure 11.5 Part of a procedure cross-reference listing.

PP 5668-958 IBM VS COBOL II Release 3.0 09/13/88 8808   ADA001   Date 12/29/88   Time 15:54:59

Context usage is indicated by the letter preceding a procedure-name reference.
These letters and their meanings are:
    A = ALTER (procedure-name)
    D = GO TO (procedure-name) DEPENDING ON
    E = End of range of (PERFORM) through (procedure-name)
    G = GO TO (procedure-name)
    P = PERFORM (procedure-name)
    T = (ALTER) TO PROCEED TO (procedure-name)
    U = USE FOR DEBUGGING (procedure-name)

Defined	Cross-reference of procedures	References
541	A000-HOUSEKEEPING.	P536
571	A100-EXIT	
543	A100-HOUSEKEEPING	
646	A105-CLOSE	G635 G642
637	A105-CONT.	G624
618	A105-INIT-VALID-CODES-TABLE.	P559
621	A105-PROCESS	G644
648	A105-XIT	E560
573	A110-INIT-SUMMARY-TABLE.	P564
588	A110-XIT	E564
590	A120-INIT-REG-TABLE.	P568
600	A120-XIT	E568
602	A121-INIT-TYPES.	P594
613	A121-XIT	E594
616	A999-EXIT	E536
650	B000-LOAD-TABLE.	P537
659	B100-EXIT	
652	B100-LOAD-TABLE	E655 G666 G676
685	B110-EXIT.	P655
662	B110-LOAD-TABLE. . . .	E537 G658
687	B999-EXIT. . . .	P538
689	C000-SORT.	
701	C100-EXIT	
691	C100-SORT	E538
703	C999-EXIT.	P695
705	D000-BUILD-SORT-RECORDS. . . .	
711	D120-EXIT	
707	D120-MAIN	E708 G716 G761
780	D130-EXIT.	P708
713	D130-READ.	P763 G786 G789
804	D140-EXIT.	P763
782	D140-TIME-PERIOD	E695 G710
806	D999-EXIT.	P696
808	E000-WRITE-REPORT. . . .	
815	E100-EXIT	
810	E100-OUTPUT	E811
827	E110-EXIT.	P811
817	E110-REPORT-ROUTINE. . . .	E825 G835
845	E120-EXIT. . . .	P825
829	E120-REPORT-MAIN	E834 E838 E843
940	E140-EXIT.	P834 P838 P843
899	E140-TYPE-BREAK. . . .	P933
942	E150-ADD-TO-SUMMARY-TABLE. . . .	E933
947	E150-XIT	

Figure 11.6   A program cross-reference listing.

```
PP 5668-958 IBM VS COBOL II Release 3.0 09/13/88 8808

 Defined    Cross-reference of programs        References

        2   ADA001 . . . . . . . . . . . .  1159
     1017   HOUSEKEEPING . . . . . . . . .  1119 543
     1039   INIT-REG-TABLE . . . . . . . .  1064 1035
     1102   INIT-SUMMARY-TABLE . . . . . .  1118 1032
     1067   INIT-VALID-CODES-TABLE . . . .  1099 1028
     1122   LOAD-TABLE . . . . . . . . . .  1158 544
 EXTERNAL   TS013A00 . . . . . . . . . . .  1014
```

the "Defined" column. The program cross-reference is printed whenever the XREF option is in effect, even if there are no contained programs and no CALLS. In such cases, it just has one line for the single program.

Names in the cross-reference listings are printed in all uppercase, even if they were written in lowercase in the source program. The compiler translates all names to uppercase internally.

MAPS

Figure 11.7 shows a VS COBOL II DATA DIVISION map. The level numbers and names are indented to show their relative levels in the structure, very much as you would normally indent them in the source. As in the cross-references, the names are in all uppercase. The leftmost column shows the line number where the name is defined in the source, making it easy to go back and forth between the map and the source without having to use the cross-reference.

There are some new types of base locators. In older compilers, the base locators in both the FILE SECTION and the WORKING-STORAGE SECTION were called BL. In VS COBOL II, a base locator for a record in the FILE SECTION is a **BLF**, and a base locator in the WORKING-STORAGE SECTION is a **BLW**. The LINKAGE SECTION still uses BLLs. The base locator for an EXTERNAL record in WORKING-STORAGE is a **BLX**.

Two different displacements are given for each field. The first, under the heading "Blk," is the displacement of the field from the base locator. This is the same as with older compilers. The next column, "Structure," is new. The **structure displacement** is the displacement of the field from the beginning of the 01 level that contains it. For example, in Figure 11.7 REPT-DAY is at displacement X'013' from BLW 0,

Figure 11.7 Part of a DATA DIVISION map.

```
PP 5668-958 IBM VS COBOL II Release 3.0 09/13/88 8808            PHONREPT  Date 01/20/89  Time 14:25:45   Page     9

Data Division Map

Data Definition Attribute codes (rightmost column) have the following meanings:
    D = Object of OCCURS DEPENDING     G = GLOBAL                               S = Spanned file
    E = EXTERNAL                       O = Has OCCURS clause                    U = Undefined format file
    F = Fixed length file              OG= Group has own length definition      V = Variable length file
    FB= Fixed length blocked file      R = REDEFINES                            VB= Variable length blocked file

Source   Hierarchy and                                        Base      Hex-Displacement  Asmblr Data                    Data Def
LineID   Data Name                                            Locator   Blk   Structure   Definition    Data Type        Attributes
     2  PROGRAM-ID PHONREPT ---------------------------------------------------------------------------------------------------------*
    14   FD CALL-DETAIL . . . . . . . . . . . . . . . . . . .           001                             QSAM             FB
    16   01 CALL-RECORD . . . . . . . . . . . . . . . . . . . BLF=0000  000               DS 0CL29      Group
    17     02 CALL-DATE . . . . . . . . . . . . . . . . . . . BLF=0000  000   0 000 000   DS 0CL4       Group
    18       03 CALL-MM . . . . . . . . . . . . . . . . . . . BLF=0000  000   0 000 000   DS 2C         Disp-Num
    19       03 CALL-DD . . . . . . . . . . . . . . . . . . . BLF=0000  002   0 000 002   DS 2C         Disp-Num
    20     02 CALL-TIME . . . . . . . . . . . . . . . . . . . BLF=0000  004   0 000 004   DS 0CL4       Group
    21       03 CALL-HH . . . . . . . . . . . . . . . . . . . BLF=0000  004   0 000 004   DS 2C         Disp-Num
    22       03 CALL-MIN. . . . . . . . . . . . . . . . . . . BLF=0000  006   0 000 006   DS 2C         Disp-Num
    23     02 CALL-EXTENSION. . . . . . . . . . . . . . . . . BLF=0000  008   0 000 008   DS 4C         Disp-Num
    24     02 CALL-NUMBER-CALLED. . . . . . . . . . . . . . . BLF=0000  00C   0 000 00C   DS 0CL10      Group
    25       03 CALL-AREA-CODE-CALLED . . . . . . . . . . . . BLF=0000  00C   0 000 00C   DS 3C         Disp-Num
    26       03 CALL-EXCHANGE-CALLED. . . . . . . . . . . . . BLF=0000  00F   0 000 00F   DS 3C         Disp-Num
    27       03 CALL-LAST-4-CALLED. . . . . . . . . . . . . . BLF=0000  012   0 000 012   DS 4C         Disp-Num
    28     02 CALL-RATE-CODE. . . . . . . . . . . . . . . . . BLF=0000  016   0 000 016   DS 1C         Disp-Num
    29     02 CALL-MINUTES. . . . . . . . . . . . . . . . . . BLF=0000  017   0 000 017   DS 2P         Packed-Dec
    30     02 CALL-COST . . . . . . . . . . . . . . . . . . . BLF=0000  019   0 000 019   DS 4P         Packed-Dec
    32   FD PHONE-REPORT. . . . . . . . . . . . . . . . . . .           001                             QSAM             FB
    35   01 REPORT-OUT. . . . . . . . . . . . . . . . . . . . BLF=0001  000               DS 132C       Display
    38   77 MORE-INPUT. . . . . . . . . . . . . . . . . . . . BLW=0000  000               DS 1C         Display
    39   88 END-OF-INPUT. . . . . . . . . . . . . . . . . . . BLW=0000  000   0 000 000
    41   01 RATE-CODE-TABLE . . . . . . . . . . . . . . . . . BLW=0000  008               DS 0CL3       Group
    42     02 RATE-CODE-VALUES. . . . . . . . . . . . . . . . BLW=0000  008   0 000 000   DS 3C         Display
    43     02 FILLER. . . . . . . . . . . . . . . . . . . . . BLW=0000  008   0 000 000   DS 0CL3       Group            R
    44       03 RATE-CODE . . . . . . . . . . . . . . . . . . BLW=0000  008   0 000 000   DS 1C         Display          O
    44          RATE-X. . . . . . . . . . . . . . . . . . . . IDX=0001  000                             Index-Name
    46   01 REPORT-LINE . . . . . . . . . . . . . . . . . . . BLW=0000  010               DS 0CL132     Group
    47     02 REPT-MONTH. . . . . . . . . . . . . . . . . . . BLW=0000  010   0 000 000   DS 2C         Num-Edit
    48     02 REPT-SLASH. . . . . . . . . . . . . . . . . . . BLW=0000  012   0 000 002   DS 1C         Display
    49     02 REPT-DAY. . . . . . . . . . . . . . . . . . . . BLW=0000  013   0 000 003   DS 2C         Disp-Num
    50     02 FILLER. . . . . . . . . . . . . . . . . . . . . BLW=0000  015   0 000 005   DS 3C         Display
    51     02 REPT-TIME . . . . . . . . . . . . . . . . . . . BLW=0000  018   0 000 008   DS 0CL8       Group
    52       03 REPT-HH . . . . . . . . . . . . . . . . . . . BLW=0000  018   0 000 008   DS 2C         Num-Edit
    53       03 REPT-COLON. . . . . . . . . . . . . . . . . . BLW=0000  01A   0 000 00A   DS 1C         Display
    54       03 REPT-MM . . . . . . . . . . . . . . . . . . . BLW=0000  01B   0 000 00B   DS 2C         Disp-Num
    55       03 FILLER. . . . . . . . . . . . . . . . . . . . BLW=0000  01D   0 000 00D   DS 1C         Display
    56       03 REPT-AM-PM. . . . . . . . . . . . . . . . . . BLW=0000  01E   0 000 00E   DS 2C         Display
    57     02 FILLER. . . . . . . . . . . . . . . . . . . . . BLW=0000  020   0 000 010   DS 3C         Display
    58     02 REPT-EXTENSION. . . . . . . . . . . . . . . . . BLW=0000  023   0 000 013   DS 4C         Disp-Num
    59     02 FILLER. . . . . . . . . . . . . . . . . . . . . BLW=0000  027   0 000 017   DS 3C         Display
    60     02 REPT-NUMB-CALLED. . . . . . . . . . . . . . . . BLW=0000  02A   0 000 01A   DS 0CL12      Group
    61       03 REPT-AREA-CODE. . . . . . . . . . . . . . . . BLW=0000  02A   0 000 01A   DS 3C         Disp-Num
    62       03 FILLER. . . . . . . . . . . . . . . . . . . . BLW=0000  02D   0 000 01D   DS 1C         Display
    63       03 REPT-EXCHANGE . . . . . . . . . . . . . . . . BLW=0000  02E   0 000 01E   DS 3C         Disp-Num
    64       03 REPT-HYPHEN . . . . . . . . . . . . . . . . . BLW=0000  031   0 000 021   DS 1C         Display
    65       03 REPT-LAST-4 . . . . . . . . . . . . . . . . . BLW=0000  032   0 000 022   DS 4C         Disp-Num
```

but its displacement from the beginning of REPORT-LINE is X'003'. The structure displacement is also useful when more than one base locator is used to address a large record. The structure displacement will show the position of each field in the record as a whole.

The last column on the right, "Data Def Attributes," replaces the old "R O Q M" flags. It provides the information given by the earlier flags, but also shows many other data characteristics. All of the attributes that can be shown in this column are listed at the beginning of the map. The code for the object of an OCCURS . . . DEPENDING ON is D instead of Q.

Notice the first line under the column headings in Figure 11.7, giving the PROGRAM-ID with a line of hyphens after it. If there are any contained programs, there will be a similar line for each one, marking in the map the beginning of the DATA DIVISION for that program.

There are no internal data-names in the map. They are no longer needed because the listing of object code for the PROCEDURE DIVI-SION now shows the actual name from the source program wherever a field is referenced, instead of the internal name. All interpretation of maps can therefore be done with source names. Figure 11.8 is part of an object code listing.

There is no significant change in the condensed PROCEDURE DIVI-SION listing, other than the name of the option to produce it. Instead of CLIST, the option is now **OFFSET**, because it shows the offset from the beginning of the module of the object code for each statement. The names of the options for the other maps are also different. The DATA DIVISION map is specified by **MAP** instead of DMAP, and the option for the full object code listing is **LIST** instead of PMAP.

Paralleling the new program cross-reference, there is also a new type of map in VS COBOL II. This is the **nested program map**, illustrated in Figure 11.9. It comes along with the MAP option, but is only produced if there are contained programs, and shows the relationship of contain-ing and contained programs. There is one line for each program in the compilation. Indentation is used to show the levels of nesting of the programs, and the numerical nesting level is also shown. The "Source Line ID" is the line number of the PROGRAM-ID paragraph. On the right are codes, explained at the top, indicating whether each program has the INITIAL or COMMON attribute, and whether it has a USING phrase in the PROCEDURE DIVISION header.

Figure 11.8 Part of an object code listing.

```
PP 5668-958 IBM VS COBOL II Release 3.0 09/13/88 8808

000085  *PRINT-REPORT-LINE
000086  MOVE                                                                    REPORT-LINE
000532         9240 8000           MVI   0(8),X'40'                REPORT-LINE+1
000536         D282 8001 8000      MVC   1(131,8),0(8)
000087  MOVE
00053C  D203 D174 A165             MVC   372(4,13),357(10)         TS2=4
000542  F211 D1FE 9000             PACK  382(2,13),0(2,9)          TS2=15
000548  960F D17F                  OI    383(13),X'0F'             TS2=24
00054C  DE03 D174 D17E             ED    372(4,13),382(13)
000552                       GN=34 EQU   *                         REPT-MONTH
000552  D201 8000 D176             MVC   0(2,8),374(13)
000088  MOVE                                                       REPT-SLASH
000558  9261 8002                  MVI   2(8),X'61'
000089  MOVE                                                       CALL-DD
00055C  D201 8003 9002             MVC   3(2,8),2(9)               REPT-DAY
000562  96F0 8004                  OI    4(8),X'F0'                REPT-DAY+1
000090  PERFORM                                                    VN=3
000566  D203 D150 D144             MVC   336(4,13),324(13)         PSV=2
00056C  4120 B1E8                  LA    2,488(0,11)               GN=20(000578)
000570  5020 D144                  ST    2,334(0,13)               VN=3
000574  47F0 B2C6                  BC    15,710(0,11)              FORMAT-TIME
000578                       GN=20 EQU   *
000578  D203 D144 D150             MVC   324(4,13),336(13)         VN=3
000091  MOVE                                                       CALL-EXTENSION
00057E  D203 8013 9008             MVC   19(4,8),8(9)              REPT-EXTENSION
000584  96F0 8016                  OI    22(8),X'F0'               REPT-EXTENSION+3
000092  MOVE                                                       CALL-AREA-CODE-CALLED
000588  D202 801A 900C             MVC   26(3,8),12(9)             REPT-AREA-CODE
00058E  96F0 801C                  OI    28(8),X'F0'               REPT-AREA-CODE+2
000093  MOVE                                                       CALL-EXCHANGE-CALLED
000592  D202 801E 900F             MVC   30(3,8),15(9)             REPT-EXCHANGE
000598  96F0 8020                  OI    32(8),X'F0'               REPT-EXCHANGE+2
000094  MOVE                                                       CALL-HYPHEN
00059C  9260 8021                  MVI   33(8),X'60'
000095  MOVE                                                       CALL-LAST-4-CALLED
0005A0  D203 8022 9012             MVC   34(4,8),18(9)             REPT-LAST-4
0005A6  96F0 8025                  OI    37(8),X'F0'               REPT-LAST-4+3
000096  IF                                                         PGMLIT AT +35
0005AA  DD00 9016 A02F             TRT   22(1,9),47(10)            CALL-RATE-CODE
0005B0  58B0 C008                  L     11,8(0,12)                PBL=1
0005B4  4770 B266                  BC    7,614(0,11)               GN=7(0005F6)
0005B8  D200 D177 9016             MVC   375(13),22(9)             TS2=7
0005BE  96F0 D177                  OI    375(13),X'F0'             TS2=7
0005C2  95F1 D177                  CLI   375(13),X'F1'             TS2=7
0005C6  4740 B266                  BC    4,614(0,11)               GN=7(0005F6)
0005CA  D200 D177 9016             MVC   375(13),22(9)             TS2=7
0005D0  96F0 D177                  OI    375(13),X'F0'             TS2=7
0005D4  95F3 D177                  CLI   375(13),X'F3'             TS2=7
0005D8  4720 B266                  BC    2,614(0,11)               GN=7(0005F6)
000099  MOVE
0005DC  F270 D170 D177             PACK  368(8,13),22(1,9)         TS2=0
0005E2  960F D170                  OI    375(13),X'0F'             TS2=7
0005E6  4F20 D170                  CVB   2,368(0,13)               TS2=0
0005EA  1A27                       AR    2,7
0005EC  D200 8029 2007             MVC   41(1,8),7(2)              REPT-RATE
0005F2  47F0 B26C                  BC    15,620(0,11)              GN=8(0005FC)     RATE-CODE()
```

Figure 11.9   A nested program map.

```
PP 5668-958 IBM VS COBOL II Release 3.0 09/13/88 8808              ADA001    Date 01/20/89

Nested Program Map

Program Attribute codes (rightmost column) have the following meanings:
    C = COMMON
    I = INITIAL
    U = PROCEDURE DIVISION USING...

Source Nesting                                                            Program
LineID Level   Program Name from PROGRAM-ID paragraph                     Attributes
    2           ADA001. . . . . . . . . . . . . . . . . . . . . . . . . . U
  1017     1      HOUSEKEEPING. . . . . . . . . . . . . . . . . . . . . .
  1039     2        INIT-REG-TABLE. . . . . . . . . . . . . . . . . . . .
  1067     2        INIT-VALID-CODES-TABLE. . . . . . . . . . . . . . . . C
  1102     2        INIT-SUMMARY-TABLE. . . . . . . . . . . . . . . . . .
  1122     1      LOAD-TABLE. . . . . . . . . . . . . . . . . . . . . . . I
```

SELECTIVELY SUPPRESSING PARTS OF THE LISTING

VS COBOL II has a new compiler-directing statement that allows the programmer to suppress the printing of parts of the compiler listing, for parts of the program. The statement is *CONTROL. (The asterisk is part of the keyword.) This statement can be used anywhere in the program, but it must be on a line by itself. It can turn off and turn on the SOURCE, MAP, and LIST options at the point in the source where the *CONTROL statement appears. For example

```
*CONTROL NOSOURCE
```

suppresses the listing of the source from that point on. Printing can be resumed by coding

```
*CONTROL SOURCE
```

More than one option can be specified in one statement. For example, before a COPY of a large record description in the DATA DIVISION you could code

```
*CONTROL NOSOURCE,NOMAP
```

This would suppress the listing of the source code, and also suppress the DATA DIVISION map for that part of the program. NOLIST and LIST can be used similarly in *CONTROL statements to suppress the object code listing for part of the PROCEDURE DIVISION. It does not affect the OFFSET listing.

The *CONTROL statement cannot turn on an option that was not in effect at the beginning of the compilation. It can only suppress the output for an option that is in effect. For example, if NOLIST is in effect for the compilation, then *CONTROL LIST and *CONTROL NOLIST have no effect. But if the LIST option is in effect for the compilation, then *CONTROL NOLIST will suspend it and *CONTROL LIST will resume the LIST output.

*CBL can be used as a synonym for *CONTROL. However, CBL (without the asterisk) is a synonym for the PROCESS statement. The similarity is likely to lead to confusion, so it is best to use the longer, more distinct keywords for both statements.

The use of *CONTROL seems attractive as a way to keep the compiler listing shorter, especially if it is to be viewed on a CRT. But it omits information that could turn out to be useful or essential for debugging or for understanding the program, and the omission is not obvious. The *CONTROL statement itself is never printed on the listing. If the NOSOURCE option is used, an informational message indicates that part of the source listing has been suppressed. Informational messages are usually not embedded in the source, however, so the message will only appear at the end of the listing, not at the point of the omission. For NOMAP and NOLIST there isn't even a message, so it might not be immediately apparent to someone looking at the listing that part of the map is missing. Because it omits potentially important information, the use of *CONTROL should be discouraged. At most, it is only suitable for temporary use during development. It should never be left in a production program, or used when the compiler listing will be filed for future reference.

Chapter 12

The Formatted Dump (FDUMP)

The **formatted dump** is a powerful debugging tool for VS COBOL II. It provides more information than the symbolic abend dump in OS/VS COBOL, in a form that is easier to use. The process of obtaining the formatted dump is also simpler. Most abends can be debugged using the VS COBOL II formatted dump alone, without looking at the MVS system dump.

HOW TO GET A FORMATTED DUMP

There are two simple requirements to get a formatted dump. When the program is compiled, specify the **FDUMP** option (if it is not the default). At run time, provide a SYSDBOUT DD statement for the dump output. This would typically be

```
//SYSDBOUT DD SYSOUT = A
```

That's all there is to it. One other requirement is that the STAE run-time option must be in effect. Since this is usually the default, normally nothing has to be done about it.

To get a formatted dump in CICS, all that is necessary is to specify the FDUMP compiler option. No DD statement is needed. The formatted dump will be written to a temporary storage queue named CEBRxxxx, where xxxx is the terminal ID of the terminal that initiated the transaction. The CEBR transaction can be used to browse the formatted dump.

In order to get a symbolic dump in OS/VS COBOL, a data set from the compilation had to be available at run time. This was a cumbersome procedure that discouraged the use of the symbolic dump. The VS COBOL II formatted dump is sure to enjoy more widespread use because it is so much easier to obtain. The need for the data set is eliminated by including in the object module all of the tables that are needed to produce the formatted dump. This does make the object program somewhat larger than it would be without the FDUMP option, but for most batch programs, the size is not a problem. It is practical to use FDUMP in production as well as for testing, which can make it much easier to debug production abends.

In CICS the size of the module may be more of a problem. Dynamic storage is usually at a premium, unless the program runs above the 16 megabyte line in an XA system. Also, CICS imposes limits on the total size of a program. Another drawback is that a formatted dump takes a lot of space in temporary storage. It is disproportionately large compared to the types of data for which temporary storage is generally used. Because of the object module size and the amount of temporary storage needed, you may not want to use FDUMP routinely in CICS.

FINDING THE FAILING STATEMENT

One of the first things that a programmer wants to know when a program abends is which statement in the program was being executed when the abend occurred. Figure 12.1 shows the beginning of a formatted dump. The fourth line after the heading answers the question with no work at all. The statement that failed is on source line 112, and it is the first verb on that line. This is the same information provided by the STATE option in OS/VS COBOL. (The "or" in the message should really be "and." Both the line number and the verb number in that line are shown.)

If the program was compiled with the OPTIMIZE option, the very handy message in Figure 12.1 is replaced by:

```
Optimization was in effect for this program.
The relative address of the next instruction to be executed:
'000004C6'
```

Finding the failing statement from this information is not quite as simple as being given the line number, but it is still very easy. It does not even require arithmetic. It is only necessary to find the relative

Figure 12.1 The first page of a formatted dump.

```
--- VS COBOL II Formatted Dump at ABEND ---

Program = 'PHONREPT'

Completion code = 'S0C7'

PSW at ABEND = '078D10080006BA8'

Line number or verb number being executed:    '0000112'/'1'

The GP registers at entry to ABEND were

     Regs  0 -  3  - '8000BE06  00051208  00000080  000511EC'

     Regs  4 -  7  - '00009440  80006716  00005FFE  00009778'

     Regs  8 - 11  - '000511E8  000096F1  00006214  0000659C'

     Regs 12 - 15  - '00006208  00009210  70036184  80036194'


Data Division dump of 'PHONREPT'
000014 FD PHONREPT.CALL-DETAIL FD
FILE SPECIFIED AS:
   ORGANIZATION=SEQUENTIAL     ACCESS MODE=SEQUENTIAL
   RECFM=FIXED BLOCKED
CURRENT STATUS OF FILE IS:
   OPEN STATUS=INPUT
   QSAM STATUS CODE=00
000016 01 PHONREPT.CALL-RECORD AN-GR
000017 02 PHONREPT.CALL-DATE AN-GR
000018 03 PHONREPT.CALL-MM 99
       DISP  ===>12
000019 03 PHONREPT.CALL-DD 99
       DISP  ===>20
000020 02 PHONREPT.CALL-TIME AN-GR
000021 03 PHONREPT.CALL-HH 99
       DISP  ===>14
000022 03 PHONREPT.CALL-MIN 99
       DISP  ===>18
000023 02 PHONREPT.CALL-EXTENSION 9999
       DISP  ===>8194
000024 02 PHONREPT.CALL-NUMBER-CALLED 9(10)
       DISP  ===>2105559786
000025 02 PHONREPT.CALL-MINUTES 999
       CMP3  ===>003
000026 02 PHONREPT.CALL-COST 9999V99
       CMP3    HEX>000F
                   0001
000027 02 PHONREPT.CALL-RATE-CODES XXXX
       DISP  ===>DXPD
               SUB(1)
       DISP  ===>E502
               SUB(2)
       DISP  ===>NW01
               SUB(3)
000027 00 PHONREPT.RCD-IND IX
       DISP  ===>2
```

INVALID DATA FOR THIS DATA TYPE

address in the PROCEDURE DIVISION map. If the program was compiled with the LIST option, just find the object instruction that is at the relative address given in the message. The immediately preceding line number and verb identify the failing statement. With the OFFSET option, if the exact relative address is not in the OFFSET listing, find the two addresses that it falls between. Figure 12.2 is an OFFSET listing for a small program. The address in the message, hexadecimal 4C6, is between 4C2 for line number 68 and 4CC for line number 69. The failing statement is the one that precedes the relative address from the message. In this example, it is the MOVE on line 68. Note that if the address in the message exactly matches an address in the OFFSET listing, or matches the first machine instruction in the LIST output for a statement, it is still the preceding statement that failed. If the address in the message had been 4CC, the MOVE on line 68, not line 69, would still be the failing statement. This is because the address in the message is the address of the next machine instruction to be executed, not the instruction that failed.

Figure 12.2 also illustrates some of the complications that can arise because of optimization. For one thing, the compiler sometimes combines the object code for two statements so that both statements have the same starting location in the PROCEDURE DIVISION map. Lines 69 and 70, for example, both have an address of 4CC. If this were the location identified as the failing statement, both MOVEs would have to be considered as possible causes of the abend.

Another complication results from the process of procedure integration, which was discussed in Chapter 2. Procedure integration moves out-of-line PERFORMed routines in-line in the object code, so the object code is not in the same sequence as the source code. This means that line numbers in the PROCEDURE DIVISION map can be out of sequence. In the program mapped in Figure 12.2, for example, line 62 PERFORMs lines 67 through 72. Because of procedure integration, the object code for lines 67 through 72 is generated between the code for line 62 and the code for line 64. The map reflects the arrangement of the object code. This does not really affect the process of determining the failing statement, but it can be puzzling if you are not prepared for it.

The beginning of the formatted dump includes some other useful information in addition to identifying the failing statement. Figure 12.1 shows that the PROGRAM-ID, the abend code, the PSW, and the contents of the general register are given. If the program does any floating-point arithmetic, the floating-point registers will be dumped as well.

Figure 12.2   An OFFSET listing for a small program.

```
LINE #  HEXLOC  VERB        LINE #  HEXLOC  VERB        LINE #  HEXLOC  VERB
000047  000404  OPEN        000049  00042C  READ        000050  00048E  SET
000052  000492  PERFORM     000059  000496  IF          000062  0004B4  PERFORM
000067  0004B4  MOVE        000068  0004C2  MOVE        000069  0004CC  MOVE
000070  0004CC  MOVE        000071  0004D2  WRITE       000072  000504  ADD
000064  000514  READ        000065  000576  SET         000054  000582  DISPLAY
000055  000596  CLOSE       000056  0005BA  STOP
```

THE DATA DIVISION DUMP

The heart, and the bulk, of the formatted dump is the DATA DIVI-
SION dump. This begins after the dump of the registers, and constitutes the remainder of the dump. It displays the contents of the current
record for each open file, preceded by some information about the
file. This is followed by the contents of the WORKING-STORAGE
SECTION and the LINKAGE SECTION.

The information for each file or data area begins with the source line
number on which it is defined, the compiler-generated relative level
number (the same as in the DATA DIVISION map), and the name
from the source. As illustrated in Figure 12.1, each name is preceded by
the PROGRAM-ID as a qualifier, with a period for a separator. If there
are nested programs, the PROGRAM-ID of the contained program is
used as an additional qualifier for names in its DATA DIVISION. For
example, if the program PHONREPT contained a program named
RATECALC, a field named BASE-RATE in the DATA DIVISION
of RATECALC would be listed as PHONREPT.RATECALC.BASE-
RATE in the dump.

For each file, the dump shows the ORGANIZATION, the ACCESS
mode, and the record format (RECFM). It also shows the mode for
which it was OPENed, if it is open, and the most recent FILE STATUS
value. After this, each field of the current record is dumped. Following
all the files, WORKING-STORAGE is dumped in the same format as
the records in the files.

All of the names from the source program are listed. A group-level
name is followed by a code indicating that it is a group level. The
code AN-GR is an abbreviation for "alphanumeric group." The first
subordinate level is on the next line. Two or more lines are printed
for each elementary item. On the first line, after the name of the item,
is its PICTURE. The next line has an abbreviation for the USAGE,
and, after the arrow, the actual contents of the field. If the field is an
internal format such as PACKED-DECIMAL or BINARY, the contents
are converted to printable form. If the contents of a field are not valid

for the definition of that field, a message is printed on the right side of the page, and the contents are shown in hexadecimal. An example of this is CALL-COST near the bottom of Figure 12.1. Sometimes a field with Xs in the PICTURE contains unprintable characters. In such cases, the contents are displayed with asterisks replacing the unprintable characters, and are also shown in hex.

For fields defined with an OCCURS clause, every occurrence is shown as a separate field in the dump. At the bottom of Figure 12.1, CALL-RATE-CODES has three occurrences. The number in parentheses after SUB is the occurrence number. If the field is INDEXED, the index itself is shown after all of the occurrences of the field. RCD-IND is the index for CALL-RATE-CODES. The value shown for the index is the occurrence number to which it is currently set.

A formatted dump can be quite large, and can become unwieldy if WORKING-STORAGE is very large, especially if there are tables with many occurrences. But debugging with a very large formatted dump is still easier than with the unformatted system dump or with no dump at all. Instead of printing a large dump, writing it to a file and viewing it on a CRT may be a better way to handle the size. A block size should be specified if SYSDBOUT is written to disk or tape, because the default is to make it unblocked. The preset DCB parameters for SYSDBOUT are RECFM = FBA and LRECL = 121. An alternative to dealing with a very large dump is to debug the program interactively with COBTEST. Commands can be used to examine only those fields that you are interested in. COBTEST is described in detail in the next chapter.

ADDITIONAL ABEND INFORMATION

Besides the formatted dump, VS COBOL II provides some additional debugging information in a data set with the DD name **SYSABOUT**. The information in this data set can save a lot of time and effort, particularly if you have to work with a system dump. All you have to do to get it is include a DD statement named SYSABOUT when the program is run. No additional overhead is incurred. The output is rarely more than one page, even for large programs. This DD statement should be included whenever a VS COBOL II program is run, both for testing and in production. It will usually simply specify SYSOUT = A. In CICS the same information is written to the CEBRxxxx temporary storage queue automatically, with no action by the programmer.

Figure 12.3 illustrates the SYSABOUT abend information. The first line gives the PROGRAM-ID and the date and time it was compiled. This date and time should always be checked against the compiler listing to make sure that the listing being used matches the program that was executed. The next line gives the address of the TGT. Like all of the addresses in the SYSABOUT information, this is the actual address in main storage, not a relative address or displacement. It can be used together with the TGT map in the compiler listing to find TGT fields in a system dump.

The next three sections of the abend information give the contents of the base locators for files, WORKING-STORAGE, and the LINKAGE SECTION. Having these addresses here eliminates having to hunt for them in the registers or in the TGT in the dump. If you need BLW = 1, for example, just look in the abend information to get its value, A778 in the example in Figure 12.3. Again, these are actual storage addresses. Additional types of base locators will be shown under the next two headings if they are used. A variably located area is a nonsubordinate area that follows an OCCURS . . . DEPENDING ON. The base locator for such an area is called a **BLV**. As mentioned in Chapter 11, an EXTERNAL record in WORKING-STORAGE is addressed by a BLX. These base locators would be shown in the same format as the more common types.

The final section of the abend information gives the value of every index in the program. The form of this information is different from the way the indexes are shown in the formatted dump. First of all, they are presented here by the internal index number—IDX = 1, IDX = 2, and so on—rather than by name. Second, the values shown in the

Figure 12.3   **Abend information in the SYSABOUT data set.**

```
--- VS COBOL II ABEND Information ---

Program = 'PHONREPT' compiled on '01/25/89' at '10:08:30'
    TGT = '00009210'

Contents of base locators for files are:
    0-000511E8        1-000096F1

Contents of base locators for working storage are:
    0-00009778        1-0000A778        2-0000B778

Contents of base locators for the linkage section are:
    0-00000000        1-00005FFE

No variably located areas were used in this program.

No EXTERNAL data was used in this program.

Contents of indexes are:
    1-00000004        2-00000002

--- End of VS COBOL II ABEND Information ---
```

abend information are displacements from the beginning of the first occurrence, not occurrence numbers. For example, IDX = 1 in Figure 12.3 is RCD-IND from Figure 12.1. (Both figures were produced by the same abend.)   The formatted dump shows that the index is set to occurrence number 2. The indexed field is four bytes long, so the second occurrence is four bytes from the first occurrence. Therefore, the actual displacement value in the index, as the abend information shows, is 4.

USER ABEND CODES FROM COBOL

When VS COBOL II detects certain types of errors during execution, it issues a user abend code in the range U1001 through U1099. Each abend code corresponds to a run-time message number IGZnnnI, where nnn is the last three digits of the abend code. For example, abend code U1006 means that message IGZ006I was issued. The message itself is printed with the allocation, step termination, and other system messages, and is also sent to the system console. The COBOL messages are documented in Appendix C of the VS COBOL II *Debugging* manual. Two abend codes, U1090 and U1091, do not have corresponding messages and are documented in Appendix D of the *Debugging* manual.

Chapter 13

The Debug
Tool (COBTEST)

The VS COBOL II debug tool, generally called **COBTEST**, is a powerful and flexible system for testing and debugging. It provides a wide variety of functions, is convenient to use, and can be used interactively at a terminal.

COBTEST is an outgrowth of OS COBOL Interactive Debug (commonly called TESTCOB) for OS/VS COBOL. Most OS/VS COBOL installations did not use Interactive Debug. The majority of VS COBOL II installations, in contrast, probably will use COBTEST. There are two reasons for this. First, COBTEST is packaged with the compiler, whereas Interactive Debug was a separate product. Second, some debugging functions that were implemented in the source language or by compiler options in OS/VS COBOL are available in VS COBOL II only by using COBTEST. VS COBOL II can be purchased with or without COBTEST. Software packages that perform similar functions can be purchased from a number of other vendors. If your installation does not have COBTEST, skip this chapter.

Many of the concepts, functions, and commands in COBTEST are similar or identical to those of Interactive Debug. However, because Interactive Debug was not widely used, most programmers are not familiar with it. This chapter, therefore, explains everything as though it were new. However, this is not by any means a complete description of COBTEST. There are so many functions, options, and variations that a book could be written on COBTEST alone. This chapter covers all of the major functions, and provides a solid base upon which the programmer can build as he or she gains familiarity with the product.

The emphasis is on controlling execution and obtaining data on the program being tested, rather than on such functions as manipulating the COBTEST environment.

THREE MODES FOR USING COBTEST

COBTEST can be used in three different modes: **batch mode**, **line mode**, and **full-screen mode**. In batch mode, all of the desired debugging commands must be entered ahead of time in a data set that COBTEST will read. The programmer has no interaction with the program or the debugging session while it is running. Batch mode can be useful for a fixed testing function, such as counting the number of times that each statement is executed. Doing this in batch mode would allow a reasonable volume of test data to be used without tying up a terminal while the test is running. However, it is very difficult to do actual debugging or problem solving with only a predetermined sequence of commands. True debugging is best done in an interactive mode.

Batch mode is the only mode that can be used to test CICS programs. The transaction being tested can be executed on-line, but the COBTEST commands must be set up in a file in advance. Because of this and other limitations, you will probably prefer using EDF or some other package for testing and debugging of CICS programs.

Line mode is interactive, but is somewhat limited. Commands and responses appear line by line on the terminal. Since the source program is not displayed, a hard copy of the compiler listing must be used to relate the line numbers in COBTEST to the source. Line mode is provided to make COBTEST functions available in installations that do not have ISPF, or where only a typewriter-style terminal is available.

The power of COBTEST is fully realized in full-screen mode under ISPF. In this mode, the screen is divided into scrollable areas or windows that display the source program, the log of COBTEST commands and responses, and, optionally, a continuous display of the contents of selected fields in the program. The debugging session is controlled by commands entered from the terminal, and PF keys can be set up for frequently used commands.

Many of the COBTEST commands are the same in all three modes. Since it will be used in full-screen mode almost all of the time, the rest of this chapter is based on that mode.

PREPARATIONS FOR A COBTEST SESSION

Before a COBTEST session can actually be started, two preparatory steps are necessary. The first is a compilation of the program specifically for COBTEST. The second is allocation of data sets.

The program must be compiled with the TEST option in order to be run under COBTEST. Because this conflicts with several other options, you will generally have to do a special compilation just for COBTEST. The TEST option forces the NOFDUMP, NOOPTIMIZE, RESIDENT, and OBJECT options. If you normally test with FDUMP, as you should, this is one reason a special compilation for COBTEST will be necessary. If the program contains a debugging section (USE FOR DEBUGGING), then the WITH DEBUGGING MODE clause must be omitted from the ENVIRONMENT DIVISION when you compile for COBTEST. If WITH DEBUGGING MODE is specified and a debugging section is present, the TEST option will be canceled.

When you run the compilation for COBTEST, the compiler listing should be written to a disk file instead of to SYSOUT. COBTEST uses this file to display the source during the debugging session. In order for COBTEST to recognize the listing file automatically, it should be named userid.program-id.LIST, and should be cataloged. The ISPF/PDF panel for running the compiler will create a file with the correct name if you enter the PROGRAM-ID in the LIST ID field. Link-edit the program as usual.

Before beginning the COBTEST session, you must also allocate all of the files that will be needed to run the program you are testing. "Allocate" in this context means to associate a data set with each FD in the program. It does not necessarily mean reserving disk space; the files may already exist on disk. Besides the files explicitly defined in the program, you must allocate any data set for which a DD statement would be needed if the program were run in a batch job. If the program uses the DISPLAY statement, you have to allocate SYSOUT or whatever other DD name is specified in the OUTDD compiler option. If the program uses the SORT statement, you also have to allocate a sort work data set, a sort message data set, and any other data sets needed by the sort. COBTEST will automatically allocate SYSABOUT and SYSDBOUT.

In a batch job, files are allocated by DD statements. In TSO, the equivalent of the DD statement is the ALLOCATE command. (In CMS it is the FILEDEF command.) You can enter each ALLOCATE command individually at your terminal. An ALLOCATE remains in effect until you log off, unless you explicitly release the file with a FREE command. It might be prudent to save the ALLOCATE commands in a CLIST in case the same program has to be tested again in a later TSO session. Information on using CLISTs can be found in the *TSO Command Language Reference* or the *TSO/E CLISTs* manual.

If you normally use ISPF/PDF, you may be unfamiliar with the ALLO-CATE command. In its simplest form it specifies the DD name, the name of an existing cataloged data set, and a status of SHR or OLD. For example,

```
ALLOC DD(INFILE) DS(AP.TEST.DATA) SHR
```

This is equivalent to the DD statement

```
//INFILE DD DSN=AP.TEST.DATA,DISP=SHR
```

This format can be used for either QSAM or VSAM. Those familiar with TSO commands often use FI (for FILE) instead of DD, and DA (for DATASET) instead of DS, but the keywords in the example are easier to remember when thinking in terms of DD names and the DSNAME or DSN parameter in DD statements.

For output data sets, to keep things simple and not have to learn all of the intricacies of the ALLOCATE command, you can create and catalog data sets with ISPF/PDF, then allocate them with a simple command like the one above. For output, specify OLD instead of SHR. You should also create disk data sets for output that would normally be printed, to allow browsing during or after the debugging session. This includes sort messages, DISPLAY output, and the like. If you allocate a file to a SYSOUT class, it remains in the SYSOUT queue until you log off. COBTEST allocates disk data sets for SYSABOUT and SYSDBOUT. These are usually named userid.SYSABOUT and userid.SYSDBOUT.

For a sort work file, an ALLOCATE command like this can be used.

```
ALLOC DD(SORTWK01) NEW SPACE(1,1) CYL UNIT(SYSDA)
```

The equivalent DD statement is

```
//SORTWK01 DD UNIT=SYSDA,SPACE=(CYL,(1,1))
```

Increase the number of cylinders in the SPACE parameter if a larger file is needed.

An output file can be allocated to DUMMY if it definitely will not need to be looked at for debugging. The ALLOCATE command would look like this.

```
ALLOC DD(OUTFILE) DUMMY BLKSIZE(2000)
```

The BLKSIZE is needed if BLOCK CONTAINS 0 RECORDS is specified in the FD, as it generally should be.

STARTING COBTEST

To begin the debugging session, select COBTEST from the ISPF menu. The standard menu option is 4.10, but this can vary from one installation to another. After selecting the proper option, you will see the VS COBOL II DEBUG INVOCATION panel shown in Figure 13.1. On this panel you identify the library and member name of the load module you are going to test. Fill in the name of the library or other partitioned data set, and the member name, just as you would on any ISPF/PDF panel. This is the only input that is always required.

If the program being tested expects to be passed a PARM value from the EXEC statement, enter the appropriate value in the field labeled VS COBOL II PROGRAM PARAMETERS. Do not put this value in quotes.

Near the bottom of the screen are two fields labeled LOG and LOG DSN which allow you to write the COBTEST log to a disk file as the debugging session proceeds. The file will be saved when you exit from COBTEST, for later review. The log contains the commands that you enter, responses to them, and other messages. It is always a good idea to write this file; it can be deleted later if not needed. Enter YES in the LOG field, and a data set name in LOG DSN. COBTEST will create the file with the name you specify, adding your TSO user ID as a high-level qualifier.

After making the appropriate entries, press ENTER to start COB-TEST. The initialization process may take a minute or so. Be patient. Normal response time will resume once the debugging session starts.

Figure 13.1   The COBTEST invocation panel.

```
------------------- VS COBOL II DEBUG INVOCATION -------------------
COMMAND ===> _

ISPF LIBRARY:
   PROJECT ===> ACCTG
   GROUP   ===> TEST
   TYPE    ===> LOAD
   MEMBER  ===> phonrept          (Blank for member selection list)

OTHER PARTITIONED DATA SET:
   DATASET NAME ===>

PASSWORD ===>                     MIXED MODE ===> NO   (YES or NO)

VS COBOL II PROGRAM PARAMETERS:
   ===> 022889
   ===>

LOG        ===> YES   (Yes or No)
LOG DSN    ===> DEBUG.LOG
RESTART    ===> NO    (Yes or No)
RESTART DSN ===>
```

THE COBTEST MAIN PANEL

When COBTEST has completed its initialization, you will see the **main panel**, illustrated in Figure 13.2. There are two main areas on the screen. The top half, called the **source area**, displays the source for the program being tested. The bottom half, called the **log area**, is the COBTEST log. A third area, the **auto monitoring area**, can be opened to display the contents of selected fields. This is discussed later in this chapter.

The top line of the panel, after the label "WHERE," shows the next statement to be executed. It gives the PROGRAM-ID, the line number, and the verb number on that line. When COBTEST is first entered, this will be the first statement in the PROCEDURE DIVISION. The next statement to be executed is also highlighted in the source listing. The second line of the panel is the command line, including a field to control scrolling, just as in ISPF/PDF. Any COBTEST command, ISPF command, or TSO command can be entered on the command line. TSO commands must be preceded by the keyword TSO.

The two areas of the main panel scroll independently of each other. When a scrolling PF key is pressed, or a scrolling command is entered, the area that scrolls is whichever one the cursor is in. If the cursor is on the command line, then the log is scrolled. This means that in order to scroll the source the cursor must be moved into the source area. An easy way to do this is to simply press the down arrow once, moving the cursor to the column-number scale at the top of the source area.

The numbers on the left side of the source area are the compiler-generated line numbers, which are used by COBTEST to identify the lines of the source program. The field containing these line numbers is called the **prefix area**. Certain commands can be entered in this area.

Much of the output from COBTEST includes line numbers of statements in the program. As in the WHERE display on the top line of the screen, the line number is always followed by a period and a one- or two-digit number for the verb within the line. Since it is good programming practice to put only one verb on a line, the verb number should always be 1. The remainder of this chapter assumes that this recommended practice is being followed, and refers to the line number and verb number as simply "line number."

COBTEST uses a separate set of PF key definitions from ISPF/PDF. The first time you use COBTEST, it will copy your PF key definitions

Figure 13.2   The COBTEST main panel.

```
COBTEST     WHERE: PHONREPT.000073.1

COMMAND ===>  _                                      SCROLL ===> PAGE
SOURCE ----+----1----+----2----+----3----+----4----+----5----+-- LINE: 70 OF 122
70  007000         10 RATE-CODE OCCURS 3 TIMES INDEXED BY RATE-X PIC X.
71  007100
72  007200 PROCEDURE DIVISION.
73  007300     OPEN INPUT CALL-DETAIL OUTPUT PHONE-REPORT
74  007400     READ CALL-DETAIL
75  007500         AT END SET END-OF-INPUT TO TRUE
76  007600     END-READ
77  007700     PERFORM UNTIL END-OF-INPUT
78  007800         PERFORM PRINT-REPORT-LINE
79  007900         READ CALL-DETAIL
80  008000             AT END SET END-OF-INPUT TO TRUE
LOG ----+----0----+----1----+----2----+----3----+----4----+----5----+----  LINE: 0 OF 3
******************************** TOP OF LOG ************************************
000001 IGZ100I PP - 5668-958 VS COBOL II DEBUG FACILITY --- REL 3.0
000002 IGZ100I (C) COPYRIGHT IBM CORPORATION 1983, 1988
000003 IGZ102I PHONREPT.000073.1
******************************* BOTTOM OF LOG *********************************
```

from ISPF/PDF. To change the COBTEST PF keys, enter the ISPF command KEYS while you are in COBTEST. This will display the same panel that is used to define PF keys in ISPF/PDF option 0.3, but these definitions are only for COBTEST. You can assign COBTEST commands to PF keys, and set up the keys as desired for COBTEST, without affecting your PF keys for ISPF/PDF. The definitions that you enter will be saved, and will take effect again each time you enter COBTEST. When you return to ISPF/PDF from COBTEST, your regular ISPF/PDF PF key definitions will be back in effect.

Commands that you enter from the terminal are preceded by an asterisk when they are listed in the log. You can copy a command from the log to the command line to avoid retyping if it is necessary to enter the same or a similar command again. To copy a command, move the cursor to the command in the log area. Make some change to it— perhaps just delete the asterisk—then press ENTER. The command will appear on the command line. Make any desired additional changes and press ENTER again to execute the command.

When you finish debugging, enter the QUIT command to exit from COBTEST. The END command (usually assigned to PF 3 or PF 15) is used in COBTEST to return to the main panel from HELP or from other auxiliary panels, but QUIT must be used to leave COBTEST.

CONTROLLING THE EXECUTION OF THE PROGRAM

COBTEST gives the programmer complete control over the execution of the program while it is being tested. You can stop execution at predetermined points, or when a certain condition occurs. Whenever execution is stopped, control returns to the terminal and you can enter commands to examine fields or perform other testing functions.

One of the most useful features of COBTEST is that it lets you set a **breakpoint** in the program. A breakpoint at a particular statement causes execution to stop when that statement is reached. This facility has many uses. If you are unsure of the effect of a particular statement or routine, you can set a breakpoint immediately after it, and examine the fields that were affected. Another common use is to set a breakpoint at a point in the program just prior to a routine that is not working properly. The program can run quickly until it stops at the breakpoint. A trace, or other detailed debugging procedures, can then be used from that point on. Breakpoints can also be used to determine which of several possible paths is being taken, by setting a breakpoint in each path and seeing which one is hit.

Breakpoints are set by the **AT** command. The simplest way to set a breakpoint is to enter the word AT in the prefix area of the line where you want the breakpoint. The AT will remain in the prefix area, replacing the line number, to indicate the presence of the breakpoint. (A verb number can be specified after AT, but this is not necessary if you code only one verb on a line.) Any number of breakpoints can be set at different statements.

To begin execution of the program, enter the **GO** command. The program will run until it reaches a breakpoint. It stops just before executing the statement at which the breakpoint is set. When execution stops at a breakpoint, the line containing the breakpoint is highlighted in the source area, and a message in the log gives the location, preceded by the word AT. Figure 13.3 shows what the screen looks like when the program has just stopped at a breakpoint. Except for the part of the message that identifies the reason, the display looks essentially like this whenever execution stops for any reason. To continue execution after a breakpoint, enter another GO command.

The AT command can also be entered on the command line, specifying the line number where the breakpoint is to be set. The effect is exactly the same as entering it in the prefix area, but additional operands can be used. When the command is entered on the command line, it can include a **command list** of one or more COBTEST commands to be executed when the breakpoint is reached. This can be used, for example, to display the contents of a certain field each time the breakpoint is reached. Unless you expect to hit the same breakpoint many times, it is just as easy, and more flexible, to enter commands from the terminal when execution stops at the breakpoint.

You may not always want to take a breakpoint the first time that the statement is reached. A program bug may occur, for example, only after a certain number of records have been processed. By entering the AT command on the command line, COUNT can be used. The following command sets a breakpoint that will cause execution to stop the tenth time that line 734 is reached.

```
AT 734 COUNT(10)
```

To stop at this line *every* tenth time, use the following command.

```
AT 734 COUNT(10,10)
```

Figure 13.3   A program stopped at a breakpoint.

```
COBTEST       WHERE:  PHONREPT.000096.1
COMMAND  ===>  _                                        SCROLL  ===> PAGE
SOURCE  ----+----1----+----2----+----3----+----4----+----5----+-- LINE: 93 OF 122
    93  009300        MOVE CALL-EXCHANGE-CALLED TO REPT-EXCHANGE
    94  009400        MOVE '-' TO REPT-HYPHEN
    95  009500        MOVE CALL-LAST-4-CALLED TO REPT-LAST-4
AT      009600        IF CALL-RATE-CODE NUMERIC
    97  009700            AND CALL-RATE-CODE >= 1
    98  009800            AND CALL-RATE-CODE <= 3
    99  009900            MOVE RATE-CODE (CALL-RATE-CODE) TO REPT-RATE
   100  010000        ELSE
   101  010100            MOVE CALL-RATE-CODE TO REPT-RATE
   102  010200        END-IF
   103  010300        MOVE CALL-MINUTES TO REPT-MINUTES
LOG    0----+----1----+----2----+----3----+----4----+----5----+---- LINE:  0 OF 6
***************************** TOP OF LOG ***************************************
000001  IGZ100I PP - 5668-958 VS COBOL II DEBUG FACILITY -- REL 3.0
000002  IGZ100I (C) COPYRIGHT IBM CORPORATION 1983, 1988
000003  IGZ102I PHONREPT.000073.1
000004  * AT 000096
000005  * go
000006  IGZ105I AT PHONREPT.000096.1
******************************** BOTTOM OF LOG ********************************
```

The specific place in the program where a problem is occurring is not always known. For example, you may know that a problem is caused by an incorrect value in a field, but you don't know what statement is putting the value there. The **WHEN** command lets a breakpoint be taken based on the contents of a field. A WHEN command looks like this.

```
WHEN  TST1  ITEM—TOTAL
```

This command will cause execution to stop whenever the value of ITEM-TOTAL changes. TST1 is a name for the WHEN breakpoint, and is used to identify it in messages and in other commands. The value in the specified field is checked before every statement. When the breakpoint is taken, a message in the log will give the WHEN name and the line number of the next statement to be executed. The statement that changed the field is the one preceding the statement identified in the message and highlighted in the source listing, because the field has already been changed when the breakpoint is taken.

The WHEN command can also be used to compare a field to a literal or to another field. For example, this command will cause a breakpoint when any statement makes the value of TABLE-INDEX greater than 49.

```
WHEN  IND TABLE—INDEX  > 49
```

An AT breakpoint is removed by the **OFF** command. Like the AT command, OFF can be entered in the prefix area of the line that has the breakpoint, or on the command line with the line number as an operand. A WHEN breakpoint is removed by the **OFFWN** command, with the WHEN name as an operand. OFF or OFFWN entered on the command line with no operand removes all breakpoints of the corresponding type.

The program being tested might, of course, abend while it is running under COBTEST. If this happens, control is returned to the terminal just as though a breakpoint had been taken. Messages in the log give the abend code and the PSW, as well as the line number of the statement that abended. In the case of an abend, unlike most times when execution stops, the statement identified by the message and the highlight is the statement that failed, not the next statement. In COBTEST, it is often possible to correct the cause of an abend and continue executing the program. Execution will resume with the statement that abended. To resume execution, enter a GO command.

Any time execution stops, you might want to start over again from the beginning of the program. The **RESTART** command accomplishes this. It first reinitializes the entire program (it actually loads a fresh copy), then immediately begins execution. It does not stop at the first statement of the program, as happens when COBTEST is first entered. If you want to stop at the first statement, enter the command "AT ENTRY program-id" before the RESTART. This sets a breakpoint at the entry to the program. RESTART is not allowed when the program is in an INPUT PROCEDURE or OUTPUT PROCEDURE for a SORT.

At some point you may want to let the program run without taking any more breakpoints. This can be done by entering the **RUN** command. Execution will continue until the program either ends normally or abends. Note that RUN does not just ignore breakpoints; it actually removes them. If you use RESTART after RUN, you must reenter any breakpoints that you want to have in effect.

DISPLAYING AND CHANGING FIELDS

One of the biggest advantages of interactive testing is the ability to examine the contents of fields when the program stops at a breakpoint. The primary command for looking at data is **LIST**. The basic format is simply the word LIST followed by the name of the field that you want to display. For example,

```
LIST ACCOUNT-TOTAL
```

The name can be subscripted or indexed to display an item in a table.

The output of the LIST command goes to the log. The contents of the field are displayed in the same format as in a formatted dump (see Chapter 12). Figure 13.4 shows the output of a LIST command. If you use a group level name in the command, each of the elementary items in the group will be listed. If you prefer to see the group level displayed as a single item, put the word GROUP after the name of the field.

```
LIST CUSTOMER-ADDRESS GROUP
```

Figure 13.4   Output of a LIST command for one field.

```
* list account-total
000069 02 PHONREPT.ACCOUNT-TOTAL S9(5)V99
       CMP3 ===> +37281.64
```

There are two shortcuts to avoid having to type long data-names in LIST commands. LIST can be used as what is called a **cursor-sensitive command**, meaning that the results of the command depend on the position of the cursor when the command is entered. In the case of LIST, the cursor can be used to point to the name of the field to be listed. On the command line, type just the word LIST, with no operands. Then move the cursor to the name of the field anywhere it appears in the source, and press ENTER. The effect is exactly the same as if you had typed the name in the command. This shortcut is much more convenient if LIST is assigned to a PF key because nothing has to be put on the command line. Simply move the cursor to the name and press the PF key to list the field.

The second shortcut works for any command where a data-name has to be entered, not just for LIST. The **EQUATE** command lets you assign a shorter name as a synonym for any data-name in the program. The command itself can also be abbreviated.

```
EQ CA CUSTOMER-ADDRESS
```

Once this command has been entered, you can type CA instead of CUSTOMER-ADDRESS in any command where the name of the field is required. You can enter as many EQUATEs as you want. They remain in effect until you exit from COBTEST, unless you cancel them with a **DROP** command. The RUN command also cancels all EQUATEs.

Another way to look at fields is to have them displayed continuously in the third area of the screen, the auto monitoring area. Auto monitoring is initiated by the **AUTO** command. This consists of the word AUTO followed by a LIST command. More than one field can be specified in the LIST command by enclosing a list of names in parentheses, with the names separated by commas.

```
AUTO LIST (REC-COUNT,ACCOUNT-TOTAL)
```

If the entire command does not fit on one line, you can continue it by typing a plus sign or a minus sign at the end of the line and pressing

ENTER. You can use as many continuation lines as needed to complete the command. Continuation can be used with any command, not just AUTO.

When the AUTO command is entered, the auto monitoring area will open on the screen, and the specified fields will be displayed in it, in the same format as produced by the LIST command. Figure 13.5 shows the main panel after an AUTO command. The auto monitoring area is near the top, above the source area. Notice that the AUTO command does not appear in the log. Commands like AUTO that affect only the display, and are valid only in full-screen mode, are not shown in the log. The auto monitoring area can be scrolled, just like the source and log areas, in order to view all of the fields. The auto monitoring area is immediately updated every time execution of the program stops. This saves entering LIST commands repeatedly when you have to keep looking at the same fields.

If you enter another AUTO command, the field or list of fields in the new command completely replaces the previous list. There is no way to add or remove individual fields. To stop monitoring and close the auto monitoring area, enter the command AUTO OFF. If you want to monitor the same list of fields again later, you can just enter AUTO ON instead of repeating the original command.

AUTO LIST ALL is a valid command that initiates auto monitoring of all of the fields defined in the program. This form of the command should not be used because it requires a tremendous amount of CPU time. (In effect it has to produce an entire formatted dump every time execution stops.) Auto monitoring works very well for a reasonable number of fields. Determine which fields you really need to see continuously, and monitor only those.

Besides *displaying* the value in a field, COBTEST also allows you to *change* the value. The **SET** command performs this function. Here are some examples.

```
SET ACCOUNT-TOTAL = 257.38
SET TABLE-CODE (4) = 'RA'
SET OUT-TOTAL = IN-TOTAL
```

A field can be set equal to a literal, a figurative constant, or another field. The assignment of the value is done according to the rules for MOVE in COBOL. The sending field or value must be a valid type for the field that is being changed. Lowercase letters in a nonnumeric literal

Figure 13.5 The main panel with auto monitoring in effect.

```
COBTEST    WHERE: PHONREPT.000079.1
COMMAND ===>                                                          SCROLL ===> PAGE
AUTO 0----+----1----+----2----+----3----+----4----+----5----+---- LINE: 1 OF 7
000001 000067 01 PHONREPT.ACCOUNT-INFO AN-GR
000002 000068 02 PHONREPT.ACCOUNT-TYPE X
000003        DISP   ===> B
000004 000069 02 PHONREPT.ACCOUNT-TOTAL S9(5)V99
000005        CMP3   ===> +37281.64
SOURCE ----+----1----+----2----+----3----+----4----+----5----+-- LINE: 76 OF 128
76 007600            10 RATE-CODE OCCURS 3 TIMES INDEXED BY RATE-X PIC X.
77 007700
78 007800 PROCEDURE DIVISION.
79 007900     OPEN INPUT CALL-DETAIL OUTPUT PHONE-REPORT
80 008000     READ CALL-DETAIL
81 008100        AT END SET END-OF-INPUT TO TRUE
82 008200     END-READ
83 008300     PERFORM UNTIL END-OF-INPUT
84 008400        PERFORM PRINT-REPORT-LINE
85 008500        READ CALL-DETAIL
86 008600           AT END SET END-OF-INPUT TO TRUE
LOG   0----+----1----+----2----+----3----+----4----+----5----+---- LINE: 1 OF 3
000001 IGZ100I PP - 5668-958 VS COBOL II DEBUG FACILITY -- REL 3.0
000002 IGZ100I (C) COPYRIGHT IBM CORPORATION 1983, 1988
000003 IGZ102I PHONREPT.000079.1
```

are not translated to uppercase. If you want uppercase letters in the field, be sure to type them in uppercase.

SET can be used to correct errors during a test by replacing incorrect or invalid data. It can also be used to set up various conditions that have to be tested, and can save a lot of time that might otherwise be spent creating and modifying test data and rerunning the program.

Testing how a program handles invalid data in a field, such as non-numeric data in a numeric field, can be done by using a hexadecimal literal in the SET command. The hexadecimal value is moved to the field as though the field were alphanumeric, regardless of its actual PICTURE or USAGE.

TRACING THE FLOW OF THE PROGRAM

Debugging often requires figuring out what path is being taken through a part of the program. The simplest way to do this in COBTEST is with the **STEP** command. The command is just the word STEP. Each time it is entered, it executes one statement in the program, then stops and returns control to the terminal. By using the STEP command repeatedly, you can execute the program one statement at a time, and actually watch the flow of control in the source area. Since you will want to issue STEP commands in rapid succession, it is a good idea to assign STEP to a PF key.

After each STEP command, a message is displayed in the log. As with all other messages issued when execution stops, the line number in the STEP message is the number of the next statement to be executed, not the statement that was just executed by the STEP. The next STEP command will execute the statement identified in the most recent message. The messages in the log constitute a detailed trace showing every statement that was executed.

The **TRACE** command, another way to follow logic flow, writes a trace of the program flow to the log while the program is running. Unlike STEP, TRACE does not show every statement that was executed. It only produces an output at each point where execution might not continue sequentially, such as in an IF or other conditional statement, or at a GO TO or the beginning of a new paragraph.

The simple command TRACE, or just T, will produce a list of line numbers. TRACE NAME will display the paragraph name in addition

to the line number when a new paragraph is entered. The names make
the output easier to use, so you should normally use this option. Points
where the flow changes within a paragraph still show only the line
number. The line number displayed for the beginning of a paragraph
is the number of the line containing the first verb in the paragraph, not
the line containing the paragraph name. Figure 13.6 is an example of
the output produced by TRACE NAME. If you are testing a program
that CALLs a number of subprograms, you can use TRACE ENTRY
to display the PROGRAM-ID each time a different COBOL program
is entered. All tracing is stopped by the command TRACE OFF, or by
a RUN command.

Even though it does not list every statement, the output of TRACE
could quickly become unreasonably large if the program is allowed to
run for any length of time. You should use breakpoints to limit the
scope of the trace to the part of the program you need to examine
in detail. Set one breakpoint just before the section you want to trace,

Figure 13.6   Output from TRACE NAME.

```
* trace name
* go
IGZ106I TRACING CBA001
IGZ109I 000830.1 E120-REPORT-MAIN
IGZ109I 000832.1
IGZ109I 000836.1
IGZ109I 000842.1
IGZ109I 000844.1
IGZ109I 000848.1 W010-WRITE-DETAIL-REC
IGZ109I 000850.1
IGZ109I 000851.1
IGZ109I 000997.1 S010-BREAK-IN-STORE
IGZ109I 000999.1
IGZ109I 001002.1
IGZ109I 001016.1
IGZ109I 001019.1 S010-EXIT
IGZ109I 000854.1
IGZ109I 000873.1
IGZ109I 000880.1
IGZ109I 000881.1
IGZ109I 000887.1
IGZ109I 000894.1
IGZ109I 000897.1 W010-EXIT
IGZ109I 000845.1 E120-EXIT
IGZ105I AT CBA001.000845.1
```

and another just after it. Enter the TRACE NAME command at the first breakpoint, and TRACE OFF at the second.

Another approach to tracing is the **FLOW** command, which records in an internal table the same line number information as TRACE, but does not automatically display it. FLOW avoids the problem of too much volume by keeping only the most recent 255 entries in the table. The command FLOW ON begins the recording of line numbers. You can display the FLOW table at any time by entering the command FLOW (n), where n is the number of entries you want to see. For example, FLOW (20) will display the last 20 entries in the table. Figure 13.7 shows what the FLOW output looks like. The line numbers are shown in reverse chronological order, with the most recent entry first. FLOW OFF stops the recording of line numbers, but it also clears the table, so you must be sure to display any FLOW information you want to look at before entering FLOW OFF. The RUN command also has the effect of FLOW OFF.

A faster (and showier) way of following the logic flow is the **VTRACE** command, which can be used only in full-screen mode. VTRACE steps through the program automatically at low speed, so you can sit back and watch the current-statement highlight move through the source. The auto monitoring area, if it is open, is also updated after each statement. The keyboard is locked out during VTRACE. Execution continues until a breakpoint is taken, the program terminates, or you interrupt it by pressing the ATTN key. You can also specify that VTRACE stop after executing n verbs by entering the command

Figure 13.7   Output of a FLOW command.

```
* flow on
* go
IGZ105I AT CBA001.000845.1
* flow (10)
 PGM=CBA001 STTMNT & VERB=000845.01
 PGM=CBA001 STTMNT & VERB=000897.01
 PGM=CBA001 STTMNT & VERB=000894.01
 PGM=CBA001 STTMNT & VERB=000887.01
 PGM=CBA001 STTMNT & VERB=000881.01
 PGM=CBA001 STTMNT & VERB=000880.01
 PGM=CBA001 STTMNT & VERB=000873.01
 PGM=CBA001 STTMNT & VERB=000854.01
 PGM=CBA001 STTMNT & VERB=001019.01
 PGM=CBA001 STTMNT & VERB=001016.01
```

VTRACE *n* instead of just VTRACE. VTRACE by itself does not produce a permanent record of the flow. If you want to be able to go back and review what happened, you must use TRACE or FLOW together with VTRACE.

The default value for the delay between statements under VTRACE is half a second. You may find this a bit too fast, especially if you are not of the video-game generation. You can enter a larger value on the profile panel, which is displayed by entering the **PROFILE** command.

COUNTING VERB EXECUTIONS

Counting the number of times that each verb in a program is executed is a useful technique for debugging, testing, and tuning. For debugging, it can identify routines that are being executed more or fewer times than they should be, compared to the number of records processed, number of entries in a table, or the like. It is often used to make sure that every line of a program is actually tested. It can also be used to identify the most frequently executed parts of a program, to determine where tuning efforts can most productively be applied.

The **FREQ** command in COBTEST initiates the counting of verb executions, which is referred to as **frequency tallying**. The command can simply be entered as FREQ, without any operands. You would normally enter this command at the beginning of the debugging session, before starting to execute the program. Entering this command in full-screen mode also opens the **suffix area** at the right side of the source area. The execution count for each verb is shown in the suffix area, as illustrated in Figure 13.8. Four periods shown instead of a number means there is no verb on that line. The counts are automatically updated as the program executes. Entering another FREQ command resets all the counts to zero. To stop counting and close the suffix area, enter FREQ ALL OFF, which also resets all the counts. A RUN command also has the effect of FREQ ALL OFF, so you must use GO rather than RUN, even if you want to count verb executions for the entire program.

The **LISTFREQ** command displays in the log the line number and number of executions for every verb in the program that has been executed at least once. Figure 13.9 shows the LISTFREQ output for a small program. At the end it shows the total number of verbs in the program, how many of them were executed, and the number executed as a

Figure 13.8   The main panel with verb frequency counts in the suffix area.

```
COBTEST      WHERE: CBA001.000539.1                           SCROLL ===> PAGE
COMMAND ===> _                                             LINE: 841 OF 1155
SOURCE ----+----1----+----2----+----3----+----4----+----5----    LINE: 841 OF 1155
  841 084100         MOVE SD-ACCOUNT TO HOLD-REGION.                     0006
  842 084200      IF SD-TYPE NOT EQUAL HOLD-TYPE                         0099
  843 084300         PERFORM E140-TYPE-BREAK THRU E140-EXIT.             0001
  844 084400      PERFORM W010-WRITE-DETAIL-REC THRU W010-EXIT.          0099
  845 084500 E120-EXIT.  EXIT.                                           0100
  846 084600                                                              . . . .
  847 084700 W010-WRITE-DETAIL-REC.                                       . . . .
  848 084800      IF LINE-CTR GREATER THAN 58                            0100
  849 084900         PERFORM H010-WRITE-HEADINGS  THRU  H010-EXIT.       0009
  850 085000      IF SD-STORE NOT EQUAL TO HOLD-STORE                    0100
  851 085100         MOVE SD-STORE TO HOLD-STORE                         0064
LOG   0----+----1----+----2----+----3----+----4----+----5----  LINE:  0 OF 6
****************************** TOP OF LOG ************************************
000001 IGZ100I PP - 5668-958 VS COBOL II DEBUG FACILITY -- REL 3.0
000002 IGZ100I (C) COPYRIGHT IBM CORPORATION 1983, 1988
000003 IGZ102I CBA001.000525.1
000004 * freq
000005 * go
000006 IGZ129I PROGRAM UNDER COBTEST ENDED NORMALLY
*************************** BOTTOM OF LOG ************************************
```

Table 13.1   Summary of COBTEST Commands

Controlling Program Execution

GO	Execute to breakpoint or end
STEP	Execute one statement
VTRACE	Visual trace to breakpoint, ATTN, or end
RUN	Execute to end; removes breakpoints, turns off TRACE, FLOW, and FREQ
RESTART	Reinitialize and execute from beginning

Breakpoints

AT	Set breakpoint at specified line
WHEN	Set breakpoint to be taken when a field changes or a comparison is true
OFF	Remove AT breakpoint(s)
OFFWN	Remove WHEN breakpoint(s)

Displaying and Changing Fields

LIST	Display contents of a field or fields
AUTO	Continuously view contents of field(s)
SET	Change the contents of a field
EQUATE	Assign short synonym for a data-name
DROP	Cancel short synonym(s)

Tracing Program Flow

STEP	Execute one statement
TRACE	Start or stop writing trace data to the log
FLOW	Start or stop recording line numbers in internal table, or display table entries
VTRACE	Start visual trace

Counting Verb Executions

FREQ	Start or stop counting verb executions
LISTFREQ	Display verb execution counts

Session Control

PROFILE	Set VTRACE speed; also sets window sizes
QUIT	End COBTEST session

Figure 13.9   Output of a LISTFREQ command.

```
* listfreq
FREQUENCY OF VERB EXECUTIONS IN PHONREPT
000073.1=1        000074.1=1        000077.1=1        000078.1=93
000079.1=93       000080.1=1        000083.1=1        000084.1=1
000086.1=93       000087.1=93       000088.1=93       000089.1=93
000090.1=93       000091.1=93       000092.1=93       000093.1=93
000094.1=93       000095.1=93       000096.1=93       000099.1=66
000101.1=27       000103.1=93       000104.1=93       000105.1=93
000107.1=93       000109.1=1        000110.1=1        000112.1=33
000113.1=33       000115.1=3        000116.1=3        000118.1=56
000119.1=56       000121.1=93       000122.1=93
TOTAL VERBS=36   TOTAL VERBS EXECUTED=35   PERCENT EXECUTED=97
```

percentage of the total. The command LISTFREQ ALL ZEROFREQ
lists the line numbers of all verbs that have not been executed.

SUMMARY

This chapter has covered all of the essential functions of COBTEST.
With this information, you should be able to accomplish just about any
debugging task. Some of the more advanced capabilities that have not
been covered here are searching and repositioning the source and log,
customizing the size and appearance of the full-screen areas, modifying
the sequence of execution, and testing calling and called programs
separately. When you are ready to explore these facilities, you can refer
to the *Debugging* manual. But you should first practice the techniques
that have been described in this chapter and be comfortable with the
basics before going on to more advanced functions.

Table 13.1 summarizes the COBTEST commands that have been discussed in this chapter.

PART III

OTHER FEATURES AND CHANGES

Chapter 14

XA Support: Running Above the Line

One of the new features of VS COBOL II is that COBOL programs can use storage above the 16-megabyte line in an XA environment making much larger storage areas available to COBOL programs.

REVIEW OF XA ADDRESSING CONCEPTS

The original architecture of the IBM System/360 and System/370 used 24 bits for the address of a location in storage. Using 24 bits, the machine could address a maximum of 2^{24} or 16,777,216 storage locations. Since the addressable unit is a byte, programs could address 16 megabytes of storage. It made no difference to any one program whether the storage in question was real or virtual. Only 16 million locations could be referred to, and this range of addresses constituted the "address space" in which a program could operate.

Extended Architecture, or XA, makes it possible to use 31 bits for a storage address, expanding the addressable area to 2,147,483,648 bytes, or two gigabytes. An XA machine can execute instructions in either of two addressing modes. In 24-bit mode it operates in the same way as the original architecture. As illustrated in Figure 14.1, a program executing in 24-bit mode can access only the first 16 megabytes of the 2-gigabyte address space. In 31-bit mode the full 2-gigabyte address space can be used. The addressing mode can be changed by non-privileged instructions, so an application program can change the addressing mode in which it is running. As a general rule, though, programs are written to be executed in one mode or the other. A given program receives control in a predetermined mode and normally remains in that mode.

Figure 14.1   Addressing modes and address space.

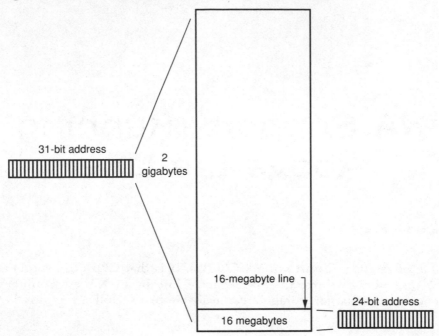

The difference in the amount of addressable storage in each of the two addressing modes gives rise to the concept of a boundary line at 16 megabytes. Programs that run in 24-bit mode can only use storage that is "below the line." Programs that run in 31-bit mode can access any part of storage, either above or below the line.

Every load module has two attributes related to addressing which are determined by the linkage editor, based on information that the compiler puts into the object module. One attribute is referred to as the AMODE, the addressing mode in which the program is to be given control when it is executed. AMODE 24 means the program will be given control in 24-bit mode; AMODE 31 means that it will be given control in 31-bit mode. The AMODE attribute can also be ANY, meaning that the program can be given control in either mode. But ANY is not a mode in which the processor can run. At run time, the program must be given control in either 24-bit mode or 31-bit mode.

The other attribute is the RMODE, which stands for residence mode. This determines in which part of storage the program can be loaded. A program with RMODE 24 must be loaded below the line. A program with RMODE ANY can be loaded anywhere, above or below the line. These are the only possible values for RMODE. A program is never required to be loaded above the line.

HOW VS COBOL II DETERMINES AMODE AND RMODE

The AMODE and RMODE of a VS COBOL II program are determined as secondary effects of certain compiler options. The RESIDENT option, usually abbreviated RES, determines the AMODE. The primary effect of the RES option is the same as in OS/VS COBOL. When RES is in effect, the COBOL library subroutines are loaded at run time. (This is sometimes referred to as the Library Management Feature.) With NORES, the library subroutines are included in the load module during link-editing. In VS COBOL II, NORES also makes the program AMODE 24, and RES makes it AMODE ANY.

A new option in VS COBOL II, the **RENT** option, makes the object program reentrant, and secondarily determines the RMODE. No changes in the source are needed for the program to be reentrant, and there are no restrictions on the use of any language features. Merely specifying the RENT option makes the compiler generate an object program that is fully reentrant. If RENT is specified, RES must also be in effect. RENT also makes the program RMODE ANY. If NORENT is in effect, the program is not reentrant, and has RMODE 24. Table 14.1 summarizes the allowable combinations of RES and RENT, and the resulting AMODE and RMODE.

Nothing in the architecture of the system requires AMODE and RMODE to be tied to the RES and RENT options. The machine and the operating system will support both static and dynamic subprogram linkage in either addressing mode. (OS/VS COBOL programs with RES still run in 24-bit mode.) Loading above 16 megabytes does

Table 14.1   Options That Determine AMODE and RMODE

	NORES NORENT	RES NORENT	RES RENT
AMODE	24	ANY	ANY
RMODE	24	24	ANY

not require that a program be reentrant. The connection between the AMODE and RMODE attributes and the RES and RENT options is simply a choice made by the designers of VS COBOL II.

THE BENEFITS OF XA SUPPORT

The possibility of running above the line, using the RES and RENT options, means that a huge amount of storage is potentially available to a COBOL program. In a complex application, multiple modules can be loaded above the line without running out of room, and overlays are unnecessary. Liberal size limits in VS COBOL II allow even a single program to take advantage of large amounts of storage. For example, an individual data item, group item, or table can be as large as 16 megabytes. The WORKING-STORAGE SECTION can be up to 128 megabytes.

Of course, very few applications require so much storage. The 16-megabyte address space and the size limitations of OS/VS COBOL have not been a problem for most batch applications. In CICS, however, even modest-sized installations have been constrained by the old limits.

The CICS dynamic storage area, or DSA, is shared by all the application programs in the CICS region. It is used both for loading programs and for work areas and buffers. With a number of terminals entering transactions, and a number of applications being used concurrently, the available dynamic storage can easily be exhausted, even in the largest possible region. One way to relieve a shortage of dynamic storage is to make use of storage above the line. VS COBOL II makes it possible for COBOL programs to do this. CICS programs written in VS COBOL II must be compiled with the RES and RENT options. This means they are always eligible to be loaded above the line, and they normally will be. Moving as many programs as possible above the line makes much more storage available to those programs and also frees up storage below the line for use by other programs that cannot be moved.

CALLS ACROSS THE LINE

CALLs between programs on opposite sides of the 16-megabyte line, or with different addressing modes, can present problems with addressing mode and with the passing of parameters. The dynamic CALL in

COBOL, which has to be used anyway to CALL a separate load module, eliminates the addressing mode problems. Any COBOL program can dynamically CALL any other COBOL program, in any combination of addressing mode and location above or below the line. This applies to OS/VS COBOL as well as VS COBOL II, including CALLs between the two versions of COBOL. An OS/VS COBOL program, of course, is always AMODE 24 and RMODE 24. Figure 14.2 illustrates the possibilities. Any needed switching of address modes is done automatically by the dynamic CALL.

Unfortunately, passing parameters is not so easy. There is no problem if a program below the line CALLs one above the line. The CALLed program above the line can address parameters that are passed to it no matter where they are in storage, as illustrated in Figure 14.3(a). But if a program that resides above the line CALLs a subprogram below the line, the subprogram has to be executing in 31-bit mode to address parameters that are above the line. A VS COBOL II program compiled with the RES option runs in 31-bit mode, so it can accept parameters that are above the line, as shown in Figure 14.3(b). However, if the subprogram is written in OS/VS COBOL, it must run in 24-bit mode. As Figure 14.3(c) illustrates, it is impossible for such a program to access parameters that are above the line. Therefore, if the subprogram is

Figure 14.2   Possible dynamic CALLs.

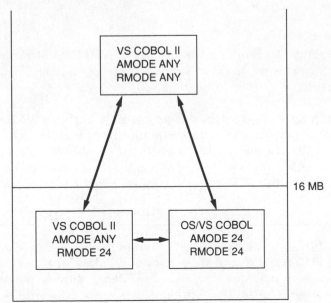

Figure 14.3   Passing parameters across the 16-megabyte line. (a) CALL from below the line to above the line. (b) CALL from above the line to VS COBOL II RES below the line. (c) CALL from above the line to OS/VS COBOL below the line.

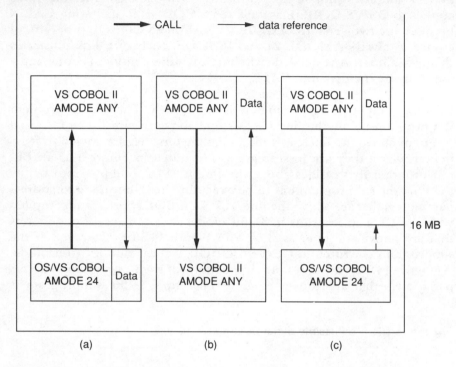

                                (a)   (b)   (c)

an OS/VS COBOL program, or any other AMODE 24 program, the CALLing program must make sure that any parameters it passes are below the line.

The new **DATA** option solves this problem by enabling a VS COBOL II program to put its data areas below the line, even though the program itself is above the line. In a program compiled with the RENT option, WORKING-STORAGE is allocated at run time and is not part of the load module. If a RENT program has to pass parameters to an AMODE 24 program, the RENT program should also have the option DATA(24). This puts the WORKING-STORAGE SECTION and other data areas below the line, and makes any passed parameters accessible to an AMODE 24 program, as shown in Figure 14.4. Specifying DATA(31) would allow storage for data areas to be obtained anywhere, above or below the line. DATA(31) should be specified if sharing data with AMODE 24 programs is not a concern, in order to

Figure 14.4   Using DATA(24) to CALL from above the line to OS/VS COBOL below the line.

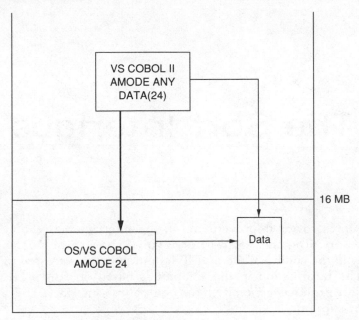

take advantage of the availability of storage above the line. The DATA option is only meaningful with RENT. NORENT programs are always loaded below the line, and all of their storage areas are part of the load module. Therefore, their storage is always below the line, and the DATA option is ignored.

QSAM can only be used in 24-bit mode, and all of its control blocks and buffers must be below the line. However, any type of file can be used in any VS COBOL II program, regardless of the program's AMODE and RMODE. VS COBOL II automatically does any necessary mode switching or other adjustments.

Chapter 15

The Sort Interface

This chapter covers improvements in the interface between COBOL and the sort program that do not involve changes in the language. Changes in the coding of the SORT statement were discussed in Chapter 6. The information in this chapter is based on IBM's DFSORT. Other sort products generally have compatible interfaces and provide the same support.

The improvements in the sort interface fall into two categories: the efficiency of input and output for the sort, and methods of specifying parameters and options for the sort.

FASTER SORT INPUT AND OUTPUT

The **FASTSRT** compiler option can improve the efficiency of input or output operations for a SORT by allowing the I/O operations on a USING or GIVING file to be done directly by the sort program instead of by the COBOL program. Without FASTSRT, even if USING is coded instead of an INPUT PROCEDURE, the COBOL compiler generates a routine to read the input file and pass the records to the sort program. The flow is illustrated by the top diagram in Figure 15.1. For output, even when GIVING is used instead of an OUTPUT PROCEDURE, a compiler-generated routine accepts the sorted records from the sort program and writes them to the output file.

When the FASTSRT option is in effect and the USING phrase is coded in the SORT statement, the input file is read by the sort program instead of by a routine in the COBOL program. The bottom diagram in Figure 15.1 shows the difference. Similarly, if GIVING is used in

Figure 15.1   Flow of sort input records.

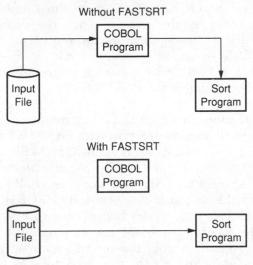

the SORT statement, FASTSRT allows the sort program to write the output file directly. FASTSRT improves performance in three ways. First, the sort performs I/O more efficiently than COBOL. Second, there is no need for the sort to move each record to or from its main storage work area. When the sort performs the I/O operations itself, it can do them directly to or from its work area. Third, FASTSRT eliminates the overhead of passing control back and forth between the sort program and the COBOL program for each record.

A number of requirements, in addition to specifying the option, must be satisfied for FASTSRT to actually take effect. The requirements are evaluated separately for the input and the output. It is therefore possible (in fact, likely) for FASTSRT processing to take place for the input to a particular SORT, but not for the output, or vice versa. The primary requirement is that USING must be specified instead of an INPUT PROCEDURE in order to use FASTSRT for the input to the sort. For FASTSRT to be used for output, GIVING must be used instead of an OUTPUT PROCEDURE. Also, there must be only a single input file or a single output file for FASTSRT to work. The *Application Programming Guide* lists a number of other requirements, all of which will generally be met by a typical SORT.

It is advisable to make FASTSRT the default option, even though many programs use INPUT PROCEDURE and OUTPUT PROCEDURE. If FASTSRT is the default, the programmer does not have to remember to specify it; it will automatically take effect for any file that meets all of the requirements. If FASTSRT is specified and a SORT input or output does not meet the requirements, the compiler issues an informational (I-level) message stating the requirement that was not met, and FASTSRT is not active for that file. If the NOFASTSRT option is in effect, the compiler issues an informational message if a file would have been eligible for FASTSRT processing.

There are two situations in which the DD statements for sort input or output files have to be slightly different with FASTSRT than without it. One is when the output of the sort is a new QSAM file, and FASTSRT is not used for the sort input (usually because there is an INPUT PROCEDURE). Under these circumstances, the DCB parameter in the DD statement for the output file must specify RECFM and LRECL as well as BLKSIZE. This is necessary because the sort program does not have access to the record format and record length information in the FD for the file. For a new file, the record characteristics are not in the file label. The sort cannot copy the characteristics of the input file because the COBOL program is handling the input file, making the output DD statement the only other source for the information.

A more unusual case in which FASTSRT requires different JCL is when USING and GIVING are specified in the same SORT statement, and the same QSAM file is used as both input and output. (A VSAM file cannot be used in this way.) There must be separate DD statements for the input file and the output file, even though they describe the same file and are identical except for the DD name. This situation affects the source program, as well as the JCL, because two different DD names are needed. There must be two FD's for the file, normally identical except for the file name, and a separate FILE-CONTROL entry for each FD, with different DD names corresponding to the two separate DD statements.

SORT PARAMETERS AND OPTIONS

All of the special registers for sorting available in OS/VS COBOL are still supported in VS COBOL II. Both VS COBOL II and DFSORT also provide control files that can be used to supply parameters and options to the sort at run time. By using one of these files, sort options can be changed without recompiling the program, and most sort options can be specified or overridden, not just those for which there is a special register. Specifying a sort parameter in any one of the control files overrides the corresponding special register, if there is one. Because of this possibility, VS COBOL II issues a warning (W-level) message if the program assigns a value to any of the special registers that can be overridden.

The control file provided by VS COBOL II uses the DD name **IGZSRTCD**. It can contain any DFSORT control statement except SORT, MERGE or RECORD, but it is normally used to supply an OPTION statement. Any OPTION parameters can be specified, except SORTIN or SORTOUT. There is also a special control statement that can only be used in IGZSRTCD. It is used instead of the SORT-MODE-SIZE special register to specify the most frequent record length for variable-length records. Here is an example of this statement, assuming that the most frequent record length is 435 bytes.

```
SMS=435
```

Most sorts probably will not need IGZSRTCD. However, every time a VS COBOL II program executes a SORT statement, it attempts to open IGZSRTCD even if the DD statement has not been coded. This causes two messages to be sent to the console: "IEC130I IGZSRTCD DD STATEMENT MISSING" and "IGZ027I The sort control data set could not be opened." To eliminate these messages, you can include an IGZSRTCD DD statement specifying DUMMY in any step that executes a VS COBOL II program with a SORT statement, if IGZSRTCD is not being used. There is no harm in including this DD DUMMY statement for programs that do not use SORT, so for simplicity, you could include it in the JCL for every COBOL program.

A new special register, **SORT-CONTROL**, lets the program specify a different DD name for IGZSRTCD.

Additional sort control statements can also be supplied in the SORT-CNTL file, which is read directly by the sort program, and is not part of VS COBOL II. Control statements in SORTCNTL override any options specified in the program (including special registers) or in IGZSRTCD. Release 11 or later of DFSORT also accepts control statements in a file with the DD name DFSPARM. This file can include options that would be coded in the PARM field of the EXEC statement for a JCL-invoked sort, as well as sort control statements. DFSPARM overrides all other sources of control information for the sort.

The SRTCDS file, which was used in OS/VS COBOL only to supply a DEBUG statement for the sort, is not supported by VS COBOL II, and is certainly not needed. There are more than enough ways to supply options and parameters to the sort.

Chapter 16

Compiler Options

Many of the new or changed compiler options in VS COBOL II have been discussed in earlier chapters in connection with the features they affect. Most of the options not discussed elsewhere are covered in this chapter. All of the options are summarized in Appendix E.

OPTIONS WITH LITTLE OR NO CHANGE

Some options are essentially unchanged from OS/VS COBOL to VS COBOL II. These are

ADV	LIB	SOURCE
APOST	OPTIMIZE	TEST
DECK	QUOTE	VBREF
DUMP	RESIDENT	ZWB
DYNAM		

Three other options are unchanged, except that the keywords are fully spelled out in VS COBOL II, instead of being abbreviated. However, the short forms used in OS/VS COBOL are also accepted by VS COBOL II. The three options are

OS/VS COBOL	VS COBOL II
NUM	NUMBER
SEQ	SEQUENCE
TERM	TERMINAL

Among the unchanged options, the OPTIMIZE option deserves special mention. Although the option is coded the same way and has the same meaning, the optimization performed by VS COBOL II is greatly improved over previous compilers. One improvement is procedure integration, which was discussed in Chapter 2. Another is the elimination of redundant calculations. That is, if the same calculation is done more than once, and the values of any variables do not change in between, the result of the first calculation will be saved so that it does not have to be recalculated. This optimization will even be performed for just part of an arithmetic expression if that part is repeated in another expression. If part of a calculation will always produce the same result, it will be calculated at compile time. Another improvement is that, where possible, VS COBOL II will combine MOVEs of adjacent fields into a single move.

The most impressive optimization, and the one that frequently surprises programmers, is the elimination of unreachable code. When the OPTIMIZE option is in effect, the compiler does extensive analysis of logic flow and conditional expressions. This analysis sometimes finds one or more statements that can never be executed, perhaps because a condition in an IF statement can never be true (or never false). When the compiler finds such a situation, it issues a warning message and does not generate object code for the statements that cannot be executed. Of course, the programmer wrote those statements for some purpose, and often does not immediately see why they cannot be reached. There is a tendency to think that it must be a bug in the compiler, but experience shows that such bugs are extremely rare. More likely explanations are a paragraph that is never PERFORMed, a conditional test of a field that always has the same value at that point, or something else along these lines. Consulting the cross-references may help to explain the problem. Until you get used to them, these situations can be disconcerting.

The additional overhead of the OPTIMIZE option at compile time is relatively small, so this option can reasonably be used all the time. It should always be used when the program is put into production. If OPTIMIZE is not used for all testing, it should be used to do final testing. Otherwise, untested code will be put into production. Although rare, the possibility of a difference in results between the optimized and unoptimized object code always exists.

The TRUNC option in VS COBOL II is very similar in function to the TRUNC option in OS/VS COBOL, but is coded in a different way and has three possible values instead of only two. TRUNC(STD) in VS COBOL II is the equivalent of TRUNC in OS/VS COBOL.

With this option, a binary receiving field is truncated to the number of decimal digits in its PICTURE. This conforms to the ANSI standard, but tends to produce inefficient object code. TRUNC(BIN) is equivalent to NOTRUNC in OS/VS COBOL. It causes binary fields to be handled according to their actual size in storage. The new option, TRUNC(OPT), always generates the most efficient code possible. However, if truncation occurs it will sometimes truncate according to the PICTURE, like TRUNC(STD), and sometimes according to the size of the field, like TRUNC(BIN). TRUNC(OPT), therefore, can safely be used only when no value in any binary field will exceed the number of digits in its PICTURE.

SOME IMPORTANT NEW OPTIONS

The new **SSRANGE** option is an important testing tool, and is one of the most valuable new features of VS COBOL II. It generates code to check whether any subscript or index goes beyond its valid range during execution of the program. It also checks for OCCURS . . . DEPENDING ON objects exceeding their defined maximum number of occurrences, and for reference modification exceeding the bounds of the field. If any of these out-of-range conditions occurs, a message is printed and the program abends. This option can eliminate many of the bewildering problems that occur when areas beyond the end of a table are modified because a subscript or index exceeds the number of occurrences in the table.

Unfortunately, the SSRANGE option has a fair amount of overhead. In a program with a lot of subscripting or indexing, using SSRANGE could cause an increase in CPU time on the order of 25%. (The increase was many times that prior to Release 3 of VS COBOL II.) For testing, the benefits far outweigh the cost of the extra CPU time. SSRANGE should always be used when testing. When a program is compiled for production, however, NOSSRANGE should be specified to eliminate the overhead.

There is also a run-time SSRANGE option. For the range checking to be performed, the program must be compiled with the SSRANGE compiler option, and the run-time SSRANGE option must be in effect when the program is executed. The run-time option is usually in effect by default. Specifying NOSSRANGE at run time disables the range checking and also eliminates most (but not all) of the overhead of SSRANGE. The SSRANGE run time option has no effect if the program was not compiled with the SSRANGE compiler option.

SSRANGE can be a problem with certain programs converted from an earlier version of COBOL. With earlier versions, for example, programmers sometimes intentionally used subscript or index values beyond the specified maximum in order to get around the limitations on the size of a table. When a program that uses this technique is converted to VS COBOL II, the out-of-range subscript will cause an abend when it is detected by the SSRANGE checking. Automated conversion programs or translators cannot easily recognize this technique, and will leave the original code unchanged. Either the changes must be made manually, or the program must be compiled with NOSSRANGE.

Another new option is **NUMPROC**, which affects the processing of signs in decimal fields. (This option was called PFDSGN in earlier releases of VS COBOL II.) It is important for programmers to understand the effect of this option. When NUMPROC(PFD) is specified, the compiler assumes that the sign in any decimal field is the correct **preferred sign**, based on the PICTURE for the field. (PFD is an abbreviation for "preferred.") For a signed field (S in the PICTURE), the preferred sign is hexadecimal C for a positive number or zero, and D for a negative number. For an unsigned field, the preferred sign is hexadecimal F. These rules apply to both external decimal (USAGE DISPLAY) and internal decimal (PACKED-DECIMAL or COMP-3) fields. Note that hexadecimal F is not a preferred sign if the field has an S in the PICTURE. By assuming that all decimal fields have preferred signs, NUMPROC(PFD) can generate very efficient object code for handling these fields. However, if the assumption is not true, statements that use decimal fields may not produce correct results.

NUMPROC(NOPFD) assumes only that decimal fields have a valid sign, that is, any hexadecimal value from A through F. The sign does not have to agree with the PICTURE. If necessary, NUMPROC(NOPFD) generates code to move the field to a temporary work area and change the sign to the preferred value before using the data.

A third choice, NUMPROC(MIG), is intended only for programs converted from OS/VS COBOL. It handles decimal signs in a manner very similar to OS/VS COBOL, and will therefore produce the same results in most cases. This setting should not be used for new programs written in VS COBOL II.

Regardless of which NUMPROC setting is used, VS COBOL II always creates preferred signs in receiving fields.

In most cases, NUMPROC(NOPFD) is the best choice. The rules for preferred signs are quite strict, and will rarely be met by existing data files. OS/VS COBOL and other languages sometimes produce non-preferred signs. NUMPROC(PFD) could be used for a new application written entirely in VS COBOL II, but fields must be defined with great care and absolute consistency. If a field is defined as unsigned in one program and signed in another program, the rules for preferred signs will unavoidably be broken in one program or the other. Careless use of REDEFINES can also cause problems. If high performance is important and the program does a lot of decimal arithmetic, the added efficiency of NUMPROC(PFD) may be worth the extra effort.

The NUMPROC option also affects the NUMERIC class condition (IF . . . NUMERIC) for a signed decimal field. If NUMPROC(PFD) is in effect, the NUMERIC test will be true only if the field has a preferred sign. With either of the other NUMPROC values, the result of the NUMERIC condition depends on another new compiler option, **NUMCLS**. This option can be specified only when the compiler is installed, and cannot be overridden at compile time. The normal setting is NUMCLS = PRIM. When this is specified, the NUMERIC condition will be true for a signed decimal field only if the sign is hexadecimal C, D, or F. This is the same rule followed by OS/VS COBOL. If NUMCLS = ALT is specified, any sign A through F is accepted as NUMERIC.

The **AWO** option has the same effect as coding APPLY WRITE-ONLY in the I-O-CONTROL paragraph of the ENVIRONMENT DIVISION. When this option is in effect, it applies to any QSAM file with blocked variable-length records, whether or not WRITE-ONLY is specified in the program. VS COBOL II, unlike OS/VS COBOL, does not require the use of WRITE . . . FROM when WRITE-ONLY is in effect.

There are two new flagging options for use when programs must be restricted to a subset of the full VS COBOL II language. **FLAGSTD** can be used to produce messages when any language element used in a program does not conform to the COBOL 85 standard. This is similar to the LVL option in OS/VS COBOL, which flagged elements not conforming to COBOL 74. Several codes can be specified in the FLAGSTD option. One code specifies which subset of standard COBOL is being used—minimum, intermediate, or high. The second code specifies whether or not use of the optional Debug or Segmentation modules is to be flagged. A third code determines whether obsolete elements will also be flagged. The other new flagging option is **FLAGSAA**, which produces a warning message for anything in the program that does not conform to SAA COBOL.

VS COBOL II provides three user exits from the compiler. The exits are useful primarily for software that interfaces with or invokes the compiler; they are unlikely to be used by an application programmer. Two of the exits can be used to supply the source program or COPY code to the compiler from user-written programs instead of from the SYSIN and SYSLIB files. The third exit can receive the print-image records for the compiler listing, instead of the compiler writing them to SYSPRINT. The **EXIT** option specifies the program name for each exit used. The exit routines can be written in COBOL.

An interesting feature of VS COBOL II is the ability to use a modified table of reserved words. The **WORD** option specifies the name of an alternate reserved word table to be used instead of the standard one. Instructions for creating an alternate reserved word table are in the *Installation and Customization* manual. The standard table is used as a base. Obviously, words that are reserved because they are part of the COBOL language cannot be made nonreserved. But one possible change is to flag any use of an existing reserved word with either an informational or an error message. For example, the table could be modified to flag the reserved word ALTER as an error, thereby preventing the use of that undesirable statement. Any word can be added to the table as a reserved word to be flagged with either an informational or an error message. Another possible modification is to add an abbreviation for an existing reserved word. For example, PK-DEC could be made an abbreviation for PACKED-DECIMAL.

There are two special compiler options to assist in the transition from Release 2 of VS COBOL II to Release 3 or later. Release 2 and earlier releases were based on the COBOL 74 standard, while Release 3 and later are based on COBOL 85. Because of this change, a few statements work slightly differently or produce different results in some cases. Most of the differences involve unusual situations or rarely used features, so the transition is not a problem for most programs. If a particular program poses a problem, it can be compiled with the **CMPR2** option. Think of this as an abbreviation for "compile like Release 2." With this option, the compiled program will produce exactly the same results as if it had been compiled with Release 2. However, when this option is in effect, most of the new features that were added in Release 3 to support COBOL 85 cannot be used. Therefore, this option should be considered a temporary expedient, not a permanent way to avoid making the transition.

The **FLAGMIG** option can be used together with CMPR2 to help the programmer modify the program to work with Release 3. FLAGMIG will produce a warning message for anything in the program that might produce different results if CMPR2 were not used. These messages show what may have to be changed to make the program operate correctly under Release 3.

Obviously there is no reason to use CMPR2 or FLAGMIG with a new program that was originally written using Release 3 or later.

DELETED OPTIONS

VS COBOL II does not have the Lister feature that was part of OS/VS COBOL. Therefore, all of the options associated with this feature are omitted. These are CDECK, FDECK, LCOL1, LCOL2, LSTCOMP, LSTONLY, L120, and L132.

The debugging options, COUNT, FLOW, STATE, and SYMDMP have also been eliminated. Substitutes for these options are discussed at the end of Chapter 10.

The following other options have also been deleted.

BATCH	VBSUM
ENDJOB	VERB
LANGLVL	XREF
MIGR	

Batch compilation can still be done with VS COBOL II, but does not have to be specified as an option. The function is always available just by including two or more programs in the input to the compiler. Each program in the batch must end with an END PROGRAM header, like a nested program. In a batch compilation, however, the END PRO-GRAM for each program comes before the IDENTIFICATION DIVI-SION header of the next program, and they are compiled as separate programs. The NAME option has the same function in VS COBOL II as in OS/VS COBOL, but it has a new suboption. If NAME(ALIAS) is specified, a linkage editor ALIAS statement is generated for each ENTRY statement in the program.

The ENDJOB and VERB functions are always in effect in VS COBOL II, so there is no need for the options. VBSUM is included in the VBREF option, as it was in OS/VS COBOL, but cannot be specified separately in VS COBOL II. Cross-reference listings in the order that the names appear in the source, as produced by the XREF option in OS/VS COBOL, are not available in VS COBOL II. The XREF option in VS COBOL II is equivalent to SXREF in OS/VS COBOL, and produces cross-references with the names sorted in alphabetical order.

The LANGLVL and MIGR options would not be appropriate in VS COBOL II. The VS COBOL II options CMPR2 and FLAGMIG, discussed above, parallel LANGLVL and MIGR, but are one generation newer. LANGLVL selects either the COBOL 68 or the COBOL 74 interpretation of certain language constructs, while CMPR2 chooses between COBOL 74 and COBOL 85. MIGR flags differences between OS/VS COBOL and VS COBOL II; FLAGMIG flags differences between Release 2 and Release 3 of VS COBOL II.

SPECIFYING OPTIONS TO THE COMPILER

There are three ways to specify compiler options. Default options are specified when the compiler is installed. These can be overridden at compile time by specifying options in the PARM field of the EXEC statement that executes the compiler, or in an on-line equivalent such as the options field of the ISPF/PDF panel that invokes the compiler.

The third way to specify options is in a **PROCESS** statement at the beginning of the source program. This overrides the other two sources. The PROCESS statement is a compiler-directing statement that must precede the IDENTIFICATION DIVISION header. It consists of the word PROCESS followed by a list of options, like this.

```
PROCESS ADV,TRUNC(BIN)
```

The PROCESS statement cannot be continued, but more than one PROCESS statement can be used.

The PROCESS statement is particularly appropriate for options that affect the results of the compiled program, such as DATA, TRUNC, ZWB, and others. Some programs may be dependent on particular settings of these options in order to execute correctly. Including the

critical options as part of the source program in such situations will
avoid errors when the program is recompiled in the future.

CBL can be used as a synonym for PROCESS. This is similar to the
CBL statement in OS/VS COBOL, but in OS/VS COBOL it was used
only in batch compilations. Using this synonym, however, could lead to
confusion because *CBL is a synonym for the *CONTROL statement
discussed in Chapter 11. Because the two shorter synonyms are similar,
it is best to use the longer, more distinct keywords for both statements.

OPTIONS THAT CANNOT BE OVERRIDDEN

There are two categories of compiler options in VS COBOL II that
cannot be specified or overridden at compile time. In the first category,
there are three options that can be specified only when the compiler
is installed. One of these, NUMCLS, was discussed above. The other
two are **ALOWCBL** and **LVLINFO**. ALOWCBL specifies whether or
not the PROCESS statement can be used. This should normally be
specified as YES because of the advantage discussed above. If CICS is
used, ALOWCBL = YES must be specified, because the CICS COBOL
translator generates a PROCESS statement.

LVLINFO is designed to help systems programmers who maintain the
VS COBOL II software. It specifies a four-character constant that can
be used to indicate the maintenance level of the compiler. This constant
is printed after the release number in the heading of the compiler
listing, and is included in the identifying information at the beginning
of the object program. If software problems arise, the constant provides
a handy record of the compiler's maintenance level at the time the
program was compiled.

The other category of options that cannot be overridden is **fixed
options**. Any of the options can be designated as fixed when the compiler is installed. This means that the default value specified during
installation cannot be overridden at compile time. Fixing options provides a way to enforce standards. For example, the APOST option
could be fixed to enforce the use of the apostrophe for enclosing
literals. However, a purchased application package, for example, might
not conform to the coding standards of the installation. The only way
to change a fixed option is to assemble another copy of the compiler
module that contains the options, and load it from a STEPLIB during
compilation. This is a lot less convenient than just putting the option
in a PARM field or in a PROCESS statement.

Chapter 17

Converting Existing Programs

Most of this book has been devoted to the use of VS COBOL II features in new programs. A major consideration for installations that are starting to use VS COBOL II is the conversion of existing programs written in an older version of COBOL. This chapter discusses the reasons for converting existing programs, strategies for planning and organizing the conversion effort, and the mechanics of converting programs.

WHY CONVERT?

As this book has shown, VS COBOL II provides a tremendous number of new features not available with older compilers. The ability to use these new features with existing programs is a major reason to convert them. One feature that can provide an immediate benefit for converted programs is the ability to run above the 16-megabyte line in an XA system. This can provide significant relief from storage constraints in CICS or other on-line systems, and it does not require any program changes beyond those that might be required for the conversion. A frequent problem area where many batch programs can benefit from conversion is in the limits on the size of tables. In VS COBOL II, the limits are so high that they amount to no limit at all in most cases.

One of the things programmers like best about VS COBOL II is that the tools for testing and debugging are much more powerful than in OS/VS COBOL or earlier versions. Subscript range checking, COBTEST, more information in the compiler listings, better dumps, and other improvements all make testing and debugging easier and faster, and thus make programmers more productive. If changes have to be made to an existing program, converting it to VS COBOL II makes all of these features available, and can shorten the testing cycle.

Converting all existing programs will eliminate the drawbacks of having two different compilers in use at the same time. As long as two versions of COBOL are in use, programmers will have to switch back and forth between the two, depending on their projects. This inevitably will result in mistakes caused by inadvertently using the syntax of one version in the other environment. This problem would more likely occur with maintenance programmers, who have to make the switch more frequently. Having two compilers also necessitates continuing to provide training for both versions. Direct costs are also higher with two compilers: license or maintenance fees must be paid for both, and both require installation, maintenance, and technical support.

Improving portability is another reason to convert existing programs. With the increasing use of personal computers, distributed processing, and equipment from multiple vendors, it becomes more important to be able to run the same program in different environments. With VS COBOL II, programs can be brought into conformance with the current standard, COBOL 85, making them more readily transportable, since a COBOL 85 compiler is available for just about any environment. VS COBOL II can also be used to bring programs into conformance with SAA if that approach to portability is chosen.

One other reason for converting existing programs cannot be ignored: sooner or later IBM will stop supporting OS/VS COBOL. While it is possible to continue using unsupported software, doing so entails the risk of encountering a problem that cannot be fixed, or of not being able to upgrade other software that interacts with the unsupported product. You may not want to take that kind of risk with a product on which a large number of your application programs depend. Nor is it advisable to delay conversion until IBM actually announces a cutoff date for support of OS/VS COBOL, since the amount of advance notice may not be sufficient for a large conversion effort. (An old IBM statement on the subject promises only one year's notice.) Also, the announcement could come at an inconvenient time, when programming resources are committed to critical projects. It seems more reasonable to at least begin the conversion effort in earnest as soon as VS COBOL II is installed.

CONVERSION STRATEGY

Once the decision is made to convert existing programs, the next question is how to go about it. Two preliminary steps will facilitate the conversion. First, as soon as VS COBOL II is installed, start using only the VS COBOL II subroutine library for execution and for new link-edits, even for OS/VS COBOL programs. The VS COBOL II library, sometimes referred to as the "compatibility library," provides full support for both versions of COBOL. Using a single library greatly simplifies link-editing, setting up execution JCL, and maintenance of the library itself. It is not necessary to relink-edit existing OS/VS COBOL programs.

The second step is to teach the new features of VS COBOL II to all of the COBOL programmers. Many of the advantages of VS COBOL II will be lost if the programmers do not use the new features. Also, the many changes will cause errors and confusion if programmers try to use the new compiler without any training. Too much new material exists to expect programmers to "pick it up" from the reference manuals. This book can be used as a training vehicle, either by itself or as a basis for classroom instruction. A classroom course takes two to three days, depending on how thoroughly the subject is covered. The new compiler should be available for practice and experimentation during training.

An obvious next step, once the programmers have been trained, is to start using VS COBOL II for all new programs. Continued development with the older language just increases the number of programs that will eventually have to be converted. Using VS COBOL II for new development makes all of the advantages of VS COBOL II available for the new programs.

The real strategy issue lies in deciding which programs to convert first. One possibility is to start with those programs that will produce the biggest benefit by being converted. For example, if you are running MVS/XA and your CICS system is encountering frequent shortages of dynamic storage, converting CICS programs to VS COBOL II can quickly relieve the situation.

Another approach is to convert any program that has to be changed in the course of regular maintenance or enhancement. As discussed later in this chapter, converting the program will usually add only a few minutes to the time needed to make and test other changes. This

approach can be used instead of or in addition to converting programs
that will benefit the most.

Converting programs as they require maintenance means that some
programs in an application will be converted before others. Because
of the "coexistence" features of VS COBOL II, this mixing of old and
new programs will not be a problem. As already mentioned, the VS
COBOL II subroutine library will support programs compiled with
either compiler. Even where one program CALLs another, it is not
necessary to convert both at the same time. VS COBOL II and OS/VS
COBOL programs can CALL each other in any combination, as long as
they are all link-edited and run with the compatibility library. Similarly,
both OS/VS COBOL and VS COBOL II programs can run in the same
CICS region. One transaction could even use a mix of both.

Whether you choose one or both of these conversion policies, there
are two types of programs for which you will want to defer conversion.
One is any program or application that is going to be replaced in the
near future. The other is programs that present particularly difficult
conversion problems, such as programs that use BDAM direct files.
Programs in the first category will probably never have to be converted,
because the replacements will be written in VS COBOL II. Programs
in the second category will eventually have to be converted, but should
be deferred until experience is gained with easier cases.

Both approaches described above will still leave a large number of
programs to be converted. Maintenance does not fall evenly on all
programs. Some programs tend to be changed frequently, while others run for years without being touched. As the number of OS/VS
COBOL programs requiring maintenance declines, programs will have
to be selected for conversion just to maintain the pace of conversion,
and some personnel will have to be devoted to the effort. Eventually,
everything that is not replaced will have to be converted.

HOW TO CONVERT A PROGRAM

Converting an OS/VS COBOL program to VS COBOL II basically
involves changing anything in the program that is not acceptable to the
VS COBOL II compiler, or that would produce different results under
VS COBOL II. The changes could be made manually, and Appendix
A could be used as a guide to what must be changed. However, doing
this manually is time-consuming, the work is tedious, and mistakes are
likely to be frequent.

A much more efficient method is to use an automated translator or conversion program, several of which are available from IBM and other companies. The translator will make most of the necessary changes automatically, and will flag anything that requires the programmer's attention. The translators handle CICS programs as well as batch, and take care of eliminating references to BLL cells. Translation is very fast. Typically, the percentage of statements that can be translated automatically is very high, and little or no manual work is needed after translation. There is enough upward compatibility between the two compilers that some programs will not require any change at all.

If an automated translator is used, the aspect of conversion that takes the most time is testing. If the program is being changed by maintenance or enhancements, it will have to be tested anyway, so converting it at the same time takes only a few extra minutes. Running the translator is simple and quick, little or no manual conversion is needed in most cases, and one set of tests can serve both purposes. The translation should be done first, then the maintenance changes should be made to the translated program.

When a program is translated just for the purpose of conversion, you will want to run at least one test to make sure that the converted program produces the same results as the original. The magnitude of the changes made by the translator may serve as a guide to the amount of testing that is appropriate. As experience is gained with the translator, you may develop enough confidence to cut corners on testing in selected cases, especially for simple or noncritical programs, or where very few changes were made.

Some programmers misunderstand the purpose of the translator. The intent of automated translation is only to change what must be changed to make the program acceptable to the VS COBOL II compiler. The translators do not attempt to use any of the new language features for their own sake, or to alter the style or structure of the code. There are software packages that restructure COBOL programs, but they do not do translation. The translators do not do restructuring. Their purpose is only to produce a program that can be compiled and run under VS COBOL II, not to produce coding that a programmer might have written if it had originally been done in VS COBOL II. The translated program will not look markedly different from the original. It may not contain any of the new statements or other features. If the original program was not structured, the translated program will not be structured either, but it will run under VS COBOL II.

SOME SPECIFIC CONVERSION PROBLEMS

One difficulty that always arises with any change to the COBOL language is the problem of new reserved words. New language features use new words, so words that previously were not reserved become reserved. Appendix C lists the new reserved words in VS COBOL II. The problem is minimized by the fact that the words used in a programming language tend not to be the sort of words that programmers use to name data fields and procedures.

Fortunately, the problem of reserved words is very easy for an automated translator to resolve. If a program contains a data-name or procedure-name that has become a reserved word, the translator will simply modify the word wherever it appears, typically by adding a predetermined prefix or suffix.

Another common difficulty is language that was accepted by the old compiler, even though it was not valid according to the language reference manual. VS COBOL II checks the syntax of the source program more stringently than OS/VS COBOL. Therefore some instances of invalid syntax accepted by OS/VS COBOL will be flagged as errors by VS COBOL II. Ideally a translator would change any such coding to make it valid for VS COBOL II. By their nature, though, many of these differences are not documented in the reference manuals because the differences are not evident from the language specifications. A translator therefore will, at best, handle those cases that the developers have discovered through experience in translating their customers' programs. Some translators assume that the OS/VS COBOL program conforms to the language specifications, and do not translate undocumented differences. This will result in diagnostic messages when the translated program is compiled with VS COBOL II.

A major concern is what to do about converting programs that use features of OS/VS COBOL not supported in VS COBOL II. The most significant omitted features were discussed in Chapter 10. Many of these are readily replaced by other language in VS COBOL II, and a translator will generate the appropriate new coding. A few major features have no direct or easy replacement. One of these is the Report Writer. The translators do not handle it, and manual conversion would be a big job. IBM offers a product called the COBOL Report Writer Precompiler specifically to take care of Report Writer. This package converts Report Writer coding to ordinary COBOL language acceptable to VS COBOL II.

There are two ways to use this product. The first way uses the Report Writer Precompiler purely as a conversion tool. The source program is run through it once, producing a new source program that will generate the same results but does not contain any Report Writer statements. This is exactly like using the regular translator, except that one package handles only Report Writer, and the other takes care of everything else. Both must be run in order to complete the translation of a program that uses Report Writer. The Report Writer coding is permanently removed from the program.

The other way of using the Report Writer Precompiler allows you to keep the Report Writer coding in the translated program. The Report Writer Precompiler is used as a "front end" to the compiler whenever the program is compiled. When it is used in this way, the Report Writer Precompiler can produce a combined listing that makes it appear as though VS COBOL II is compiling the Report Writer coding.

ISAM is another feature not supported in VS COBOL II. In the case of ISAM, the changes to the source program are the easiest part of the conversion. The translator will convert ISAM language in the program to VSAM. The problem is that the file itself must also be converted to a VSAM KSDS. This means all of the programs that access any one file will have to be converted at the same time. All JCL that references the file will have to be changed, and a one-time job to convert the file will have to be run. The conversion of the file can be accomplished by writing the records to a sequential file with the IEBISAM utility program, then copying them to the new VSAM file with the IDCAMS utility program. No programming should be needed to convert the file.

BDAM also is not implemented in VS COBOL II. The BDAM file can be converted to a VSAM file, but the conversion may not be quite as easy as for an indexed file. The organization and processing logic of a BDAM relative file is very similar to that of a VSAM relative file (RRDS). Converting a relative file is therefore fairly straightforward. The changes in the source are not major, but the translator may leave more to be done manually than it would for ISAM. As with ISAM, JCL will also have to be changed. A direct file is a much bigger problem. VS COBOL II has no equivalent of the track and key addressing used in a BDAM direct file, so a straight conversion is impossible. The file will have to be redesigned as either an indexed or a relative file.

The Communication Feature is also omitted from VS COBOL II. The only substitute is use of a different communications monitor, such as CICS, which obviously involves a major rewriting of the program.

The features that are most difficult to convert, such as direct files and the Communication Feature, are not used very much, and therefore will not be a problem for most installations. This is small comfort, however, if your installation is one of the few with a major application that uses one of these features. As noted above, the conversion of these particular programs can, and should, be deferred, but it cannot be avoided indefinitely.

Conversions are unpleasant but necessary for the continued advancement of technology. Converting to VS COBOL II is a manageable job that has some benefits. Using some of the suggestions in this chapter can minimize the difficulty and the cost.

APPENDICES

Appendix A

Differences Between VS COBOL II and OS/VS COBOL

The following table lists all COBOL language elements and briefly indicates anything that is new or changed in VS COBOL II. The column on the right shows the chapter in which the new or changed element is discussed. The table includes changes that are not discussed in the text. The comparison is between VS COBOL II Release 3 with the NOCMPR2 option and OS/VS COBOL Release 2.4 with the LANG-LVL(2) option. Formats of all new and changed clauses and statements are in Appendix B.

Language Element	New or Changed in VS COBOL II	Chapter
General Items:		
Lowercase letters	Allowed anywhere in source.	6
Reserved words	Additions and deletions.	App. C
Nested programs	New feature.	8
Nonnumeric literal	Can be up to 160 bytes long.	
Hexadecimal literal	New feature.	5
DBCS literal	New feature.	
NULL figurative constant	New figurative constant used with ADDRESS OF and POINTER.	7
DBCS	New feature.	5

Language Element	New or Changed in VS COBOL II	Chapter
Special registers:		
ADDRESS OF	New.	7
CURRENT-DATE	Deleted.	10
DAY-OF-WEEK	New.	6
LENGTH OF	New.	5
LINE-COUNTER	Deleted. (Report Writer)	10, 17
PAGE-COUNTER	Deleted. (Report Writer)	10, 17
SHIFT-IN	New. (DBCS)	5
SHIFT-OUT	New. (DBCS)	5
SORT-CONTROL	New.	15
TIME-OF-DAY	Deleted.	10
WHEN-COMPILED	Different format and length.	
All other special registers	No change.	
IDENTIFICATION DIVISION		
PROGRAM-ID paragraph	New attributes COMMON and INITIAL.	8, 7
REMARKS paragraph	Deleted.	10
All other paragraphs	No change.	
ENVIRONMENT DIVISION	Optional.	8
CONFIGURATION SECTION	Optional.	8
SOURCE-COMPUTER	No change.	
OBJECT-COMPUTER	No change.	
SPECIAL-NAMES	New function-names. Report code deleted (Report Writer). Word ALPHABET required. New character set names.	
SYMBOLIC CHARACTERS	New clause.	5

Language Element	New or Changed in VS COBOL II	Chapter
CLASS	New clause.	6
CURRENCY SIGN	Can specify the letter L.	
INPUT-OUTPUT SECTION		
FILE-CONTROL clauses:		
SELECT	OPTIONAL allowed for all files except output.	
ASSIGN	Organization codes D, W, R, and I deleted. (BDAM and ISAM)	10, 17
RESERVE	ALTERNATE not supported.	
ORGANIZATION	Word ORGANIZATION is optional.	
ACCESS	No change.	
RECORD KEY	No change.	
ALTERNATE RECORD KEY	No change.	
ACTUAL KEY	Deleted. (BDAM)	17
NOMINAL KEY	Deleted.	
RELATIVE KEY	New clause for relative file.	
PASSWORD	No change.	
FILE STATUS	New codes. Additional field for VSAM.	6
TRACK-AREA	Deleted. (ISAM)	10, 17
TRACK-LIMIT	Deleted. (BDAM)	10, 17
PADDING CHARACTER	New clause. (No effect on processing.)	
RECORD DELIMITER	New clause. (No effect on processing.)	
I-O-CONTROL clauses:		
RERUN	No checkpoint taken on first record.	
SAME	No change.	
MULTIPLE FILE	No change.	

Language Element	New or Changed in VS COBOL II	Chapter
APPLY WRITE-ONLY	Does not require WRITE FROM. Can be specified by AWO compiler option.	16
All other APPLY formats	Deleted. (BDAM and ISAM)	10, 17
DATA DIVISION	Optional.	8
FILE SECTION	No change.	
WORKING-STORAGE SECTION	No change.	
LINKAGE SECTION	No change.	
REPORT SECTION	Deleted. (Report Writer)	10, 17
COMMUNICATION SECTION	Deleted. (Communication Feature)	17
FD and SD clauses:		
EXTERNAL	New clause in FD.	7
GLOBAL	New clause in FD.	8
LABEL RECORDS	Optional in FD. Not allowed in SD. TOTALING and TOTALED deleted.	
RECORD CONTAINS	Interpreted differently when only one integer is specified.	5
RECORD IS VARYING	New clause.	5
REPORT	Deleted. (Report Writer)	10, 17
All other FD and SD clauses	No change.	
Data description clauses:		
Data-name	May begin in Area A for 01 or 77.	
FILLER	Word FILLER optional.	5
EXTERNAL	New clause for 01 in WORKING-STORAGE.	7
GLOBAL	New clause for 01 level.	8
OCCURS	Up to seven dimensions allowed. With DEPENDING ON minimum number of occurrences can be zero. VALUE allowed with OCCURS.	5

Language Element	New or Changed in VS COBOL II	Chapter
PICTURE	Last character can be period or comma. Letter G represents a DBCS character.	
SIGN	Allowed at group and elementary levels in same hierarchy.	
USAGE	New USAGEs PACKED-DECIMAL, BINARY, POINTER, and DISPLAY-1.	5, 7
VALUE	Allowed with OCCURS.	5
All other data description clauses	No change.	
PROCEDURE DIVISION General:	Optional.	8
Arithmetic expressions	Figurative constant ZERO can be used.	
Class condition	Meaning of ALPHABETIC changed. New classes ALPHABETIC UPPER, ALPHABETIC-LOWER, DBCS, KANJI, and programmer–defined CLASS.	6
Relation condition	New relational operators > = and < =.	6
Other conditions	No change.	
Subscripting	Up to seven dimensions allowed. Relative subscripting allowed. Subscripts and indexes can be mixed in one multidimension reference.	5
Reference modification	New feature.	5
END PROGRAM	New element for nested programs or batch compilation.	8, 16
Statements:		
ACCEPT	DAY-OF-WEEK. SYSIPT synonym for SYSIN. MESSAGE COUNT deleted (Communication Feature).	6
ADD	Explicit scope terminator END-ADD. NOT ON SIZE ERROR phrase. TO allowed with GIVING.	3, 6

Language Element	New or Changed in VS COBOL II	Chapter
ALTER	No change.	
CALL	BY REFERENCE and BY CONTENT phrases. Literals as parameters. ON EXCEPTION and NOT ON EXCEPTION phrases. ON OVERFLOW executed for any EXCEPTION condition. Explicit scope terminator END-CALL. Procedure name not allowed as parameter.	7, 3
CANCEL	No change.	
CLOSE	REEL/UNIT, FOR REMOVAL, and NO REWIND allowed for any QSAM file; REEL/UNIT FOR REMOVAL always treated as comment.	
COMPUTE	Explicit scope terminator END-COMPUTE. NOT ON SIZE ERROR phrase.	3
CONTINUE	New statement.	3
DELETE	Explicit scope terminator END-DELETE. NOT INVALID KEY phrase.	3
DISABLE	Deleted. (Communication Feature)	17
DISPLAY	NO ADVANCING phrase. SYSLIST and SYSLST synonyms for SYSOUT.	
DIVIDE	Explicit scope terminator END-DIVIDE. NOT ON SIZE ERROR phrase.	3
ENABLE	Deleted. (Communication Feature)	17
ENTRY	No change.	
EVALUATE	New statement.	4
EXAMINE	Deleted.	10
EXHIBIT	Deleted.	10
EXIT	No change.	
EXIT PROGRAM	Does not have to be only statement in paragraph. In subprogram, resets exits from uncompleted PERFORMs.	
GENERATE	Deleted. (Report Writer)	10, 17

Language Element	New or Changed in VS COBOL II	Chapter
GOBACK	In subprogram, resets exits from uncompleted PERFORMs.	
GO TO	No change.	
IF	Explicit scope terminator END-IF. OTHERWISE deleted.	3
INITIALIZE	New statement.	5
INITIATE	Deleted. (Report Writer)	10, 17
INSPECT	Unlimited number of REPLACING or TALLYING comparands. CHARACTERS phrase can be repeated. BEFORE and AFTER can be used together. CONVERTING phrase.	5
MERGE	Paragraph names for OUTPUT PROCEDURE. More than one file in GIVING.	6
MOVE	De-editing. Improvement in MOVE of group containing OCCURS DEPENDING ON.	5
MULTIPLY	Explicit scope terminator END-MULTIPLY. NOT ON SIZE ERROR phrase.	3
NOTE	Deleted.	10
ON	Deleted.	10
OPEN	EXTEND allowed for indexed and relative files. REVERSED not allowed for multireel files. LEAVE, REREAD, and DISP deleted.	
PERFORM	In-line format with explicit scope terminator END-PERFORM. TEST AFTER and TEST BEFORE phrases. Up to six AFTER phrases (total of seven dimensions). Different sequence of incrementing multiple identifiers when they are interdependent. In subprogram, exit from uncompleted PERFORM is reset by GOBACK or EXIT PROGRAM.	2, 5

Language Element	New or Changed in VS COBOL II	Chapter
READ	Explicit scope terminator END-READ. NOT AT END and NOT INVALID KEY phrases.	3
READY TRACE	Deleted.	10
RECEIVE	Deleted. (Communication Feature)	17
RELEASE	No change.	
RESET TRACE	Deleted.	10
RETURN	Explicit scope terminator END-RETURN. NOT AT END phrase.	3
REWRITE	Explicit scope terminator END REWRITE. NOT INVALID KEY phrase.	3
SEARCH	Explicit scope terminator END-SEARCH.	3
SEEK	Deleted. (BDAM)	
SEND	Deleted. (Communication Feature).	17
SET	Condition-name TO TRUE. ADDRESS OF or POINTER. UPSI switch ON or OFF.	6, 7
SORT	Paragraph names for INPUT or OUTPUT PROCEDURE. DUPLICATES IN ORDER. More than one file in GIVING.	6
START	Explicit scope terminator END-START. NOT INVALID KEY phrase. USING deleted.	3
STOP	No change.	
STRING	Explicit scope terminator END-STRING. NOT ON OVERFLOW phrase. Group level allowed as receiving (INTO) field.	3
SUBTRACT	Explicit scope terminator END-SUBTRACT. NOT ON SIZE ERROR phrase.	3
TERMINATE	Deleted. (Report Writer)	10, 17
TRANSFORM	Deleted.	10, 5

Language Element	New or Changed in VS COBOL II	Chapter
UNSTRING	Explicit scope terminator END-UNSTRING. NOT ON OVERFLOW phrase. All subscripts evaluated before any data movement.	3
WRITE	Explicit scope terminator END-WRITE. NOT INVALID KEY and NOT END-OF-PAGE phrases. POSITIONING deleted. Not allowed for QSAM file OPENed I-O.	3, 10
Compiler-directing statements:		
BASIS	No change.	
*CONTROL	New statement.	11
COPY	Nesting allowed.	6
DEBUG	Deleted. (Debugging packet)	10
DELETE	No change.	
EJECT	No change.	
ENTER	No change.	
INSERT	No change.	
PROCESS	New statement.	16
REPLACE	New statement.	6
SERVICE LABEL	New statement. (CICS)	9
SERVICE RELOAD	Deleted. (CICS)	9
SKIP1/2/3	No change.	
TITLE	New statement.	
USE AFTER EXCEPTION/ERROR	Can specify GLOBAL. GIVING deleted.	
USE AFTER STANDARD LABEL	Can specify GLOBAL. BEFORE deleted.	
USE FOR DEBUGGING	Only for procedures, not for data-names or files.	10
USE BEFORE REPORTING	Deleted. (Report Writer)	10, 17

Appendix B

New or Changed Language Formats

This appendix contains format diagrams for all of the language elements that are new or changed in VS COBOL II. The formats are shown in the new "railroad-track" style used in the *Language Reference* manual. This new type of diagram is explained at the end of Chapter 6.

COBOL Source Program

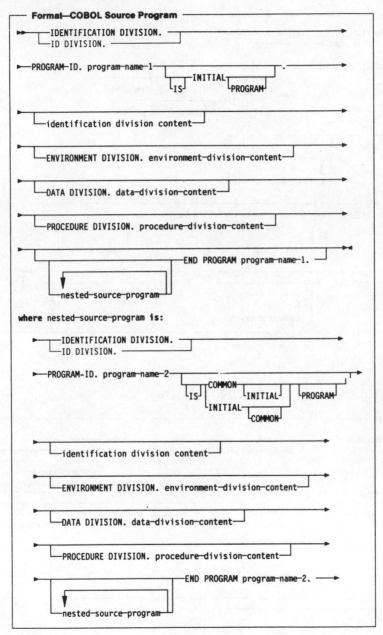

IDENTIFICATION DIVISION

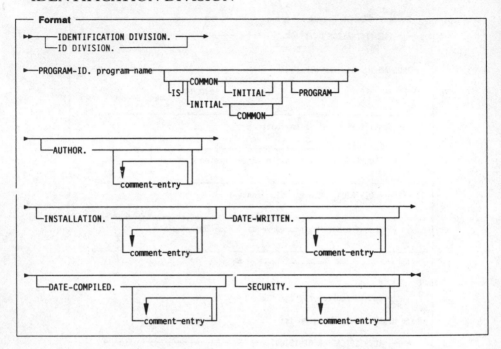

ENVIRONMENT DIVISION

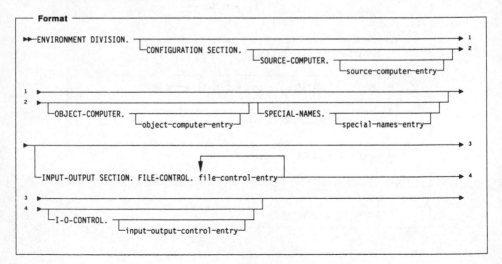

SPECIAL-NAMES Paragraph

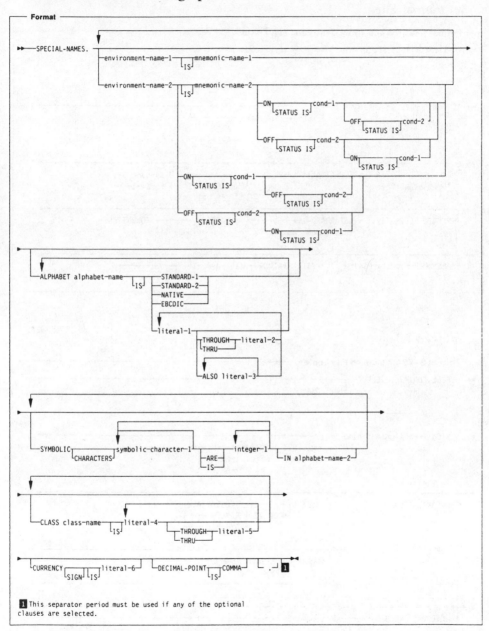

1 This separator period must be used if any of the optional clauses are selected.

FILE-CONTROL Paragraph
Sequential File

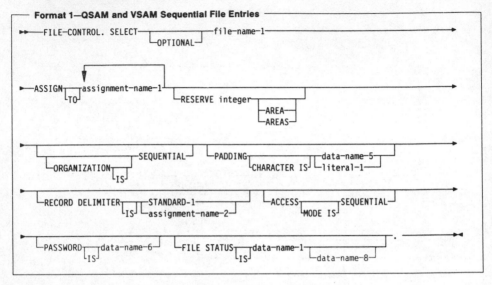

Indexed File

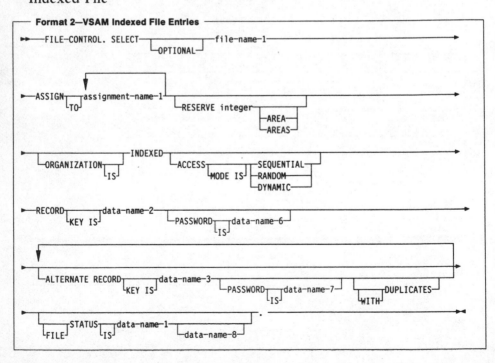

Relative File

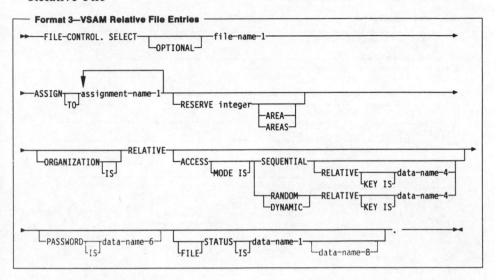

DATA DIVISION
File Description Entry
Sequential File

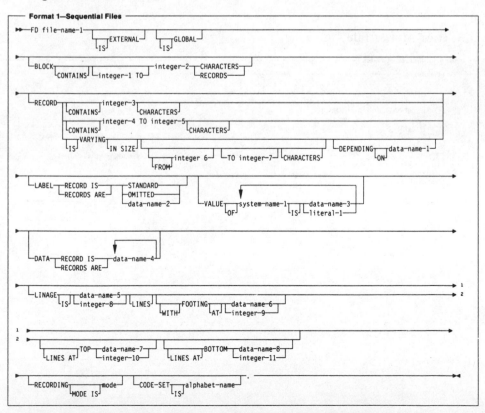

Indexed or Relative File

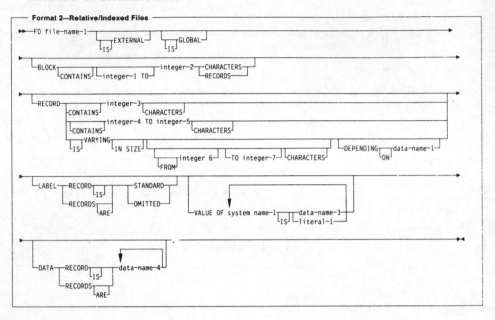

Sort or Merge File

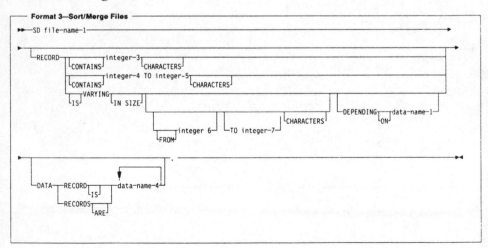

Data Description Entry

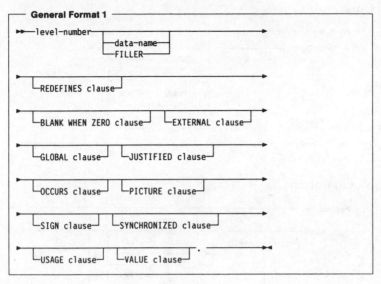

USAGE Clause

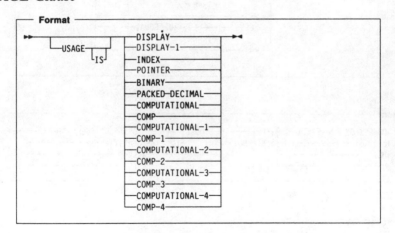

PROCEDURE DIVISION
Class Condition

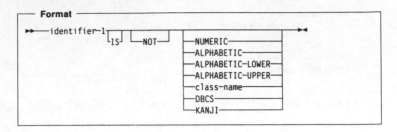

Relation Condition

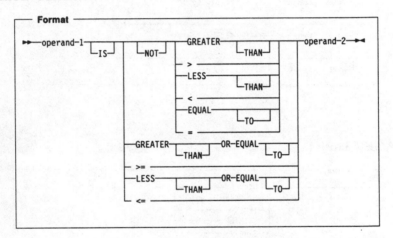

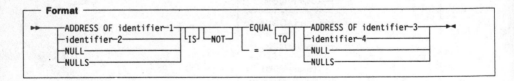

Subscripting

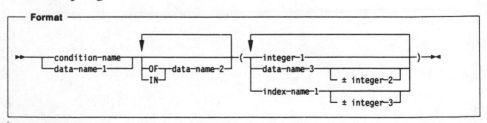

Reference Modification

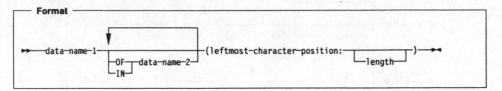

PROCEDURE DIVISION Statements

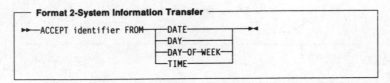

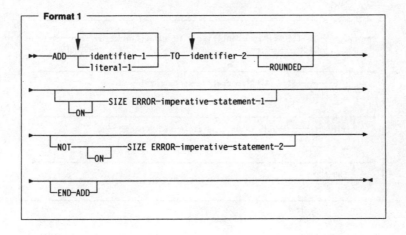

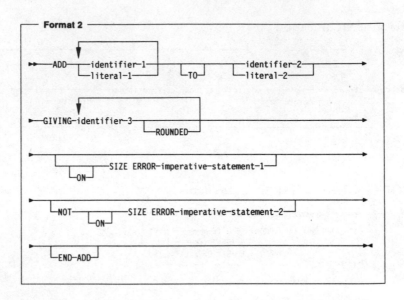

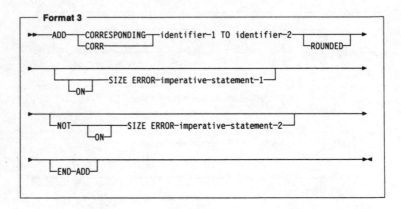

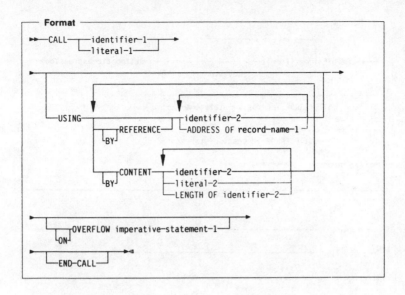

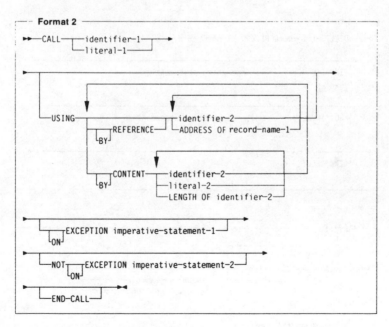

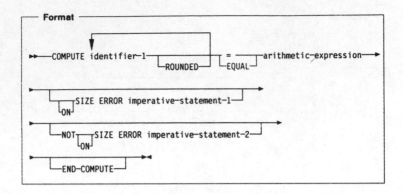

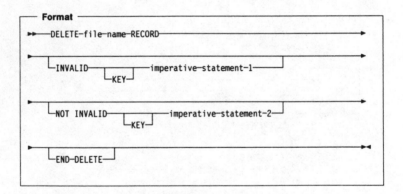

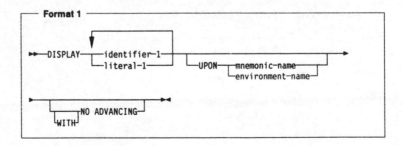

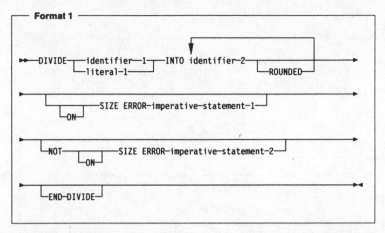

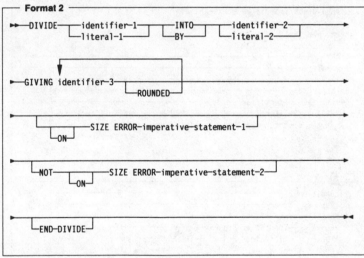

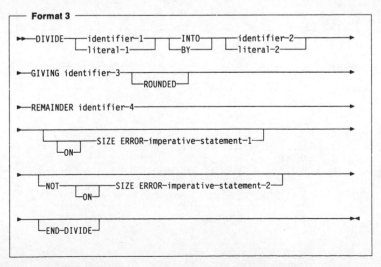

Format

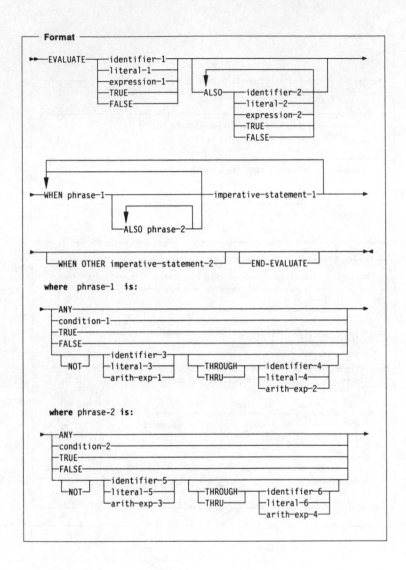

where phrase-1 is:

where phrase-2 is:

Format

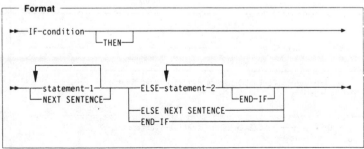

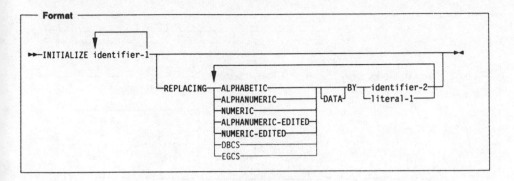

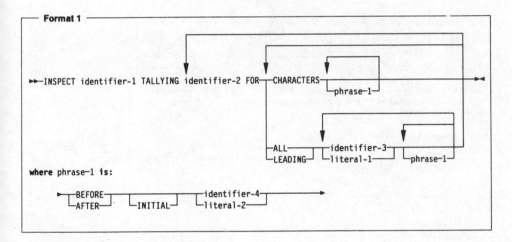

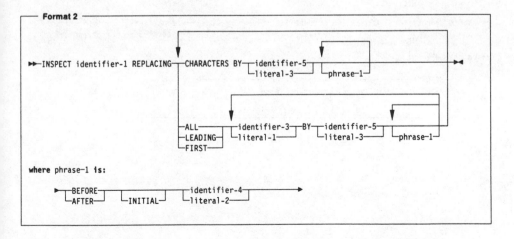

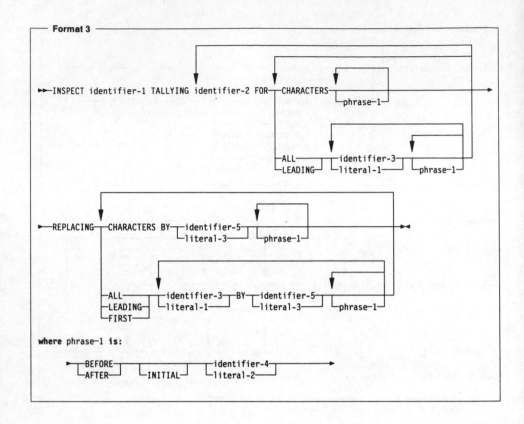

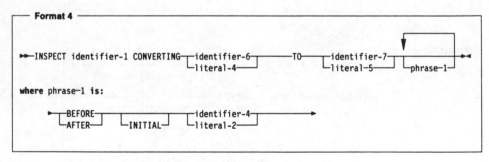

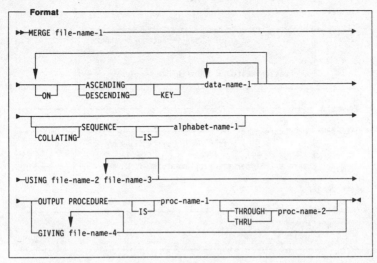

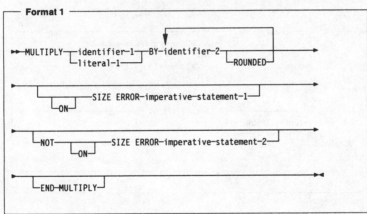

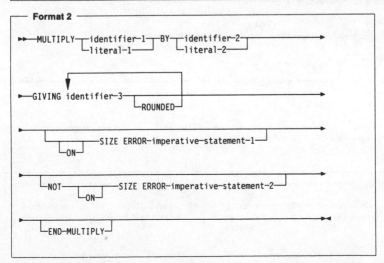

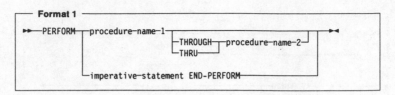

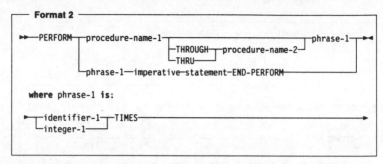

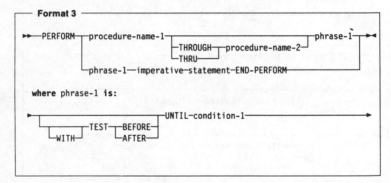

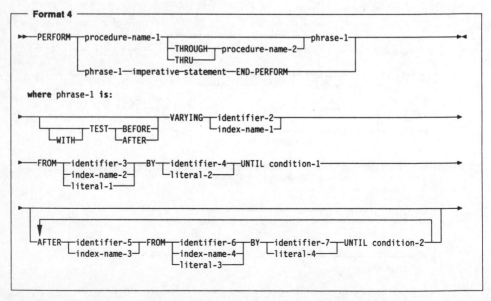

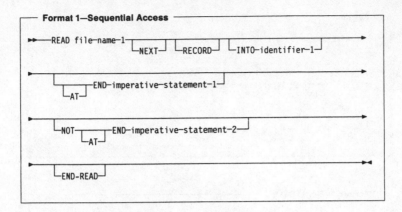

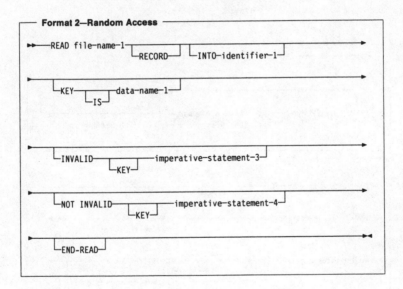

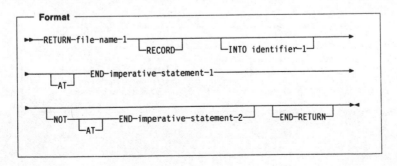

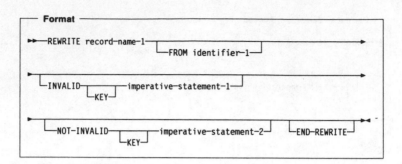

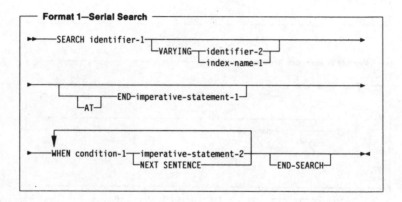

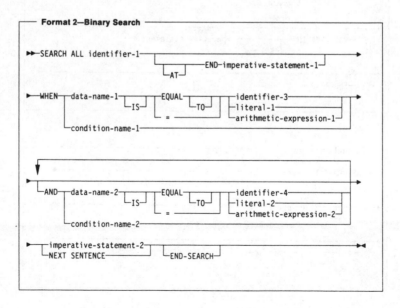

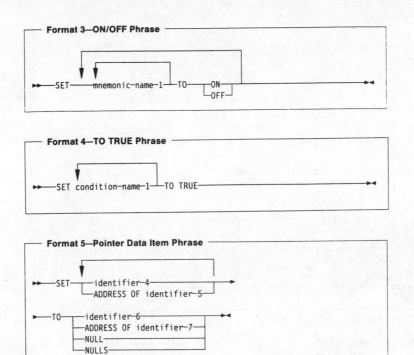

Format 3—ON/OFF Phrase

Format 4—TO TRUE Phrase

Format 5—Pointer Data Item Phrase

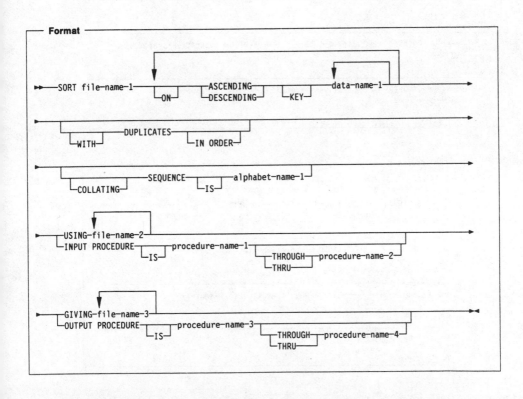

Format

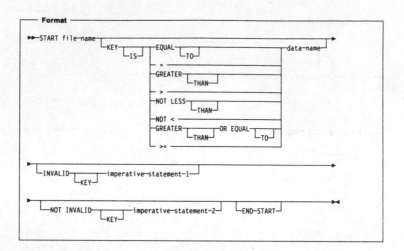

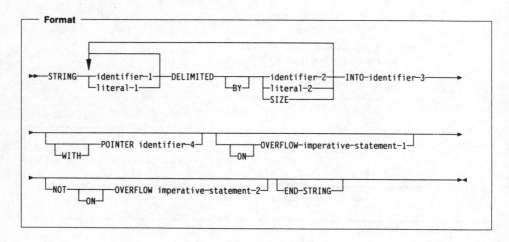

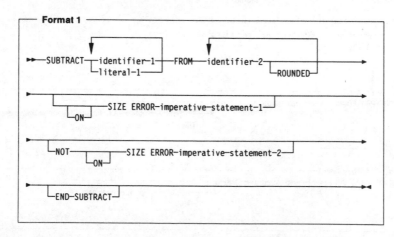

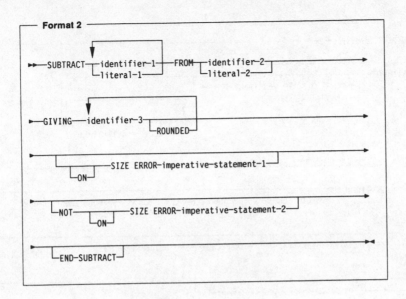

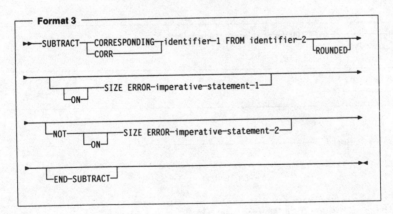

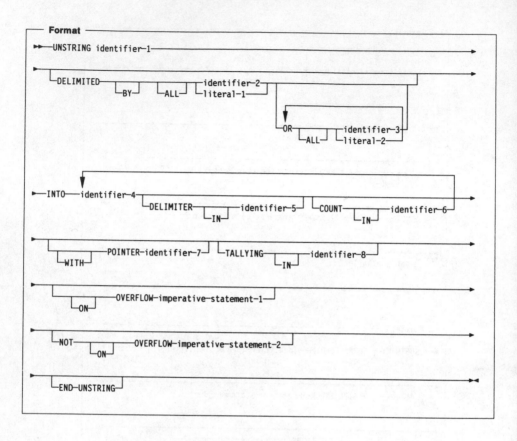

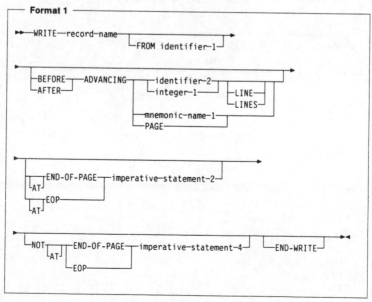

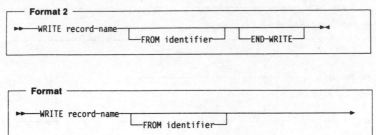

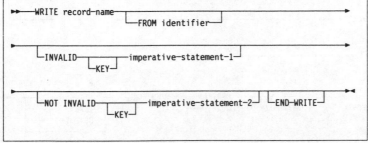

Compiler-directing Statements

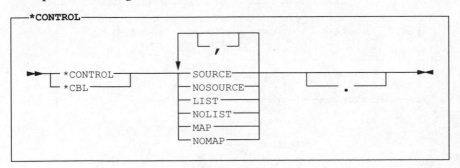

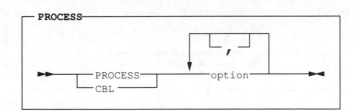

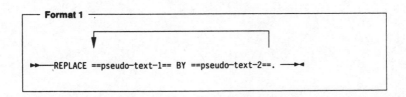

Format 2

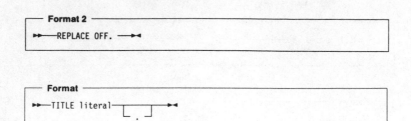

Format

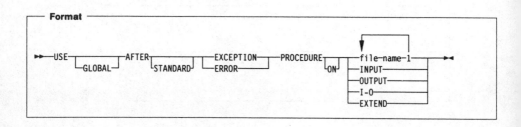

Format

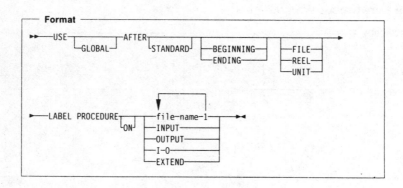

Format

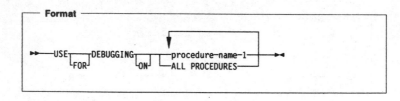

Appendix C

New and Deleted Reserved Words

NEW RESERVED WORDS

The following are new reserved words in VS COBOL II. They were not reserved in OS/VS COBOL.

ALPHABET
ALPHABETIC-LOWER
ALPHABETIC-UPPER
ALPHANUMERIC
ALPHANUMERIC-EDITED
ANY
BINARY
CLASS
COBOL
COM-REG
COMMON
CONTENT
CONTINUE
CONVERTING
DAY-OF-WEEK
DBCS
DISPLAY-1
EGCS
END-ADD
END-CALL

END-COMPUTE
END-DELETE
END-DIVIDE
END-EVALUATE
END-IF
END-MULTIPLY
END-PERFORM
END-READ
END-RECEIVE
END-RETURN
END-REWRITE
END-SEARCH
END-START
END-STRING
END-SUBTRACT
END-UNSTRING
END-WRITE
EVALUATE
EXTERNAL
FALSE

GLOBAL	PURGE
INITIALIZE	REFERENCE
KANJI	REPLACE
NULL	SHIFT-IN
NULLS	SHIFT-OUT
NUMERIC-EDITED	SORT-CONTROL
ORDER	STANDARD-2
OTHER	TEST
PACKED-DECIMAL	TITLE
PADDING	TRUE
PRINTING	

DELETED RESERVED WORDS

The following are reserved words in OS/VS COBOL that are not reserved in VS COBOL II. A number of these words are still used as environment-names in the SPECIAL-NAMES paragraph and the ACCEPT and DISPLAY statements, but are no longer reserved.

ACTUAL	LABEL-RETURN
CHANGED	LEAVE
CONSOLE	NAMED
CORE-INDEX	NOMINAL
CSP	NOTE
CURRENT-DATE	OTHERWISE
C01	POSITIONING
C02	PRINT-SWITCH
C03	RECORD-OVERFLOW
C04	REMARKS
C05	REORG-CRITERIA
C06	REREAD
C07	SEEK
C08	SELECTIVE
C09	SYSIN
C10	SYSIPT
C11	SYSLST
C12	SYSOUT
DEBUG	SYSPCH
DISP	SYSPUNCH
DISPLAY-ST	S01
EXAMINE	S02
EXHIBIT	TIME-OF-DAY
FILE-LIMIT	TOTALED
FILE-LIMITS	TOTALING

TRACK	UPSI-2
TRACK-AREA	UPSI-3
TRACK-LIMIT	UPSI-4
TRACKS	UPSI-5
TRANSFORM	UPSI-6
UPSI-0	UPSI-7
UPSI-1	

CODASYL RESERVED WORDS

The following are reserved words in CODASYL COBOL. They are not reserved in VS COBOL II, but are flagged with an informational (I-level) message. These words are likely to be used for new features in future versions of COBOL.

ARITHMETIC	DB-STATUS
B-AND	DEFAULT
B-EXOR	DISCONNECT
B-LESS	DISPLAY-2
B-NOT	DISPLAY-3
B-OR	DISPLAY-4
BIT	DISPLAY-5
BITS	DISPLAY-6
BOOLEAN	DISPLAY-7
COMMIT	DISPLAY-8
COMP-5	DISPLAY-9
COMP-6	DUPLICATE
COMP-7	EMPTY
COMP-8	END-DISABLE
COMP-9	END-ENABLE
COMPUTATIONAL-5	END-SEND
COMPUTATIONAL-6	END-TRANSCEIVE
COMPUTATIONAL-7	EQUALS
COMPUTATIONAL-8	ERASE
COMPUTATIONAL-9	EXACT
CONNECT	EXCEEDS
CONTAINED	EXCLUSIVE
CURRENT	FETCH
DB	FIND
DB-ACCESS-CONTROL-KEY	FINISH
DB-DATA-NAME	FORMAT
DB-EXCEPTION	FREE
DB-RECORD-NAME	FUNCTION
DB-SET-NAME	GET

INDEX-1
INDEX-2
INDEX-3
INDEX-4
INDEX-5
INDEX-6
INDEX-7
INDEX-8
INDEX-9
KEEP
LD
LOCALLY
MEMBER
MODIFY
NONE
ONLY
OWNER
PARAGRAPH
PRESENT
PRIOR
PROTECTED
REALM

RECONNECT
RECORD-NAME
RELATION
REPEATED
RETAINING
RETRIEVAL
ROLLBACK
SESSION-ID
SHARED
STANDARD-3
STANDARD-4
STORE
SUB-SCHEMA
TENANT
TRANSCEIVE
UNEQUAL
UPDATE
USAGE-MODE
VALID
VALIDATE
WAIT
WITHIN

Appendix D

Obsolete Language Elements

This appendix lists the language elements implemented in VS COBOL II that are designated as obsolete in the COBOL 85 standard. The use of these elements should be avoided because they will be deleted from the COBOL language in the next standard.

ALL literal used with a numeric or numeric-edited field, when the literal is more than one byte.

All IDENTIFICATION DIVISION paragraphs except PROGRAM-ID. (That is, AUTHOR, INSTALLATION, DATE-WRITTEN, DATE-COMPILED, and SECURITY.)

MEMORY SIZE in the OBJECT-COMPUTER paragraph of the ENVIRONMENT DIVISION.

RERUN in the I-O-CONTROL paragraph of the ENVIRONMENT DIVISION.

MULTIPLE FILE TAPE in the I-O-CONTROL paragraph of the ENVIRONMENT DIVISION.

LABEL RECORDS, VALUE OF, and DATA RECORDS in an FD or SD.

The ALTER statement, and the GO TO statement without a procedure-name (that is, an ALTERable GO TO).

The ENTER statement.

OPEN . . . REVERSED.

STOP literal.

Segmentation.

Debugging sections (USE FOR DEBUGGING).

Appendix E

Summary of Compiler Options

The following table lists all of the VS COBOL II options that can be specified at compile time. For each option, it gives the corresponding OS/VS COBOL option, if there is one, and a brief description of what the option does. The description indicates whether the option is new or changed in VS COBOL II. The column on the right shows the chapter in which the option is discussed. OS/VS COBOL options not implemented in VS COBOL II are listed and discussed in Chapter 16.

In VS COBOL II, options that specify a value put the value in parentheses after the keyword, whereas OS/VS COBOL generally used an equal sign after the keyword. For example, in VS COBOL II specify SIZE(640K) instead of SIZE = 640K.

VS COBOL II Option	OS/VS COBOL Option	Description	Chapter
ADV	ADV	No change. Carriage control character not defined in the output record.	16
APOST	APOST	No change. Apostrophe used as delimiter for literals.	16
AWO		New. APPLY WRITE-ONLY for all VB files.	16
BUFSIZE	BUF	In VS COBOL II, buffer size for each work file. In OS/VS, total for all files.	

VS COBOL II Option	OS/VS COBOL Option	Description	Chapter
CMPR2		New. Compatibility with VS COBOL II Release 2.	16
COMPILE	CSYNTAX, SYNTAX, SUPMAP	Complete compilation despite errors. NOCOMPILE(x) specifies error level to suppress object code.	
DATA		New. With RENT, location of data areas.	14
DBCS		New. Interpret X'0E' and X'0F' in literals as shift codes.	
DECK	DECK	No change. Write object module to SYSPUNCH.	16
DUMP	DUMP	No change. Produce dump for debugging compiler problem.	16
DYNAM	DYNAM	No change. Make CALL literal dynamic.	16
EXIT		New. User exits for compiler input and output.	16
FASTSRT		New. SORT I/O done by sort instead of COBOL program.	15
FDUMP	SYMDMP	Formatted dump for abend. Other SYMDMP functions deleted.	12, 16
FLAG	FLAGE/W	Level of diagnostic messages to print. In VS COBOL II, also level of messages to embed in source.	11
FLAGMIG		New. With CMPR2, flag differences between Release 2 and Release 3.	16
FLAGSAA		New. Flag language elements not defined in SAA COBOL.	16
FLAGSTD	LVL	Flag language elements not defined in specified subset of ANSI COBOL 85. Can also flag obsolete elements. LVL in OS/VS flags according to COBOL 74.	16

VS COBOL II Option	OS/VS COBOL Option	Description	Chapter
LANGUAGE		New. Language for compiler listings and messages. For English, also specifies mixed case or uppercase.	11
LIB	LIB	Source contains COPY, BASIS, or REPLACE statements.	16
LINECOUNT	LINECNT	Number of lines per page in compiler listing.	11
LIST	PMAP	Print full object code listing.	11
MAP	DMAP	Print DATA DIVISION map.	11
NAME	NAME	Produce linkage editor control statements with object module.	16
NUMBER	NUM	No change. Use source line numbers in messages and maps.	16
NUMPROC		New. Specifies decimal sign handling.	16
OBJECT	LOAD	Write object module to SYSLIN.	
OFFSET	CLIST	Print condensed object code map.	11
OPTIMIZE	OPTIMIZE	No change. Optimize object code. VS COBOL II has improved optimization.	16, 2
OUTDD	SYSx	DD name for DISPLAY output. In VS COBOL II, entire name can be specified.	
QUOTE	QUOTE	No change. Quotation mark used as delimiter for literals.	16
RENT		New. Make object program reentrant and able to load above 16-meg line.	14
RESIDENT	RESIDENT	Load COBOL library routines at run time, and object program can run in either addressing mode.	14
SEQUENCE	SEQ	No change. Check sequence of source lines.	16

VS COBOL II Option	OS/VS COBOL Option	Description	Chapter
SIZE	SIZE	No change. Amount of main storage for compiler. VS COBOL II minimum size is larger.	
SOURCE	SOURCE	No change. Print source listing.	16
SPACE	SPACE1/2/3	No change. With SOURCE, spacing of source listing.	
SSRANGE		New. Check for subscript out of range at run time.	16
TERMINAL	TERM	No change. Write messages to SYSTERM.	16
TEST	TEST	No change. Object program to be run under COBTEST.	13
TRUNC	TRUNC	Specifies truncation of binary fields.	16
VBREF	VBREF	No change. Print verb cross-reference and counts.	16
WORD		New. Use modified reserved word table.	
XREF	SXREF	Print sorted cross-reference listings.	11
ZWB	ZWB	No change. Make zoned decimal field unsigned when comparing to alphanumeric.	

Appendix F

Annotated Bibliography of IBM Publications

This appendix lists all of the IBM publications for VS COBOL II, with a short description of each one. The list is based on VS COBOL II Release 3. Each new release has eliminated a manual and added one or more new ones, so this list is subject to change.

Three reference manuals should be at the desk of every programmer who uses VS COBOL II:

Application Programming: Language Reference, GC26-4047.
  The definitive description of the language.

Application Programming Guide, SC26-4045.
  The "programmer's guide." Valuable information on coding techniques, interfaces with the operating system, and so on.

Application Programming: Debugging, SC26-4049.
  The primary reference for COBTEST. Also describes the compiler listing and dumps and includes a description of the run-time environment and control blocks.

If you are using VS COBOL II under CMS, add to the above list:

Application Programming: Supplement for CMS Users, SC26-4214.
  This is a supplement to the *Application Programming Guide.*

Other publications:

Application Programming: Reference Summary, SX26-3721.
  Not a pocket-sized "reference card," but a 270-page handbook. Complete formats of COBOL language and COBTEST commands

(one format per page—that's why it is so large), plus some other reference material. All this information is also in the first three manuals listed above. Think about how often you need to look up just a format, with no explanation.

OS/VS COBOL to VS COBOL II Migration Guide, GC26-4524.
Detailed descriptions of source language differences and compiler options. Some guidance on strategy and methods for conversion. Not needed by programmers using automated translator, but should be available for reference to the person providing technical guidance for the conversion.

General Information, GC26-4042.
Useful summary of new features for those who are just beginning to consider VS COBOL II. Basically a sales pitch.

Guide to Publications, GC26-4189.
A small reference card that lists all of the VS COBOL II publications, with a sentence or two describing each one. You have the same list here, with clearer descriptions.

Licensed Program Specifications, GC26-4044.
A carefully worded legal document, not a technical reference. This leaflet is the official warranty for the product.

Directory of Programming Interfaces for Customers, GC26-4550.
Another legal document. No technical information. Consists of nine pages of tables listing each part of the *Language Reference* and *Application Programming Guide* that defines a "Programming Interface for Customers," but doesn't explain why you need to know.

Manuals for the systems programmer:

Installation and Customization for MVS, SC26-4048.
Installation and Customization for CMS, SC26-4213.
Procedures for installing and tailoring the product. An appendix lists the function of each library module.

Diagnosis Reference, LY27-9522.
Control-block layouts and general descriptions of logic for both the compiler and object programs. Useful for troubleshooting.

Diagnosis Guide, LY27-9523.
How to choose keywords for searching the Info/MVS or Info/Access data base. Experienced systems programmers shouldn't need this.

Index